W9-CUB-380

FAILED

FAILED

What the "Experts" Got Wrong about the Global Economy

MARK WEISBROT

OXFORD
UNIVERSITY PRESS

OXFORD
UNIVERSITY PRESS

Oxford University Press is a department of the University of Oxford. It furthers
the University's objective of excellence in research, scholarship, and education by
publishing worldwide. Oxford is a registered trade mark of Oxford University Press in
the UK and certain other countries.

Published in the United States of America by
Oxford University Press
198 Madison Avenue, New York, NY 10016

Library of Congress Cataloging-in-Publication Data
Weisbrot, Mark.
Failed : what the "experts" got wrong about the global economy / Mark Weisbrot.
pages cm
Includes bibliographical references and index.
ISBN 978–0–19–517018–4 (hbk.)
1. Financial crises—European Union countries.   2. Economic forecasting.
3. Economic policy.   4. International Monetary Fund.   I. Title.
HB3782.W45 2015
330.94′0561—dc23
2015014988

9 8 7 6 5 4 3
Printed in the United States of America
on acid-free paper

To Francesca.

Contents

Preface | ix
Acknowledgments | xv

Introduction | 1

1. Troubles in Euroland: When the Cures Worsen
   the Disease | 20

2. This Time Could Be Different: The Aftermath
   of Financial Crises | 56

3. Untold History, Unsolved Mystery: The Long-Term
   Economic Growth Failure | 83

4. The Misunderstood Role of the International
   Monetary Fund | 125

5. The Latin American Spring | 167

Conclusion: Looking Ahead | 234

BIBLIOGRAPHY | 243
INDEX | 275

Preface

The history of economics and especially of economic policy has often been rewritten beyond recognition. The history of economic development is filled with episodes of industrialization through protective tariffs, import bans, state-owned enterprises, government subsidies for exports and favored industries, regulation and control over foreign investment and ownership, as well as foreign exchange, and the careful, often prolonged nurturing of infant industries. My own country, South Korea, went from a desperately poor country with per capita income half that of Ghana in 1961, to reach European living standards half a century later. It used all of these policy tools and more to defy the odds and become of one of the few developing countries in the past 70 years to make it into the club of high-income countries.

In my books and research I have shown that it is not only the late-comers like South Korea that have violated the "creation myths" of modern (and especially neoliberal) economics along the road to a developed economy. On the contrary, protection and state-sponsored development were essential to the success of almost all of today's high-income countries. The first British Prime Minister, Robert Walpole, protected the British woolen industry with high tariffs from the 1720s onward, while making sure that the colonies (including America) would supply raw materials and not compete with British industry. When America was freed from British domination, its first Treasury Secretary, Alexander Hamilton, became the world's leading protagonist of protecting "infant industries," advocating tariffs, subsidies, import bans, and other such measures. Abraham Lincoln succeeded in raising US tariffs to unprecedented levels—they remained the highest in the world while the United States was the fastest-growing economy in the world, from the end of the Civil War to World War I. The conflict between Northern industrial interests—who favored protectionism—and the Southern slave-holding champions of "free trade" was possibly at least as important to the people who decided to wage the Civil War as was the question of slavery. The Americans, like the British before them, only supported "free trade"—and a more limited version than the British—when they could do so and still dominate the world economy.

Yet most of this history doesn't trickle down to students of economics who influence or even decide policy in the real world of today. So who will object if more recent and even current events can be reshaped to fit a familiar, fictional narrative?

This book seeks to interrupt that process and cure or prevent some of the accumulating historical amnesia. It takes a closer look at some of the most profound economic failures of recent years and decades, and the institutions and politics involved in them. It begins with the ongoing spectacle of the eurozone, which many have reported as a morality play, a debt crisis, or a culture clash between lazy Greeks and industrious Germans (never mind that Greeks on average put in 47 percent more hours than Germans do in a working year). It is really none of those things, the author argues, but the prolonged recession and stagnation over the past seven years may have something to do with the desire of some unelected authorities to remake the more vulnerable countries of the eurozone into something with considerably less of a welfare state—or less of a state entirely. The author takes advantage of some thousands of pages of documentation of this elite consensus for change, thanks to the regular consultations that all European governments undertake, and report, with the International Monetary Fund (IMF).

As someone who has focused more on developing countries, I find it ironic to see high-income countries in Europe getting the Third World treatment that had previously been reserved for lower- and middle-income countries. But crises present irresistible opportunities for social engineers, especially if the authorities can be insulated from accountability to an electorate, as in the eurozone—where the IMF has rather quickly found itself with the vast majority of its loan portfolio.

The IMF is merely the junior partner in the "troika," but it has a checkered history as the leading protagonist of another "unholy trinity"—with the World Bank and the World Trade Organization—that has been steering the global economy toward neoliberalism for decades (the WTO just since 1995). It was a long, failed experiment, in dozens of countries, and this book makes a contribution by examining some of the details of that failure, too. It provides a valuable review of some of the IMF's operations in developing countries—and perhaps even more important, some of the changes that have taken place since the IMF lost most of its influence, during the twenty-first century.

In 2002, in the middle of Brazil's historic presidential campaign, the IMF sat down with Lula da Silva's Workers' Party and its neoliberal opposition, and negotiated an agreement that would determine the government's most important economic policies for the next couple of years, no matter who won the election. That will never happen again. A few years later, the IMF would be out of the picture in Brazil, as well as most of the region, and most of the middle-income countries in which the Fund—and therefore also Washington—had for decades exerted enormous influence. This is a major change in global economic relations and deserves very much the attention that it receives in this book, despite having been mostly ignored by the "experts" and most of the international media.

The author notes the irony that "after 20 years of nearly worldwide neoliberal reforms and economic failure, the one big country that chose a sharply different economic path became the world's largest economy, and helped pull dozens of countries out of their long slump in its wake." That was China, and it indeed contributed significantly to the rebound that the majority of low- and middle-income countries experienced in the twenty-first century. We do not even have to ask where China, and the hundreds of millions of people who have been pulled out of poverty there, would be today if the government had pursued its transition from a planned economy along the lines recommended by the "unholy trinity."

Unlike many Western observers, Weisbrot sees China's rise and increasing world influence as a positive development. On the basis of the long-term failures, reversals, and trends described in the book, he concludes that the steady erosion of the current international system—in which the same countries, allied with Washington, have controlled the most important institutions of global governance—is key to opening up new possibilities for the vast majority of the world. This includes, crucially, opening up more economic policy space for developing countries. Weisbrot cites the BRICS (Brazil, Russia, India, China, and South Africa) countries' creation of a new Currency Reserve Arrangement and Development Bank, as well as other recent developments, as evidence that these trends are beginning to accelerate. I would add, in just the past months, the unprecedented diplomatic coup that China pulled off in getting the United States' closest allies—including the United Kingdom, Germany, and France—to ignore Washington's entreaties and to join 40 countries in founding China's $100 billion Asian Infrastructure Investment Bank. This is clearly a major new development.

We are not heading toward the "end of history," in which Washington remakes the planet in its own image; but neither will we see China simply replace the United States as the world's hegemon, as many (often conveniently) fear. Rather, the author argues, it will be a more multipolar world in which the institutions of global governance are more pluralistic, the rule of international law plays a greater role, and the military force of great powers increasingly less. I certainly hope that he turns out to be right.

Ha-Joon Chang
Faculty of Economics
University of Cambridge

Acknowledgments

This book draws on more than a decade of research. Many people, especially my colleagues at the Center for Economic and Policy Research, contributed to the research and ideas as they evolved over the years, some through published works that are cited in the book. Among them are Dean Baker, Dan Beeton, Keane Bhatt, Kunda Chinku, Alan Cibils, Jose Antonio Cordero, Samantha Eyler-Driscoll, Peter Hayakawa, Deborah James, Jake Johnston, Sara Kozameh, Stephan Lefebvre, Alex Main, Juan Antonio Montecino, Robert Naiman, Arthur Phillips, Rebecca Ray, David Rosnick, Joe Sammut, Luis Sandoval, and John Schmitt. Many thanks to Jerry Epstein, Scott Parris, Dan Beeton, and Eileen O'Grady for their excellent reads and helpful comments; to Cathryn Vaulman for very helpful editorial assistance; and to Ha-Joon Chang for the preface.

Introduction

This is a book about failed economic policies and how they are implemented, and the role of deeply flawed economic ideas and institutions in this process. Wading through this kind of wreckage could be a depressing venture, but I have also tried to show that there are alternatives to the rollbacks and lost opportunities of recent years and decades, and that some of these more hopeful reforms are actually being implemented in the twenty-first century. Indeed, one of the central theses of this book is that there are always alternatives to prolonged high unemployment and recession or stagnation, as we have seen in Europe since the Great Recession, or decades without economic and social progress, as we saw in Latin America and much of the developing world in the last two decades of the twentieth century. And these are not necessarily radical alternatives—which are always available in theory—but practical, feasible alternatives that can often be implemented with existing institutional capacity and with the support of public opinion. This shouldn't be surprising; even after a financial crisis or recession strikes, a country will still have the same resources, human skills, and physical capital stock that existed some months prior. As such, there pretty much has to be a way to put all the pieces back together, as Keynes noted more than 80 years ago. Economic development is a more complicated challenge, but here, too, there is plenty of long-held knowledge that is not being put to use.[1]

---

1. See, for example, Ha-Joon Chang, *Kicking Away the Ladder: Development Strategy in Historical Perspective* (New York: Anthem Press, 2002); and *Bad Samaritans: The*

So why is economic policy failure so common? When Dorothy scolded the Wizard of Oz for the problems he had caused, his defense was that he was not a "very bad man," just "a very bad wizard." Behind almost every prolonged economic malfeasance there is some combination of outworn bad ideas, incompetence, and the malign influence of powerful special interests. Identifying these problems can be important to both recovery and the prevention of recurring nightmares. Lessons are of course learned, but not necessarily by the people who call the shots. In April 2014, German Finance Minister Wolfgang Schäuble audaciously told the press that Greece could serve as a model for Ukraine.[2] Greece, which lost a quarter of its output over more than six years of recession[3] and threw more than a quarter of its labor force and half of its youth out of work[4]—how exactly is that a model for anyone? And yet it could become one for Ukraine under International Monetary Fund (IMF) and European Union (EU) tutelage as the economy sinks further into recession, exacerbated by bad macroeconomic policy that got a head start on the civil conflict.

The first two chapters of this book deal with the unnecessary tragedy of Europe over the past six years, a drama that has upended

Myth of Free Trade and the Secret History of Capitalism (New York: Bloomsbury Press, 2007).

2. Ranier Buergin and Patrick Donahue, "Germany's Schaeuble Says Greece Could Be Model for Ukraine Aid," Bloomberg, March 24, 2014. Retrieved February 5, 2015, from http://www.bloomberg.com/news/articles/2014-03-26/germany-s-schaeuble-says-greece-could-be-model-for-ukraine-aid.

3. EL.STAT., "02. Quarterly GDP—Seasonally Adjusted, Current Prices and Chain-Linked Volumes Reference Year 2010 (1st Quarter 1995–3rd Quarter 2014) (Provisional Data)," n.d., Hellenic Statistical Authority. Retrieved February 10, 2015, from http://www.statistics.gr/portal/page/portal/ESYE/PAGE-themes?p_param=A0704&r_param=SEL84&y_param=TS&mytabs=0.

4. EL.STAT., "Population 15+ (Employment Status, Age, Sex (Greece, Total)) (1st Quarter 2001–3rd Quarter 2014)," n.d., Hellenic Statistical Authority. Retrieved February 10, 2015, from http://www.statistics.gr/portal/page/portal/ESYE/PAGE-themes?p_param=A0101&r_param=SJO01&y_param=TS&mytabs=0.

and in many cases ruined the lives of millions of people. It is also important for the outsized role it has played in slowing the global economy since 2010, contributing to increased poverty and unemployment worldwide.

It is ironic that the governments of what used to be some of the world's most advanced social democracies, with powerful trade unions and varying degrees of developed welfare states, could inflict such prolonged punishment on their citizens. Whereas in the United States, whose Congress is now controlled by a party of climate change deniers, flat-taxers, and devotees of Ayn Rand, the Great Recession—for all the scandalous regulatory failures that preceded it and the inadequate responses that followed—lasted for 18 months, officially ending in June 2009. And this was the epicenter of the world financial crisis and recession, brought on by the bursting of an $8 trillion housing bubble.

By contrast, the eurozone, after a recession of about the same duration (five quarters from the first quarter of 2008), lapsed into recession again after the first quarter of 2011. By the end of 2014, it was still not clear if, or when, the eurozone had emerged from recession.[5] There were still near-record levels of unemployment—at 11.4 percent,[6] about twice the rate of the United States. How does this happen? At the political level, it is clear that this can only occur in countries where the population has little or no say over their governments' most important macroeconomic policies. Even if the Republicans had controlled the US presidency and the Congress from 2008 onward, they would not have dared to do what eurozone governments have done, for fear of losing power. Yet more

5. Euro Area Business Cycle Dating Committee, "June 2014—Euro Area Mired in Recession Pause," Centre for Economic Policy Research, June 2014. Retrieved February 5, 2015, from http://www.cepr.org/content/euro-area-business-cy cle-dating-committee.

6. European Commission, Eurostat Database, n.d. Retrieved February 5, 2015, from http://ec.europa.eu/eurostat/data/database.

than 20 governments in Europe fell, essentially committing political suicide, rather than take the measures necessary for economic recovery. This is the eurozone: it looked like a great idea when the economies were booming with bubble-driven growth in the early and mid-2000s. But as the billionaire investor Warren Buffett famously said, "you only find out who is swimming naked when the tide goes out."

It was not just the bubble growth and the imbalances between the various eurozone countries, as many economists have pointed out, that took Europe down the path to prolonged recession and stagnation. The problem was built into the structure of the eurozone, and especially the European Central Bank (ECB), which billed itself as a central bank for all the member countries but turned out to be nothing of the sort. It was not a lender of last resort to the sovereigns in crisis; unlike the central banks of the United States, the United Kingdom, and Japan, it was not willing to use its power to create money to even stabilize the eurozone economies in turmoil, much less to stimulate a recovery.

The whole episode should have been a historic lesson about the importance of national and democratic control over macroeconomic policy—or at the very least, not ceding such power to the wrong people and institutions. But mediated by the mass media, it's not clear that such insights have been won. Instead, we have been treated to many reports and articles about a "debt crisis," or "financial crisis," in which sovereign debt and financial markets were the main problems. This is where public education on macroeconomic issues, or the lack of it, plays such a vital role. For as we shall see in the pages that follow, the European authorities—including most importantly the ECB—had the ability to overpower financial markets at any time. Instead, they played a precarious four-way game of chicken with the bond and currency markets and the governments whose policies they wished to transform. This went on for two years, with even the continued existence of the euro at times falling into question, until ECB President Mario Draghi finally uttered his famous statement: "Within our mandate, the ECB is ready to do whatever it takes to preserve the euro. And believe me, it will be enough."[7]

And then as if by magic, the financial crisis receded and the bond yields of the crisis countries began a steady downward path, without the ECB even having to follow up on its threat. The way in which Draghi so easily and quickly put an end to the financial component of Europe's crisis should have provoked a storm of controversy over why it had not been done sooner, sparing Europe from an additional two years of recession, hundreds of billions of dollars of lost output, and the misery of millions of lost jobs. But that controversy never materialized; so its story is thus part of this book.

Of course those who were watching closely could see what was really happening in the actions and reactions, statements and policies, of European officials over the prior two years. The European authorities—which came to include not only the ECB and the European Commission, but also the IMF—were using the crisis, pushing the eurozone repeatedly to the brink of financial meltdown in order to force governments to implement economic and social policies that the electorate in these countries would never vote for. It turns out that there is a paper trail of thousands of pages to supplement the moments of candor by eurozone officials that were captured in the first draft of history. The IMF has what are called "Article IV consultations" with member governments regularly, with a resulting paper on each country's economy and economic policy. There were 67 such reports produced for the eurozone countries during the four years of 2008 through 2011, and they show a consistent pattern: calls for fiscal consolidation, with spending cuts in pensions, healthcare, and other social expenditures;

7. Mario Draghi, "Verbatim of the Remarks Made by Mario Draghi," Speech presented at the Global Investment Conference in London, July 26, 2014. Retrieved February 5, 2015, from http://www.ecb.europa.eu/press/key/date/2012/html/sp120726.en.html.

reducing public sector employment, increasing labor supply, and reducing employment protections; and other measures that would be expected to reduce labor's bargaining power and redistribute income upward. The Article IV papers also contain statements indicating that the authors saw the eurozone crisis as the best time to implement certain unpopular "reforms."

The Article IV consultations include not just IMF recommendations but a consensus reached between the Fund, some part of the eurozone governments, and the European directors who represent the region on the IMF's executive board. They represent an elite consensus of sorts, which can differ greatly from the views of the electorate.

And so it should not be surprising that the kinds of "reforms" envisioned in the Article IV papers were the ones implemented under pressure from the European authorities since the Great Recession, especially in the most vulnerable countries, such as Greece, Spain, Portugal, and, to a lesser extent, Italy. These included layoffs of government workers, cuts in healthcare expenditures, reduced eligibility for pensions and unemployment compensation, and reduced employment protections.

Was any of this prolonged unemployment and regressive reform necessary? Those who say yes maintain either that recoveries following financial crises are inherently slow, or that there were no feasible macroeconomic alternatives within or outside the eurozone. It is easy to see that the European authorities, with the ECB in particular, could have prevented most of the damage with the proper monetary and fiscal policies. But given their refusal to do so, could the troubled eurozone countries have recovered faster if they had left the euro? This has been mostly a taboo subject, with even the leftist parties that shot up in popularity in Greece (Syriza) and Spain (Podemos) shying away from it. And it is a difficult issue for a number of reasons. One problem is that any politician or party that has a chance of coming to power runs the risk of causing a financial crisis if they convince the financial markets that they might actually leave the euro—thus marginalizing them before they could even be in a position to do anything.

But in Chapter 2, I argue that given the intransigence of the European authorities, and their political agenda from the beginning of the Greek crisis in 2009, any of the troubled eurozone economies would almost certainly have recovered faster outside the euro. The fact that this option was never on the table was not just due to deep historical and political reasons, including the association of the euro with democracy and internationalism, especially in the former dictatorships of Spain, Greece, and Portugal. It was also due to a widespread lack of understanding of the economic issues involved. An exit from the euro by any member country would likely have triggered some kind of financial crisis, but it is difficult to see how it could have caused the kind of damage that we have seen in the last six years from the policies that the European authorities imposed. Indeed, we can look at the worst financial crises of the past 20 years associated with devaluations, and there is nothing comparable to what has recently happened to Greece, Spain, Portugal, or even Italy, in terms of the length of the recession or the time it took to return to pre-recession levels of output or unemployment.

The comparison to Argentina has sometimes been made, due to its financial collapse, default, and huge devaluation in December 2001–January 2002. There was a deep crisis, but it only lasted for one quarter, and then the economy began a robust recovery that saw a 63 percent jump in GDP, a nearly two-thirds reduction in poverty, and a rapid expansion of employment over the next six years until the world financial crisis and recession hit. Most people believe that this was the result of a "commodities boom," and was driven by the direct impact of the devaluation on the trade balance, but in fact it was not. Rather, it was led by domestic consumption and investment, and was facilitated by a set of heterodox macroeconomic policies that were sharply different from the ones that (like in the eurozone) had pushed the country into a deep recession. It was this about-face in macroeconomic policies, from IMF austerity to a pro-growth agenda, that turned Argentina around. A similar policy shift in Greece or Spain—available only if they had left the euro—would have allowed these countries to avoid prolonged unemployment and stagnation. On the rare occasions when these questions came up, many people would say, "but what would Greece export?" not knowing that Greek exports were in fact twice as high, as a percent of GDP, as Argentina's during its crisis. Or that exports, while important for avoiding balance of payments crises or constraints on growth, were not the engine of Argentina's recovery. It is also very likely that, were Greece or Spain to leave the euro, they would face less difficult obstacles than those that Argentina confronted after its default and devaluation. The alternatives are there, but there is almost no public discussion that could lead to the political consensus necessary to chart a different course. This book attempts to offer some of that discussion.

Chapters 3 and 4 deal with two of the most important developments in the international economy of the past three decades, which have, inexplicably, gone largely unnoticed. One of them is another example of large-scale neoliberal policy failure, this time in the low- and middle-income countries, and a subsequent recovery. The last two decades of the twentieth century saw a sharp slowdown in the growth of per capita GDP for the vast majority of low- and middle-income countries. Perhaps not surprisingly, there was also greatly reduced progress on social indicators such as life expectancy, and infant and child mortality.[8] This is because economic growth

8. As explained in the chapter, this is measured by comparing countries that started the 1980–2000 period with a certain level of per capita income or health indicator (e.g., life expectancy) with countries that started out in 1960 at the same level. We would expect, for example, faster progress from a life expectancy of 55 to 65, than 65 to 75.

By comparing the progress of different countries starting at the same level, we avoid the problem of diminishing returns, i.e., that progress in economic or social indicators will slow as a country reaches a higher level.

over long periods of time is generally associated with progress on social indicators, and also because the growth slowdown—a collapse in many countries—also starves government budgets of the funds needed for social spending, such as healthcare and education. The economic failure was striking: if we compare, for example, the second lowest-income quintile of countries (which started each period with a per capita income between $1,429 and $3,103, in 2005 dollars), their GDP per person grew by 61 percent from 1960 to 1980, but only by 15 percent from 1980 to 2000.

A generation of billions around the globe lost an opportunity to raise its living standards and, for many, to live a longer and healthier life. But hardly anyone has asked why it happened. Normally, we would expect that a country starting out at the same level of income in 1980 as another country had reached in 1960 would have more opportunities to grow and develop, since there had been many advances in science and technology, public health, and other areas of applied knowledge to draw upon from the prior 20 years. Yet the opposite happened, for the vast majority of countries in the world. Did it have anything to do with the economic policy changes of this era? In dozens of developing and "emerging market" countries, there was a shift to tighter fiscal and monetary policies, sometimes even during economic slowdowns or recessions. Central banks were made more "independent"—that is, unaccountable to elected governments—and more likely to prioritize lower inflation over employment, economic growth, and development. Governments that had pursued industrial and development strategies abandoned them, often opening their economies indiscriminately to international trade and de-regulated, volatile capital flows. There were massive privatizations of state-owned enterprises, and other forms of deregulation, including in labor markets; although protectionism in one area that benefited higher income groups in the rich countries, "intellectual property," was sharply increased. These policy changes are commonly described as "neoliberal," and they constitute the defining features of neoliberalism in this book.[9]

Of course some of these policy changes were appropriate in some circumstances. But as a package—especially a one-size-fits-all package, as they were often implemented—they do not seem to have worked for the vast majority of countries. China, of course, is one big exception—but it seems to be the exception that proves the rule. A government that is still dominated by state-owned enterprises and that controls most of the banking system and investment is a wholly different animal from the neoliberal states fashioned during the last two decades of the twentieth century. Even China's transition to a mixed and globalized economy since the 1980s was engineered in a gradual, state-directed, and vastly different manner than the failed experiments that prevailed in most countries. Foreign investment was carefully managed to fit in, rather than interfere, with the government's development planning.

China's unorthodox policies brought the fastest growth in world history, and it is now the largest economy in the world on a purchasing-power-parity basis. But perhaps the biggest irony is what happened to the vast majority of countries in the twenty-first century: the growth slowdown of the prior two decades was finally reversed. How did it happen? A huge part of the story was China, which increased its imports from developing countries from a negligible 0.1 percent of their GDP in 1980 to 3 percent in 2010.[10]

---

9. Many observers use the label "free-market" or "market fundamentalism" to describe this package of policy changes, and/or to describe neoliberalism. As explained in Chapter 3, this book avoids these labels because some of the most important neoliberal policies have involved the opposite of "free market" reforms (e.g., tightening intellectual property).

10. International Monetary Fund. No date. "Direction of Trade Statistics." Online database, accessed November 1, 2011, http://elibrary-data.imf.org/; and World Bank, 2010, "Quarterly Update." Beijing: World Bank, November, http://siteresources. worldbank.

In other words, after 20 years of nearly worldwide neoliberal reforms and economic failure, the one big country that chose a sharply different economic path became the world's largest economy, and helped pull dozens of countries out of their long slump in its wake. This 50-year economic history, examined in Chapter 3, should be enough to make anyone question the conventional wisdom that the neoliberal reforms of the last two decades of the twentieth century were largely a success.

There were other reasons for the twenty-first century turnaround of the low- and middle-income countries, which included some shifts toward more sensible macroeconomic policies, especially the counter-cyclical policies that were implemented in many countries—including China, which by itself contributed enormously to world economic growth in 2009, and India, which had its own unprecedented growth spurt from 2003 to 2010.

Economic growth is understandably underappreciated by many at a time when greenhouse gas emissions are on a path to cause irreparable and probably catastrophic damage to the earth's ecosystem and population. But economic growth is a combination of population and productivity growth. In Chapter 3, I argue that while population growth is wholly negative in its impact on the climate and the environment, productivity growth—which is, for the most part, the per capita GDP growth that we are talking about—will have an important role to play in any solutions to climate change at the same time that it is essential to social and economic progress.

Chapter 4 discusses one of the most important changes in the governance of the international financial system that has taken place since the collapse of the Bretton Woods system of fixed exchange rates in 1973, which has also gone largely unnoticed. That is the IMF's loss of influence in middle-income countries, which happened to occur just before the majority of the Fund's lending shifted to high-income countries, that is, Europe. Of course the IMF until the past decade was much more powerful than it could have been on the basis of its own lending. This was due to its role as a "gatekeeper," or head of a creditors' cartel. By an informal arrangement, governments in financial trouble who did not sign an IMF agreement would generally not be eligible for loans from the (then larger) World Bank, regional development banks, and sometimes even the private sector. And since the IMF was also the United States' most important means of influence over economic policy in low- and middle-income countries, Washington lost some of this authority.

This turned out to be for the best; the Fund's policies were often wrong. A review of 41 countries with IMF agreements during the 2009 world recession found that 31 of them included pro-cyclical monetary or fiscal policies (in 15 cases, both were present).[11] Although some of these pro-cyclical policies prescribed by the IMF during the global downturn were later loosened, they did considerable damage and there was really no excuse for recommending them once the US recession was underway and the writing was on the wall. Of course, the Fund—despite spending hundreds of millions of dollars on research annually, and charged with the responsibility of monitoring the global economy—missed the two biggest asset bubbles in world history: the US stock market bubble, which peaked in 2000, and the $8 trillion housing bubble, which peaked in 2006.

The IMF began to lose influence in the wake of the Asian crisis that began in 1997. There the Fund failed to act as a lender of last resort, allowing the panic and crises to get out of control before it made any loans. When it did intervene, its policy prescriptions—including budget cuts and interest rate hikes—seemed to make the crisis worse. Even the Fund's own Internal Evaluation Office would later

11. Mark Weisbrot, Ray R. Johnston, J. Cordero, and J. A. Montecino, "IMF-Supported Macroeconomic Policies and the World Recession: A Look at Forty-one Borrowing Countries," Center for Economic and Policy Research, October 2009. Retrieved February 5, 2015, from http://www.cepr.net/index. php/publications/reports/imf-supported-macroeconomic-policies-and-the-world-recession.

note that in Indonesia it was "difficult to argue that things would have been worse without the IMF. . . . "[12] The entire mess convinced the affected countries—Indonesia, Malaysia, the Philippines, Thailand, and South Korea—to "self-insure" by piling up reserves so that they would never have to borrow from the IMF again. And other middle-income countries, some of which had suffered similar experiences, followed suit. Theoretically, if a country is hit by a sudden reversal of capital flows—as happened during the Asian crisis, and spread to other developing countries—we would want the Fund to provide loans that would ease the adjustment process, if the country has to reduce its imports because of a shortage of hard currency. But all too often the Fund—like the European authorities that it would later join in the eurozone crisis—would seize the crisis as the perfect moment to force the structural reforms that it saw as the solution to the borrowing country's problems. The illustrative example of the Fund's intervention in Argentina's 1998–2002 recession is also described in detail in Chapter 4.

Argentina eventually stood up to the IMF, even temporarily defaulting to the Fund in September 2003—something that no one but "failed states" like Iraq and Chad had ever done. It was an extraordinarily gutsy move by President Néstor Kirchner, and no one knew what would happen—the IMF at that time had the ability to initiate a cutoff of day-to-day credits for trade. But the Fund backed down and rolled over Argentina's debt. Argentina's demonstration that it could defy the IMF in the midst of a severe crisis, with no outside help, and live to tell about it, contributed not only to Argentina's rapid recovery but also to other escapes from IMF influence—including that of Brazil just a few years later. The Fund's loss of power opened up policy space in many countries, and

12. IEO, *The IMF and Recent Capital Account Crises: Indonesia, Korea, Brazil* (Washington, DC: Independent Evaluation Office, International Monetary Fund, 2003), p. 38. Retrieved February 5, 2015, from http://www.imf.org/external/np/ieo/2003/cac/pdf/all.pdf.

probably contributed to the twenty-first century growth rebound in middle-income countries described earlier.

That rebound came to Latin America in the last decade and is the subject of this book's perhaps most hopeful chapter (Chapter 5). This region was in many ways prototypical of neoliberal failure, with GDP per person growing a meager 5.7 percent over 20 years from 1980 to 2000. This compares with 91.5 percent during 1960–1980, a time when industrial and development policies that are now widely disrespected were the norm.[13] The 1980–2000 drop-off was the worst long-term economic failure in the region for at least a century, and it led to a revolt at the ballot box that put left-wing governments in charge of most of Latin America: Venezuela, Brazil, Argentina, Bolivia, Ecuador, Chile, Uruguay, and Paraguay in South America; El Salvador, Nicaragua, and Honduras in Central America. Almost no one in major media or foreign policy circles drew the connection between the dismal economic growth of the two prior decades and the electoral "pink tide" that began in 1998—despite the fact that most of the successful presidential candidates publicly stated their opposition to what they called "neoliberalismo."

Economic growth in the region rebounded, with per capita GDP growing 1.8 percent annually for 2000–2014, despite the world financial crisis and recession and a number of external shocks. This was not close to the 3.1 percent annual growth for the 1960–1980 period, but it was a huge improvement over the 0.3 percent annual average for the prior 20 years. More important, from 2002 to 2013, poverty in the region declined from 44 to 28 percent; over the previous two decades it had actually increased.[14]

13. Mark Weisbrot and Rebecca Ray, "The Scorecard on Development, 1960–2010: Closing the Gap?" Center for Economic and Policy Research, 2011, p. 8. Retrieved February 6, 2015, from http://www.cepr.net/documents/publications/scorecard-2011-04.pdf.

14. ECLAC, CEPALSTAT Database, United Nations Economic Commission for Latin American and the Caribbean, n.d. Retrieved February 7, 2015, from http://

As noted above for Argentina, the regional growth rebound was not the result of a "commodities boom." The increase in the price of oil, minerals, and agricultural commodities did help some countries, but it was not an export-led growth experience. What the trade surpluses did mostly was to help these countries, at least until the last couple of years, to avoid balance of payments problems as they allowed their economies to grow faster.

But even in Bolivia, which depends on hydrocarbons—mostly natural gas—for most of its export revenue, the sevenfold increase in government revenues from hydrocarbons between 2006 and 2014 was mainly a result of policy changes, not price increases.[15] Bolivia re-nationalized its hydrocarbon industry in May 2006, just a few months after its leftist and first indigenous president, Evo Morales, took office. This was a move that would not have been possible during the previous two decades, when the government operated under IMF agreements for virtually the entire period. When Morales was elected, GDP per person was below its level of 28 years earlier.[16]

Over the next eight years, the Bolivian government would raise the real minimum wage by 88 percent, lower the retirement age and increase public pension coverage, and more than double public

estadisticas.cepal.org/cepalstat/WEB_CEPALSTAT/estadisticasIndicadores. asp?idioma=i.

15. Revenues increased sevenfold: Ministerio de Hidrocarburos y Energía, Separata Nacional, May 2014, http://www2.hidrocarburos.gob.bo/index. php/prensa/separatas.html?download=388:separata-nacional-ministerio-de-hidrocarburos-y-energia-1ro-de-mayo-2014.

Production doubled: Andres Schipani, "Bolivia Facing Up to Lower Gas Export Prices,"FinancialTimes,October23,2014.RetrievedNovember28,2014,fromhttp:// blogs.ft.com/beyond-brics/2014/10/23/bolivia-facing-up-to-lower-gas-expo rt-prices/?Authorised=false.

Prices actually fell: EIA, "Henry Hub Natural Gas Spot Price 1997–2013," n.d. Retrieved February 12, 2015, from http://www.eia.gov/dnav/ng/hist/rngwhhdA.htm.

16. IMF, "World Economic Outlook October 2014," October 2014. Retrieved February 6, 2015, from http://www.imf.org/external/pubs/ft/weo/2014/02/weodata/ index.aspx.

investment as a percent of the economy. The government also redistributed more than 5 million hectares of land,[17] one of the biggest land reforms relative to cultivated land in recent memory in the region. A large stimulus at just the right time gave Bolivia about the highest growth rate in Latin America in 2009, when most of the rest of the hemisphere lapsed into recession.

Ecuador's President Rafael Correa, first elected in 2006, also showed that even small developing countries could now chart a different course that had not previously been an option for progressive governments. The government took control of the central bank, required private banks to repatriate a large portion of their foreign holdings, adopted a number of sweeping financial and regulatory reforms, and achieved large reductions in poverty and inequality. At the same time, Correa infuriated foreign investors by keeping an election campaign promise to not pay foreign debt that was found to be illegitimately or illegally contracted, thereby defaulting on a third of Ecuador's foreign debt. It seemed once again that the prevailing wisdom of most economists and the business press—that developing countries must prioritize the demands of foreign investors—was wrong. And the widely accepted notion that "globalization" severely constrained the macroeconomic and development policy options available to developing countries proved to be somewhat exaggerated, to say the least. Ecuador has done quite well so far under its "New Deal": GDP per person grew at a 2.8 percent annual rate in 2007–2014, the poverty rate was reduced by 30 percent, and inequality also fell sharply.

Brazil's Workers' Party (PT), coming to power in 2003 with the election of Luiz Inácio Lula da Silva, pursued a more gradualist approach than the Andean countries and Argentina, but

17. See Juan Carlos Rojas Calizaya (Director of the National Institute for Agrarian Reform [INRA], 2006–2011), "Agrarian Transformation in Bolivia at Risk," Bolivia Information Forum Bulletin, September 2012.

still managed to accomplish a great deal over 12 years. A country that had a total of just 3 percent per capita GDP growth over 23 years[18]—that's total, not annual—started growing again and was able to reduce poverty by 55 percent and extreme poverty by 65 percent from 2003 to 2012.[19]

Unemployment fell to record low levels and the income gains during the past decade were distributed far more equally than previously; the real minimum wage was raised by about 90 percent. A healthy stimulus helped speed the recovery from the world recession in 2009, although a premature tightening of monetary and fiscal policy contributed to sluggish growth after 2010. But there were structural changes in the labor market, and real wages continued to rise even as the economy slowed.

Even in Venezuela, the most maligned of the leftist governments, there was a large rise in living standards after the government of Hugo Chávez gained control over the all-important oil industry in 2003.[20] Although Venezuela would run into problems with high inflation, currency misalignment, and balance of payments troubles toward the end of 2012, the achievements of the post-2003 Chávez era were comparable to those of the other left-wing governments; there were large reductions[21] in poverty (42 percent), extreme poverty (53 percent),[22] and inequality, and

18. Per capita GDP growth 1980–2003: IMF, "World Economic Outlook," October 2014.

19. http://www.cepr.net/publications/reports/the-brazilian-economy-in-transition-macroeconomic-policy-labor-and-inequality.

20. As explained in Chapter 5, the proper starting point for measuring progress so as not to begin from the deep hole of the oil-strike/recession would be 2004, when the economy had caught up with its pre-recession level of GDP.

21. 2004–2013.

22. From the last half of 2004 to the last half of 2013. INE, "Pobreza por línea de ingreso, 1er semestre 1997–2do semestre 2013," *Instituto Nacional de Estadísticas*, n.d. Retrieved February 5, 2015, from http://www.ine.gov.ve/index.php?option=com_content&view=category&id=104&Itemid=45#.

greatly expanded access to education, public pensions, and health-care.[23] Especially when compared to the 20 prior years of actually negative per capita income growth, the economic and social indicators of the past decade help explain why the governing party was able to win 13 of 14 national elections and referenda. It remains to be seen if the government can overcome the current crisis and preserve those gains.

Most of the leftist governments, including Brazil, had run-ins with the United States, which had traditionally had a heavy hand in the region's politics and economic policy. They had to fight for what has become known as Latin America's "second independence," even forming new multilateral organizations such as the Community of Latin American and Caribbean States (CELAC), which includes the entire hemisphere except for the United States and Canada. The CELAC was a response to Washington's manipulation of the Organization of American States in the aftermath of the 2009 military coup in Honduras, which the leftist governments, together with almost every government other than the United States and Canada, vigorously opposed. The end result of these struggles was a sea change in US-Latin American relations, in which international institutions and norms were changed for everyone, including the non-left governments. These political changes were the *sine qua non* of many of the economic and social policy changes described in Chapter 5. Hence the chapter also looks at some of the political developments that transformed hemispheric relations over the past decade and a half.

The case studies, economic decision-making and results, and institutions examined in this book show that much of the world has paid a high price for failed economic policies and ideas over the past 35 years. Many of these failed policies and ideas continue to

---

23. See Chapter 5.

enjoy widespread support among policymakers and the press. At the same time, the experience of the twenty-first century thus far also shows that there are viable and practical alternatives, and that these can be implemented if governments possess the political will and support to do so. Whether we see more of these changes going forward may depend on how well the public, as well as the policymakers themselves, understand the available choices. I hope that this book can contribute to that understanding.

1

Troubles in Euroland

When the Cures Worsen the Disease

Of all the examples of neoliberal policy failure since the Great Recession, the eurozone crisis stands out as a work of art. The European authorities who made this mess—the European Commission, the European Central Bank (ECB), and the International Monetary Fund (IMF)—known as "the troika"—provide one of the clearest, large-scale demonstrations in modern times of the damage that can be done when people in high places get their basic macroeconomic policies wrong. That it has happened in a set of high-income economies with previously well-developed democratic institutions makes it even more compelling.

It is necessary to say "previously well-developed" democratic institutions because the eurozone countries surrendered their sovereign rights to control their most important macroeconomic policies: first monetary and exchange rate policy, and then increasingly fiscal policy for the so-called PIIGS countries (Portugal, Italy, Ireland, Greece, and Spain). As we will see, this was a profound loss of democratic governance, and one for which tens of millions of eurozone residents would pay dearly in the years following the world financial crisis and recession of 2008–2009, and for as yet untold years to come.

Most citizens of the euro area did not understand what they were losing when the Maastricht Treaty was signed in 1992, and the euro was introduced in 1999. You couldn't see it until there was a serious recession—when the government really needed to use expansionary macroeconomic policies to restore growth and employment. Then we discovered that not only was the fate of most Europeans in the hands of people who were almost completely unaccountable to the electorate; it was worse than that. Power was now in the hands of people who had their own political and economic agenda, and who, as we shall demonstrate, saw the crisis as an opportunity to implement changes that could never be won at the ballot box.

To see the world of difference between unaccountable and partially accountable economic authorities, we need only compare the economic performance of the eurozone with that of the United States in the six years following the collapse of Lehman Brothers in October 2008. The United States, which was the epicenter of what would become a world recession, had a downturn that lasted officially 18 months; its recession was declared over in June of 2009. To be sure, it was the worst US recession since the Great Depression, and more than four years after the recession ended, employment levels were almost the same as they were at the depth of the recession. The US recovery was nothing to brag about; only the vastly worse results in the eurozone could make it look good. By February 2014, the eurozone was still close to record unemployment of 12 percent (as compared with 6.7 percent in the US); and GDP had fallen in both 2012 and 2013. And in the harder hit countries like Greece and Spain, unemployment had passed 27 and 26 percent, respectively, while youth unemployment surpassed 58 and 53 percent.[1]

---

1. Eurostat, "Unemployment Rate by Sex and Age Groups—Monthly Average, %," 2014. Retrieved May 2014 from http://appsso.eurostat.ec.europa.eu/nui/show. do?dataset=une_rt_m&lang=en.

By 2013 more than 20 governments had fallen in the euro area, but austerity was still the order of the day. This could never happen in the United States, where even if the deficit hawk Republican Mitt Romney had been elected in 2012, he would not have dared plunge the US economy back into recession. His first goal, like that of most politicians, would be re-election, and there would be no external authorities that could force him to commit political suicide.

Then there is the vast difference between monetary policy in the two economies. Although by law the Fed and the ECB are both independent, there are degrees of independence and some would say, dogma; and the Fed turned out to act quite differently than the ECB in the past five years. The US Federal Reserve, which had lowered its policy lending rate to zero at the end of December 2008, kept it at or near zero for the next six years. As a way of providing further stimulus through influencing expectations, the Fed also made it clear that these "exceptionally low" rates would continue for "an extended period."[2]

By contrast, the ECB actually raised rates twice in mid-2011, to 1.5 percent, despite the weakness of the eurozone economy. But even more important was the Fed's policy of more than $2.3 trillion of quantitative easing (QE), which the ECB had refused to consider, despite the fact that it was so drastically more necessary in Europe—given the vicious cycle of rising borrowing costs that threatened to spiral out of control in the weaker economies, including the "too-big-to-fail" countries of Italy and Spain. With QE, as we will see, Europe could have recovered as quickly as the United States, and of course much more quickly if the member countries had the ability and the will to engage in expansionary fiscal policy. The ECB, like the Federal Reserve, controls a hard currency and can create money. As such, it had the ability to prevent the sovereign

2. Board of Governors of the Federal Reserve System, "FOMC Statement," March 18, 2009. Retrieved May 12, 2014, from http://www.federalreserve.gov/newsevents/press/monetary/20090318a.htm.

debt of eurozone countries from ever becoming a crisis in the first place. It actually had the ability to keep long-term borrowing costs for eurozone countries, including even Greece, as low as it wanted—as the Fed did in the United States while the US federal budget deficit soared to a post–World War II record of more than 10 percent of GDP.

The Fed's QE also provided some funding for the government to stimulate the economy through spending and tax cuts, without increasing its net debt burden. This is not magic but just the rules of accounting, combined with the economics of a weak economy. When the Fed creates money through QE, and uses it to buy long-term US Treasury bonds, it refunds the interest payments on these bonds to the Treasury. This means that the government is getting the equivalent of an interest-free loan, and its net debt burden does not rise. It can then use this money for anything—building a more energy-efficient infrastructure, for example, or any kind of expansionary fiscal policy. Unfortunately, in the United States, the federal government did not take advantage of this "free money" as much as it could have. And yes, it really is free money—with consumer price inflation at 0.8 percent for 2014 in the United States and negative 0.2 percent in the eurozone, there is no downside to this money creation, since there is no significant risk that inflation will become too high.

I remember speaking about these matters with a group of German members of parliament, from all of the major political parties, in September 2011. One of them objected that it would be impossible to sell the idea of expansionary macroeconomic policies, and especially those involving money creation, to a German public that still had historical memories of the devastating hyperinflation of the 1920s. I couldn't speak to that—not being an expert on German public opinion—but my response was that if this was indeed the case, it indicated a problem of public education, not an economic problem.

And public education is a big part of this story. It is a story in which most of the public—in Europe, the United States, and much of the world—has been continually misled as to the nature and causes of a festering economic problem. How else to explain how a crisis that originated from over-borrowing by the private sector was sold to the public as a problem caused by governments refusing to live within their means? It was then exacerbated by fiscal tightening, to the point of pushing the regional economy into years of recession and stagnation. The worsening crisis was then used to justify still more neoliberal policies—including cutting public pensions, shrinking the public sector, privatizations, and making it easier for employees to be fired. This sequence of escalating misery caused by government policy—accompanied by regressive structural reforms—can only happen if a broad swath of the public, including many journalists and politicians, is seriously confused as to what has gone wrong and what feasible economic alternatives are available.

But to understand how it happened we must also look at how the decision-makers—in this case the so-called troika—made their decisions, in large part independently of the citizenry's views of what is right and wrong. For that we must turn to the financial crisis that began in early 2010.

Crisis as Opportunity: The Troika Seizes the Moment to Reshape Europe

The crisis in eurozone financial markets began as a problem with Greek sovereign debt that could have been easily managed. Greece's economy is less than 2 percent of the GDP of the now 19-member eurozone, and the other euro countries had set aside vastly more than enough resources to resolve Greece's problems in early 2010 when Greek debt first began to disturb the financial markets. But before it was over, the crisis would push the eurozone into its longest recession and record-high unemployment, and make Europe the biggest drag on the world economy.

By the end of 2011, the so-called BRICS countries—Brazil, Russia, China, India, and South Africa—were being recruited to help Europe by buying some of their bonds or with contributions channeled through the IMF. What is wrong with this picture? India has a per capita income of $3,400,[3] less than one-ninth of the eurozone; Brazil has 42 million people living on less than $4 a day.[4] Even China, although it has more than $3.6 trillion in reserves, has only about one-fourth of the per capita GDP of the euro area.[5] And as noted above, a eurozone recovery has always been feasible without any outside help.

The eurozone crisis is most commonly described in the media as a "debt crisis," or more specifically as a "sovereign debt crisis." But this is very misleading. If we look at the numbers and recent history, we see a crisis that has been fundamentally caused and deepened by bad policy. Of the PIIGS countries, only Greece can be said to have built up a potentially unsustainable debt burden before the financial crisis and world recession of 2008–2009 hit Europe. The others actually reduced their debt-to-GDP ratios during the boom years of 2003–2008.[6] Spain's net public debt, for example, fell from 41.3 to 30.6 percent of GDP during these years.[7] Italy's was larger,

---

3. In purchasing power parity terms.

4. Socio-Economic Database for Latin America and the Caribbean (CEDLAS and the World Bank), "Poverty." Retrieved May 2014 from http://sedlac.econo.unlp.edu.ar/eng/statistics.php.

5. The Euro area's PPP per capita GDP is $34,016, while China's is $9,844. See International Monetary Fund, "World Economic Outlook April 2014," April 2014, http://www.imf.org/external/pubs/ft/weo/2014/01/weodata/index.aspx.

6. See Mark Weisbrot, "What Next for the Eurozone? Macroeconomic Policy and the Recession," Center for Economic and Policy Research, April 17, 2013, http://www.cepr.net/events-archive/what-next-for-the-eurozone-macroeconomic-policy-and-the-recession.

7. IMF, "World Economic Outlook April 2014," April 2014, http://www.imf.org/external/pubs/ft/weo/2014/01/weodata/index.aspx.

at 89.3 percent of GDP,[8] but with a low budget deficit and low interest rates there was not any reason for such debt to be seen as unsustainable until the mismanagement of the eurozone economy sent Italy's borrowing costs much higher.

Even Greece, when it was negotiating its first agreement with the IMF in May 2010, had a debt of 130 percent of GDP,[9] which could have been manageable with low interest rates, and with the debt burden reduced over time with reasonable growth. Seventeen months later, after shrinking its economy at the behest of the European authorities, its debt had increased to 170 percent of GDP.[10] By this time, even when the European authorities reached a tentative agreement on October 26, 2011, for a 50 percent "haircut" for bondholders—that is, a 50 percent reduction in the principal of the Greek public debt held by private bondholders—it was still not enough to put Greece on a sustainable debt path. A problem that could have been resolved with—at most—just a few percent of the funds that the European authorities had set aside for this purpose had morphed into a financial crisis that threatened the health of the whole European economy. This was one result of what economists call pro-cyclical macroeconomic policy—shrinking the economy when it was already weak or in recession.

8. Net debt to GDP in 2008. IMF, "World Economic Outlook October 2014," October 2014. Retrieved February 6, 2015, from http://www.imf.org/external/pubs/ft/weo/2014/02/weodata/index.aspx.

9. IMF, "World Economic Outlook October 2014," October 2014. Retrieved February 6, 2015, from http://www.imf.org/external/pubs/ft/weo/2014/02/weodata/index.aspx.
   The IMF Request for Standby Arrangement from May 2010 puts the 2009 debt at "over 115 percent" of GDP. IMF, "Greece: Request for Stand-By Arrangement," May 10, 2010. Retrieved February 11, 2015, from http://www.imf.org/external/pubs/ft/scr/2010/cr10111.pdf.

10. IMF, "World Economic Outlook October 2014," October 2014. Retrieved February 6, 2015, from http://www.imf.org/external/pubs/ft/weo/2014/02/weodata/index.aspx.

From the beginning of this crisis, the European authorities had the power, resources, and ability to bring about a robust recovery of growth and employment. It was the will that was lacking. Most commentators and analysts have emphasized the difficulties of coordinating fiscal policy—especially the spending that would be needed to put the eurozone economy back on track. A narrative of hard-working, thrifty Germans and other northern Europeans reluctant to subsidize the lazy and indulgent habits of their southern neighbors became a common theme in the media. Of course most of this has no basis in reality. For example, Greeks, on average, put in considerably more hours on the job than their German counterparts—about 2,037 per year as compared to 1,388 in Germany.[11] Greeks also retire later than Germans do. And if we look at the problem in terms of who has benefited most from the good years of the euro, it is not so clear: more than 100 percent of Germany's growth in the expansion from 2002 to 2008 came from exports, the majority of which went to Europe. Germany's export-led growth also enabled them to increase productivity and competitiveness in manufacturing. Over the long run, this is much better than the bubble-driven growth that countries like Spain and Ireland experienced in the run-up to the crisis.

This is not to deny that there are serious problems of tax evasion for high-income earners and business owners in Greece and Italy, or that popular sentiments in countries like Germany or Finland can make it more difficult to assist other eurozone countries in crisis. But the eurozone crisis was not brought on by public sector over-borrowing. And even "anti-bailout" sentiment in the richer countries is often oversimplified—much of it is not just national prejudice against southern Europeans, but also includes more legitimate popular resentment against bailing out European banks.

---

11. OECD, "Level of GDP per Capita and Productivity," 2012. Retrieved May 2014 from http://stats.oecd.org/Index.aspx?DataSetCode=PDB_LV.

But all of these problems are secondary compared to the fundamental and deeply misunderstood problem of flawed macroeconomic policy. If not for the economic damage inflicted by the European authorities in 2010–2013, the Europeans could have had a number of years to try to correct the structural and political problems of the eurozone—if that was what the people and their elected representatives wanted to do. It is of course possible that the political will would not be there to make the changes that would be necessary to preserve the common currency over the long run. But for more than four years (and still going), the European authorities successively implemented policies that slowed the eurozone economy and, for most of that time, additional policies that caused serious financial crises. This would make it increasingly difficult, if not impossible, to address problems of policy coordination or other structural problems of the eurozone.

As noted above, Greece's debt situation was transformed from something that could have been resolved relatively simply, and with few resources, into an intractable and contagious mess. And the acute crisis that the eurozone suffered from July 2011 until August 2012 was based on the worries in financial markets that the European authorities might do to Italy what they did to Greece. When the IMF had to lower its growth projections for the Italian economy, between its April and September forecasts in 2011,[12] it was a direct result of the $74 billion austerity package that the European authorities forced on the Italian government.

In May 2010, the Greek government was the first to receive money from the European authorities to finance the rollover of its debt because it was no longer feasible to borrow from financial markets. "Together with our partners in the European Union, we

---

12. The April 2011 World Economic Outlook had forecast GDP growth of 1.1 percent in 2011, 1.3 percent in 2012, and 1.4 percent in 2013. In September, these were revised down to 0.6 percent, 0.3 percent, and 0.5 percent.

are providing an unprecedented level of support to help Greece in this effort and—over time—to help restore growth, jobs, and higher living standards," said IMF Managing Director Dominique Strauss-Kahn in announcing the agreement for 110 billion euros to be disbursed over the next three years.[13]

The key words were "over time." The IMF and its partners knew that the fiscal tightening would make things worse. "Real GDP growth is expected to contract sharply in 2010–2011," said the Fund, but it added that "from 2012 onward, improved market confidence, a return to credit markets, and comprehensive structural reforms, are expected to lead to a rebound in growth."[14]

The first part of that prediction came true, with GDP falling by 11.7 percent during 2010–2011.[15] But the second part was a pipe dream. By December 2011, the Organisation for Economic Co-operation and Development (OECD) was forecasting a further decline of 3 percent for 2012,[16] which turned out to be 7 percent.[17]

It was not surprising, given that the Greek government committed to cutting $28.3 billion, or 12 percent of GDP, from its budget through 2015, and laying off 20 percent of its public sector workforce

13. IMF, "IMF Approves €30 Bln Loan for Greece on Fast Track," IMF Survey online, May 9, 2010, https://www.imf.org/external/pubs/ft/survey/so/2010/NEW050910A.htm.

14. IMF, "Greece: Staff Report on Request for Stand-By Arrangement," p. 140. Retrieved February 6, 2015, from http://www.imf.org/external/pubs/ft/scr/2010/cr10110.pdf.

15. IMF, "World Economic Outlook, October 2014," October 2014. Retrieved February 6, 2015, from http://www.imf.org/external/pubs/ft/weo/2014/02/weodata/index.aspx.

16. OECD, "Greece," in *OECD Economic Outlook*, Vol. 2011, Issue 2 (Paris: OECD Publishing, 2011).

17. IMF, "World Economic Outlook, October 2014," October 2014. Retrieved February 6, 2015, from http://www.imf.org/external/pubs/ft/weo/2014/02/weodata/index.aspx.

over the next four years.[18] Who is going to invest in a country that has committed to years of recession?

The IMF justified these measures partly on the grounds that the alternative—a debt restructuring—carried too much risk of contagion to the rest of Europe, where banks held hundreds of billions of dollars of Greek debt. But because the "bailout" package destabilized the Greek economy and thereby increased the risk of a chaotic default, their preferred solution actually worsened the contagion.

Fears that Greek bondholders would end up taking losses, and that Portugal, Ireland, and possibly even Spain would follow the path of Greece began to seep into financial markets. On May 9, 2010, the ECB said that it would intervene in sovereign bond markets, reversing a decision just four days earlier that had sent markets tumbling.[19] It was a concession by the ECB, but it was much too small to arrest the financial crisis that the European authorities had set in motion. Fears that a Greek default and its aftermath would result in a breakup of the euro began to move the markets.

The next day, the European authorities (including the IMF) reached an agreement on a trillion-dollar fund that was intended to "shock and awe" the financial markets into believing that default by any of the eurozone governments on their bonds was not possible.[20] Stock and financial markets initially soared in response, but there was a terrible hangover as reality set in the next morning. At this point the debt of Italy, which was considerably larger than that

18. Greek Ministry of Finance, "Greece: Medium-Term Fiscal Strategy 2012–15," June 2011, http://www.minfin.gr/sites/default/files/financial_files/MTFS.pdf.

19. European Central Bank, "ECB Decides on Measures to Address Severe Tensions in Financial Markets," May 10, 2010, http://www.ecb.europa.eu/press/pr/date/2010/html/pr100510.en.html.

20. Julien Toyer and Ilona Wissenbach, "'Shock and Awe' Euro Rescue Lifts Global Markets," Reuters, May 10, 2010, http://www.reuters.com/article/2010/05/10/us-eurozone-idUSTRE6400PJ20100510.

of all the other troubled eurozone economies combined, was not yet considered to be at risk.

But even for the others, including Spain, it was already clear to many that without a commitment by the ECB to keep borrowing costs down to sustainable levels, a "bailout" fund would only enable the governments to pile up more debt, on which they would eventually have to default. The European authorities were still not ready to consider any practical solution. By establishing fiscal tightening as a requirement for access to any European/IMF funding, they had guaranteed that the debt problems would only grow worse.

At this point, even the bond markets, which traditionally rally when governments commit to budget tightening, started to become strangely Keynesian: bond prices would sometimes fall on news that Greece, for example, would implement further austerity.

In November 2010, the Irish government became the second eurozone economy to sign an agreement with the IMF and the European authorities, after their 10-year bond yield had passed 8 percent. Portugal would be third, in May 2011. The dreaded agreements that had been, in past decades, the punishment meted out to low- and middle-income countries with balance of payments problems, had now become the fate of high-income European nations. It was an artificial and unprecedented kind of "balance of payments" crisis: these were, after all, governments with a hard currency that could be created by "their" central bank. But the central bank wasn't really theirs, unfortunately, and it wasn't going to do what the central bank of the United States or even the United Kingdom was willing to do in order to contain the crisis: most importantly, contain the sovereign borrowing costs of the vulnerable countries.

The crisis scenario that began in July 2011 went like this. The austerity, in combination with the slowing regional economy, was causing the Italian economy to grow slower or even shrink.[21]

21. Italy's quarterly GDP began to shrink in the third quarter of 2011. See OECD, "Quarterly Growth Rates of Real GDP, Change over Previous Quarter." Retrieved May 2014 from https://stats.oecd.org/index.aspx?queryid=350#.

Slower economic growth causes government revenues to fall (and some spending to automatically increase), and so the promised deficit targets are even more difficult to reach. The government is then pressured to take more steps to cut spending (and/or increase taxes). This further reduces economic growth. The process continues in a downward spiral, as happened in Greece. And Italy's debt, then at $2.6 trillion, was more than five times the size of Greece's.[22] The European authorities had not managed to put together the resources to deal with a possible default of this magnitude; hence the series of crises in financial markets.

As the downward spiral began to look critical, investors sold off Italian bonds, pushing down their price. This has two destabilizing results. First, as a matter of accounting, the yield on long-term bonds moves in the opposite direction of their price. So, as Italy's bond prices fell, the yield moved up to record levels. This means that as Italy refinanced its debt, it would have to pay higher interest rates, which increases its debt burden and makes it even more difficult to meet the budget targets. The second result of the fall in prices of Italian bonds (and other eurozone bonds, including the then $1 trillion Spanish debt) was that the European banks holding these bonds suffered a loss in the value of their assets. This also contributed to the instability in Europe's banking system. According to press reports,[23] speculators exacerbated the problem during the summer of 2011 by shorting European banks' stocks.[24]

22. IMF, "World Economic Outlook October 2014," October 2014. Retrieved February 6, 2015, from http://www.imf.org/external/pubs/ft/weo/2014/02/weodata/index.aspx.

23. Dan McCrum, "European Banks Face Shortsellers' Fire," *Financial Times*, August 8, 2011, http://www.ft.com/intl/cms/s/0/21550128-bf9b-11e0-90d5-00144feabdc0.html?siteedition=intl#axzz2zGm4N52N.

24. Shorting, or short-selling, an asset such as a stock involves borrowing and selling the asset, making a bet that the asset is going to fall in price. If it does, the investor then buys the borrowed stock at a lower price and profits from the

Apparently they had figured out that shorting the euro itself would have been riskier, because the ECB could and did intervene in currency markets, when it chose to do so, to push up the value of the euro. And the United States had repeatedly shown a willingness to lend or swap dollars with the ECB since the financial crisis of 2008–2009. It was thus unlikely that the ECB would run out of the dollars needed to buy up euros. As such, the speculators went after the banks instead.

An episode from the summer of 2011 illustrates the role of under-regulated financial markets and speculation in the European financial crisis at that time. As the crisis unfolded, bond traders and speculators began to short Italy's bonds, driving interest rates up further and reducing the value of the bonds held by European banks. A bond trader described the process from his point of view on August 4:

> "The SMP [the ECB's Securities Market Program, which buys eurozone government bonds] is back but it's not in the right places, what's going to stop us attacking Spain and Italy over the summer months, cause I can't think of anything," said a trader in London.
>
> "There is no buying of Italy and Spain going on and there won't be, so why can't we push these markets to 7 percent yields, I think we can quite easily," the trader said.[25]

The trader was betting that by shorting Italian bonds, yields could be pushed up to the breaking point, where markets would see

---

difference between the sale of the borrowed stock and the later purchase price. In some markets the same bet can be made without having to actually borrow the stock (these are called "naked shorts").

25. Ana Nicolaci Da Costa, "Investors Snub ECB Liquidity Promises, Bund Rallies," Reuters, August 4, 2011, http://www.reuters.com/article/2011/08/04/markets-b onds-euro-idUSL6E7J42I620110804.

the resulting additional burden on Italy as too big to sustain. This would cause a crisis in which yields would skyrocket, as they did in Greece, and speculators would profit enormously.

Of course this kind of unrestricted speculation has been a significant part of the problem. But the first sentence in the above quote is the most important one. Here the trader was describing what had opened up his opportunity at that moment: the ECB was threatening not to buy Italian bonds in order to pressure the Italian parliament into more budget tightening. When the ECB did intervene, Italian bond yields fell quickly (and prices rose), and the speculators got burned—until the process started again a month or so later. The problem was not that bond markets were so powerful that they could force governments to cut their budgets even when it was irrational to do so, as many observers thought they saw. In fact, the ECB could easily overpower any movement in the bond markets by private actors.

This is what almost all of the analysis and commentary missed: that the European authorities, regardless of political concerns within the member states, repeatedly allowed the region to slip to the edge of a financial meltdown in an effort to force the weaker eurozone governments to make more concessions. These concessions included deficit cuts, which when enacted worsen the economic and debt problems, as described above. They also included a number of regressive political reforms that the electorates of these countries would probably never vote for. Such "reforms" as raising the retirement age (in Italy, Greece, and Spain) or making it easier for employers to fire workers (in Spain and Italy) are among the numerous examples of the European authorities taking advantage of the situation to partially dismantle or remake the welfare state and economic structure of the borrowing countries in ways that are more to their liking, and more neoliberal. As we will see, this is not just a crime of opportunity, but one that has deep roots in the thinking of the European authorities, including the IMF.

Most of the game of brinkmanship that caused repeated crises in Europe during 2010–2012 was about squeezing budgets. From July to December 2011, there were repeated crises caused by the European authorities trying to force more concessions from the governments of Greece and Italy. One of them, in September 2011, was caused by the IMF refusing to release an 8 billion euro installment on a loan to Greece, unless Greece implemented further budget tightening.[26] It seems incredible that European officials—who have the final say on IMF decision-making—were willing to put the entire European economy at risk for such a relatively small amount of money. But they did. Not only was the 8 billion euros a tiny fraction of the hundreds of billions that they had available to prevent financial contagion, but Greece was within 0.8 percent of GDP of the budget targets that it had accepted. This is another indication of the ideological and political stubbornness of the people in charge, and their willingness to expose the region to enormous risks in order to make sure that a good crisis did not go to waste.

It goes without saying that these "reforms" are politically unpopular; when Greek Prime Minister George Papandreou proposed in late October 2011 that Greece hold a referendum on the austerity package then pending,[27] he came under such pressure from the European authorities (including French President Nicolas Sarkozy and German Chancellor Angela Merkel) that he was forced to back down and then resign. The resignation of Prime Minister Silvio Berlusconi of Italy followed within days. These were the third and fourth governments to fall as a result of the

26. Graeme Wearden, "EU Debt Crisis: Greece Forced to Wait for Crucial Bailout Funds—as It Happened," *The Guardian*, September 16, 2011, http://www.theguardian.com/business/2011/sep/16/euro-debt-crisis-finance-ministers.

27. Niki Kitsantonis and Rachel Donadio, "Anxieties Stir as Greece Plans Referendum on Latest Europe Aid Deal," *New York Times*, October 31, 2011, http://www.nytimes.com/2011/11/01/world/europe/greece-to-hold-referendum-on-new-debt-deal.html.

crisis and austerity, having been preceded by Ireland and Portugal. The Spanish government, led by Socialist Workers Party Prime Minister José Luis Rodríguez Zapatero, which had presided over pro-cyclical austerity policies there, went down in electoral defeat a few weeks later.

European officials were beginning to live up to the reputation for which their troika partner, the IMF, had become notorious, having toppled more governments than Marx, Lenin, Mao, and Che Guevara combined. Between May 2010 and December 2011 there were eight aid packages assembled by the European authorities in their attempts to prevent the crisis from worsening, while still forcing the policy changes that they wanted to see. The sums of money increased, as did the authorities' commitment to the common currency. But despite all of these efforts, the crisis grew increasingly worse, to the point where it threatened not only the region and the common currency but the world economy.

On November 9, 2011, the nightmare scenario that markets had feared since July seemed to have materialized. Italy's 10-year bond yields soared past 7 percent,[28] the dreaded level that had pushed Ireland and Portugal out of the financial markets and into receivership from the IMF and European authorities. The situation worsened when Europe's largest clearing house, LCH Clearnet, increased the collateral requirements that had to be posted in order to trade Italy's bonds. The euro and world stock markets fell, and fear-driven money poured into US treasuries, pushing the yield on the 10-year note below 2 percent—which had, until the worsening euro crisis of the preceding months, been the historic low set after the collapse of Lehman Brothers in 2008.

There was some mathematical basis for the markets' fears, given the ECB's unwillingness to intervene. One year prior, Italy could

28. Neal Armstrong, "Italian Bond Yields Surge Past 7 Percent," Reuters, November 9, 2011, http://www.reuters.com/article/2011/11/09/markets-bonds-euro-close-idUSL6E7M95J020111109.

borrow at 4 percent for 10-year bonds. On November 9, these yields went as high as 7.5 percent.[29] Multiply this difference, 3.5 percent, times the 325 billion euros that Italy was scheduled to refinance over the next year.[30] That's 11.3 billion euros in additional borrowing costs, or about 1 percent of Italy's GDP.

Italy had already agreed to deficit reduction of 3.9 percent of GDP by 2013, with about 1.7 percent of it coming over the first year. Prime Minister Silvio Berlusconi's resignation on November 12, 2011, had mainly been a result of the perceived political difficulty of undertaking this budget tightening in a weak economy. Now add another 1 percent of GDP to meet the same goal—and the goal posts would be expected to move because the economy could be expected to shrink further. It was easy for the financial markets to calculate that Italy was not going to make these targets.

With Italy's $2.6 trillion debt exceeding that of Ireland, Portugal, Greece, and even Spain combined, the ECB decided that it could not allow the sell-off of Italy's bonds to escalate any further. The Central Bank intervened heavily, buying Italy's bonds and pushing yields back down to 6.45 percent within the next two days.[31]

---

29. High of 7.483 on November 9, 2011. Bloomberg, "Italy Generic Government 10Y Yield," n.d. Retrieved February 10, 2015, from http://www.bloomberg.com/quote/GBTPGR10:IND/chart.

30. Tesoro, "Departamento del Tesoro, Outstanding of Public Securities (Breakdown by Maturity)" Rome: Ministero dell'Economia e delle Finanze, December 31, 2011. Retrieved February 10, 2015, from http://www.dt.tesoro.it/export/sites/sitodt/modules/documenti_en/debito_pubblico/scadenze_titoli_suddivise_per_anno/Outstanding_public_securities_31-12-2011_GPO.pdf; http://www.dt.tesoro.it/export/sites/sitodt/modules/documenti_en/debito_pubblico/scadenze_titoli_suddivise_per_anno/Outstanding_public_securities_31-10-2011_GPO.pdf.

31. Paul Dobson, "Italian Bonds Rise on ECB Debt Purchases; French Spread Widens," Bloomberg, November 10, 2011. Retrieved February 10, 2015, from http://www.bloomberg.com/news/articles/2011-11-10/italian-5-year-government-notes-drop-yield-rises-to-euro-era-record-7-80-

But this did not resolve the problem. The ECB was still not making any commitment to avoid the next crisis, which was therefore inevitable. Just a week earlier, the new ECB president, Mario Draghi (who took office on November 1, 2011), dismissed the idea of the Central Bank playing the role of lender of last resort for sovereign debt.[32]

Over the next few weeks, the pattern of the prior year and a half would be repeated, with the European authorities taking bigger steps to try to calm the markets as the crisis deepened. But in December 2011, a dynamic that had been mostly in the background started to become clearer: European governments' collective and individual efforts were not aimed so much at assuaging the markets, which had become increasingly difficult to satisfy through austerity commitments or even actual fiscal deficit reduction. Rather, they were trying to satisfy the ECB, in order to convince it to keep long-term interest rates from reaching meltdown levels.

It had already become clear to many observers that the ECB was the only source of funds that could actually resolve the crisis, as a minority of economists (including this one) had been saying all along. But on December 1, 2011, Draghi suggested that the Central Bank "could increase its support for the European economy if political leaders took more radical steps to enforce spending discipline among members."[33] Draghi even hinted at a new rationale for such intervention, which the ECB had previously maintained was a violation of the treaty that established its mandate: The ECB, he said, had a mandate to ensure price stability "in either direction." The

32. Mark Weisbrot, "Italy Pushed to the Brink by ECB Fiscal Orthodoxy." *The Guardian*, November 9, 2011, http://www.theguardian.com/commentisfree/cifamerica/2011/nov/09/italy-pushed-brink-ecb-fiscal-orthodoxy.

33. Jack Ewing, "Central Bank Chief Hints at Stepping Up Euro Support," *New York Times*, December 1, 2011, http://www.nytimes.com/2011/12/02/business/global/draghi-hints-again-at-rate-cut-in-europe.html?pagewanted=all.

idea was that a severe recession could push Europe into deflation—a possibility that at the time was rather remote—and the Bank had a mandate to prevent that. This was a rather transparent excuse for a 180-degree turnaround from the ECB's prior position on its legal mandate—but would it actually happen?

The statements were widely interpreted as an offer to bring down, and possibly keep down, the interest rates on Italian and Spanish bonds—the very actions that were needed to resolve the crisis. The reaction in the bond markets was large and immediate; within a day, Italian 10-year bond yields fell from well over 7 percent to under 6 percent.[34] Spanish bond yields also fell.[35] Why not buy Italian and Spanish bonds at these rates, if—as just a year ago was the conventional market wisdom—the risk of default was negligible?

The news was yet too good to be true. Draghi walked back from his remarks the next week, and Italian (and Spanish) bond yields shot back up, though not to peak levels.

The results were pretty clear for anyone who wanted to see. The ECB—the one institution with the power to end the crisis—quite literally and intentionally did not want to end it—not even with words, let alone deeds.

In other words, for the ECB and its allies, most importantly in the German government, the crisis was an opportunity: to force the weaker eurozone governments to institute "reforms" that their electorates would never vote for. And as much as the troika feared the possibility of a devastating financial crisis or a prolonged recession, they were even more averse to resolving the crisis and taking the pressure off the besieged governments.

---

34. Bloomberg, "Italy Generic Government 10Y Yield," n.d. Retrieved February 10, 2015, from http://www.bloomberg.com/quote/GBTPGR10:IND/chart.

35. Bloomberg, "Spain Generic Government 10Y Yield," n.d. Retrieved February 10, 2015, from http://www.bloomberg.com/quote/GSPG10YR:IND/chart.

As a result, there were more financial crises in 2012, including one in July that sent the yield on 10-year Spanish bonds to a new high of 7.6 percent.[36] Finally, on July 26, 2012, Draghi uttered the famous words that would put an end to the recurring crises of the euro:

> Within our mandate, the ECB is ready to do whatever it takes to preserve the euro. And believe me, it will be enough.[37]

And it was indeed enough, especially when the ECB followed up with a new program, called "Outright Monetary Transactions," a few weeks later. There were significant differences between this program and the Securities Market Program (SMP), noted above, that the ECB had used previously to stabilize sovereign bond yields. Most importantly, there was no limit on the amount of money that the ECB could deploy. Since the ECB can create euros, that was a pretty clear message to anyone betting on the collapse of the euro that "whatever it takes" was no empty threat. The prior SMP program was seen as limited and temporary; although it was used to resolve some of the crises described above, they kept coming back.

The ECB's new commitment in July and August 2012 was so widely believed that after more than two years, it had never been used. By finally making the commitment to do at least some of what a normal central bank (e.g., the US Fed or the Bank of England) does as a lender of last resort for sovereign debt, the ECB convinced the

36. Lucy Meakin and Emma Charlton, "Spanish Yield Reaches Euro-Era Record on Regional Concern," Bloomberg, July 23, 2012, http://www.bloomberg.com/news/2012-07-23/german-bonds-rise-on-debt-crisis-as-spanish-yield-reaches-record.html.

37. European Central Bank, "Verbatim of the Remarks Made by Mario Draghi," July 26, 2012, https://www.ecb.europa.eu/press/key/date/2012/html/sp120726.en.html.

financial markets that the euro would not break up—or at least, that it would not break up due to the kind of rising interest rates, self-reinforcing spiral that had happened repeatedly over the prior three years. There were still other risks that contributed to the spread that remained between Spanish or Italian bonds, on the one hand, and German bonds on the other. But the ECB's commitment got rid of most of the speculative risk, and thereafter kept Spanish and Italian bond yields within sustainable levels.

The ECB had, for all these years, the ability to resolve the acute crisis. But they refused to use it until July 2012. As argued above, this was mainly because the troika wanted to use the recurring crises to force unwanted political changes in the more vulnerable eurozone countries. So why did the ECB finally relent? It is difficult to say—there are a number of possible contributing factors. Perhaps Draghi and others got tired of the near-death experiences. Or perhaps they thought that they had squeezed most of what was possible in terms of "reforms" out of the vulnerable countries, and the rest could be gotten through loan conditionalities and reviews. The political climate had also changed, with the fall of many governments, including Sarkozy's in France, whose successor, François Hollande, was elected on an anti-austerity campaign. There were also some indications that the US government was lobbying the troika for stability, as the repeated euro-crisis and threat of a financial meltdown were seen by some in the Obama administration as a potential threat to the US president's re-election in November 2012.

Whatever the reasons for the policy turnabout, it worked. From that point on, the main threat to European recovery would come from fiscal austerity, without the threat of financial meltdown or the breakup of the euro playing a prominent role.

On the positive side, the fiscal consolidation, or budget tightening, was winding down: from about 1.5 percent of GDP in 2012, to 1.1 percent in 2013, to .035 percent in 2014. However, even the IMF's analysis in its July 2013 Article IV consultation was rather

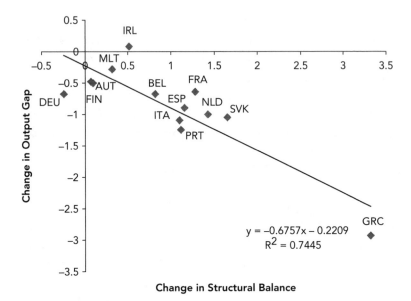

FIGURE 1.1 Euro Area Countries—Pro-cyclicality of Fiscal Policy, 2013 (Output Gap and Fiscal Impulse Changes from 2012)

Source: IMF, "Euro Area Policies: 2013 Article IV Consultation," July 25, 2013, http://www.imf.org/external/pubs/cat/longres.aspx?sk=40820.0.; and IMF, "World Economic Outlook, October 2014," http://www.imf.org/external/pubs/ft/weo/2014/02/weodata/index.aspx.

gloomy.[38] "Fiscal policies remain pro-cyclical with widening output gaps," the Fund noted—in other words, the budget tightening is pushing the eurozone farther from its potential output. The IMF recognized the clear relationship between the eurozone's austerity and its reduced growth and loss of potential GDP, as shown in Figure 1.1.

Furthermore, the Fund also recognized that after nearly four years of "internal devaluation," the economic strategy had not

38. IMF, "Euro Area Policies: 2013 Article IV Consultation," July 25, 2013, http://www.imf.org/external/pubs/cat/longres.aspx?sk=40820.0.

succeeded. The idea of an "internal devaluation" is that if you create enough mass unemployment and push wages down far enough, the economy can become more competitive due to lower labor costs. This allows exports to grow, and import-competing industries to also do better, improving the trade balance. Since exports add to economic growth and employment, and reduced imports do the same, the economy can recover in this scenario due to increasing net exports (exports minus imports). Normally this could be attempted through a devaluation of the currency. But the troika has only recently shown any intention of trying to push the euro's value down against external trading partners; and of course since it is a common currency, the more depressed economies within the currency union can't devalue against the others (e.g., Spain versus Germany). This leaves "internal devaluation" as the remaining hope for recovery for countries such as Spain, Greece, and Portugal. In other words, despite the negative impact of the fiscal austerity, the theory is that "internal devaluation" based on lower labor costs can drive recovery based on the growth of net exports.

But it took years to reach this point[39]—despite crushing levels of unemployment and mandated reductions in the social wage (e.g., pensions and healthcare). The Fund finds that from 2008 to 2012, there was "limited evidence of re-allocating resources from non-tradable to tradable sectors." In other words, even with some internal devaluation taking place, it wasn't nearly enough to have the hoped-for impact of increasing production or employment in the tradable goods' sector.

Given this policy failure, and with no major political forces presenting a strategy of exit from the euro (see Chapter 2), the

39. In June 2014, the IMF acknowledged that Greece had still not been able to increase its exports. See Weisbrot et al., "The Greek Economy: Which Way Forward?" Center for Economic and Policy Research, January 2015, http://www.cepr.net/index.php/publications/reports/the-greek-economy-which-way-forward.

eurozone economy's recovery has remained weak and uncertain. It could take many years to reach normal levels of employment. It will most likely depend on how fast the European authorities move away from the fiscal austerity that has kept the eurozone in recession for most of the past four years, as well as external forces (e.g., demand for exports) outside its control. And that, in turn, will depend on how much political resistance there is to continued stagnation and attacks on the living standards of the majority of eurozone residents.

The Troika's Political Agenda

The foregoing discussion provides evidence that Europe's "sovereign debt crisis," as it is so often described, has been badly misnamed, and that there was a political agenda that kept the ECB and its troika partners from ending the threat to the euro for most of three years. Indeed, it is hard to imagine otherwise, given that they could have avoided so much economic damage at the outset by simply resolving Greece's debt problems in early 2010—for a small fraction of the hundreds of billions of euros eventually spent (and lost by creditors), and allowing the eurozone to grow its way out of its budget deficits, as the United States did.[40] But for those who might find plausible the "austerian"[41] argument that the European authorities were actually just trying to put the eurozone

---

40. The Congressional Budget Office projected the US budget deficit at 2.8 percent of GDP for 2014. Of course there were much better alternative fiscal policies that would have restored full employment in the United States, and these, too, were feasible in Europe.

41. Paul Krugman coined this term to describe pro-austerity economists and policymakers. See, e.g., "Osborne and the Stooges," *New York Times*, December 19, 2013. http://www.nytimes.com/2013/12/20/opinion/krugman-osborne-and-the-stooges.html?hp&rref=opinion.

on a sustainable debt trajectory, there is another paper trail that reveals their political agenda.

The IMF conducts regular consultations with member governments and produces a report that includes recommendations on major policy issues, including fiscal, monetary, and exchange rate policy; healthcare and pensions; labor market policy (including wages, unemployment compensation, and employment protections); and numerous other policy issues. These are called "Article IV" consultations because it was under this part of the IMF's original Articles of Agreement that the Fund's surveillance duties (and concomitant obligations of the member countries) were specified.

A review of Article IV reports for European Union countries for the years 2008–2011—these four years include the world financial crisis, recession, and recovery—reveals a remarkably consistent and disturbing pattern.[42] This review covers 67 agreements with 27 countries. In all of the countries, the IMF recommends fiscal consolidation. Spending cuts in the public sector are generally favored over tax increases; these include reducing public employment and the rate of growth of wages for government workers, as well as reduced social spending.

The IMF's recommendations were generally not good for labor. Centralized collective bargaining was to be discouraged, while measures that increase labor supply were recommended. These included lowering the age of retirement, reducing eligibility for benefits such as disability payments and unemployment insurance. The desire to increase labor force participation did not seem to be related to actual participation rates; an increase was deemed appropriate even for countries with some of the highest labor force

---

42. For more details see Mark Weisbrot and Helene Jorgensen, "Macroeconomic Policy Advice and the Article IV Consultations: A European Union Case Study." Center for Economic and Policy Research, January 2013. http://www.cepr.net/index.php/publications/reports/macroeconomic-policy-advice-and-the-article-iv-consultations.

participation rates in Europe, including Austria, Denmark, and the Netherlands. The rate of unemployment didn't seem to matter either. In all of the countries for which the IMF made recommendations for labor—about half of the 27 countries—the advice went in the same direction.

The same is true for healthcare, which the IMF tended to see as a place for fiscal consolidation. In 14 of the 15 countries for which it made recommendations for healthcare, the IMF counseled spending cuts. For pensions, even more: 22 countries with recommended cuts.

On the other hand, there were very few recommendations for measures to reduce poverty. Although some northern European countries had been more successful than the European average in achieving high levels of employment and other social and even fiscal indicators, the IMF didn't seem interested in whether they had any "best practices" that might be relevant to other countries.

The likely impact of this pattern of recommendations, to the extent that they are followed, is pretty clear. It is a society with less bargaining power for labor and lower wages, more inequality and poverty, and a smaller government and social safety net. The fiscal consolidation would also generally tend to reduce growth and employment. These are not outcomes that the residents of these countries would generally vote for.

Perhaps most tellingly, European Article IV consultations also contained further evidence that the Fund—like its troika partners—saw the crisis as an opportunity to get the policy changes it had always wanted: "historical experience indicates that successful fiscal consolidations were often launched in the midst of economic downturns or the early stages of recovery," was the refrain from a 2009 Article IV consultation with France.[43] Or perhaps

43. IMF, "France: 2009 Article IV Consultation—Staff Report; Public Information Notice on the Executive Board Discussion; and Statement by the Executive Director for France." (Washington, DC: International Monetary Fund, 2009), p. 20.

more clearly, "empirical evidence also suggests that recoveries from economic crises often serve as an opportunity for reform," from a 2010 consultation with Spain.[44]

This is an opportunity, indeed, for the social engineers who want changes that could never be won at the ballot box. But it is a brutal assault from the viewpoint of the victims.

In Naomi Klein's comprehensive work, *The Shock Doctrine*, she provides detailed historical examples of how various authorities have taken advantage of crises to remake economies and societies, bringing them more into line with a neoliberal vision.[45] Much of the eurozone's recent history would fit well within her thesis.

These Article IV papers are the most comprehensive and damning evidence of the political agenda behind the prolongation and abuse of Europe's misnamed "sovereign debt crisis." Although the recommendations come from the IMF, the Fund is not an independent entity. It has an Executive Board made up of representatives from the member countries; and although the US Treasury Department may be the decider of IMF policy for many developing countries, the European governments make the decisions for Europe, in coordination with the IMF's troika partners, the European Commission and the ECB. So the policies elaborated in the Article IV reports for European or eurozone countries represent, more or less, the same balance of forces as those within the troika. Of course some governments (e.g., Germany) are more equal than others. The IMF papers detail the agenda of Europe's decision-makers, and they have accomplished quite a bit of it over the past five years.

---

44. IMF, "Spain: 2010 Article IV Consultation—Staff Statement; Staff Supplement; Staff Report; Statement by the Executive Director for Spain; and Public Information Notice on the Executive Board Discussion" (Washington, DC: International Monetary Fund, 2010), p. 13.

45. Naomi Klein, *The Shock Doctrine* (New York: Metropolitan Books/Henry Holt, 2007).

Structural Problems of the European Monetary Union

Ever since the troubles of the eurozone began to gather steam, as reported in the international press in 2010, a number of economists and commentators cast doubt on whether the euro was sustainable as a common currency for the member countries. Some of these observers, dubbed "euroskeptics," had made this argument from the beginning of the monetary union a decade earlier. These problems are important, but are they the main cause of the eurozone's depressed economy over the past six years, and its still rather bleak prospects going forward?

The main economic argument of the euroskeptics revolves around the productivity differences between the richer and the less competitive countries in the monetary union. If there are large differences in productivity relative to wages in the member countries, then the countries with higher productivity relative to wages[46] will tend to run trade (and current account) surpluses with the others. If the countries have different currencies, the country that is running a trade deficit would normally expect its currency to depreciate, thus making its exports cheaper and its imports more expensive. This would generally be expected to improve its trade balance.[47] But with a common currency, this adjustment cannot take place through currency depreciation. For these reasons, it is argued, Spain ran current account deficits averaging about 5 percent of GDP from 1999 to 2007, while Germany ran current account surpluses.

46. Another way of saying this is that these countries have lower unit labor costs.

47. Technically, this depends on the elasticities of supply and demand for the country's imports and exports—i.e., how much these quantities change with price. We are assuming here that these are, at least over time, sufficient to reduce the trade deficit when the currency depreciates.

The current account story was similar for Portugal and Ireland. Germany relied heavily on exports to other European countries for its growth during the expansion of 2002–2007. It didn't help that Germany increased its competitiveness by keeping wage growth to a minimum.[48] Clearly these differences in productivity relative to wages are a structural problem for the eurozone. But is it inherently fatal to the monetary union? And is this why the eurozone crisis has been so persistent and damaging in the past five years? To attempt to answer these questions, it is necessary to think about the alternatives—both within and outside the monetary union.

If countries such as Spain and Greece were not in the eurozone, they could have increased their competitiveness through currency depreciation. But what does it mean to have a persistent current account deficit when an economy (in its private and public sectors) is borrowing in a common currency? The big borrowing in the run-up to the crisis was taking place in the private sector. In other words, there was a good deal of (mostly private) over-borrowing from other countries—along with bubble growth, over-leveraged banks, and the other financial excesses associated with the expansion prior to the 2008–2009 crisis and world recession. But the United States and the United Kingdom, with their own currencies and not members of any currency union, also had the same set of problems. These were massive in the United States, with an $8 trillion housing bubble that caused the Great Recession when it burst. In the eurozone, of course, the common currency contributed to the bubble growth and over-borrowing in the private sector of the weaker eurozone economies by allowing for cross-border borrowing at low interest rates. The PIIGS countries could borrow at rates similar to France and Germany,

---

48. Out of 23 European countries for which data are available, Germany had the second slowest increase in hourly labor costs from 2002 to 2007. See Eurostat, "Hourly Labour Costs." Retrieved May 2014 from http://epp.eurostat.ec.europa.eu/portal/page/portal/labour_market/labour_costs/database.

because creditors perceived the country risk to be basically the same throughout the common currency area. They were to find out later that this assumption was wrong. There were important differences between the run-up to the crisis in the eurozone and in the United States, some of them due to the structural problems that were specific to the eurozone.

But the more important difference between what happened to the eurozone and the United States or the United Kingdom was the eurozone's failed macroeconomic policies after the crash. The European authorities—especially the ECB—were not willing to take the necessary measures to prevent the economy from lapsing into a second recession—on the contrary, they brought it on. As noted above, if these authorities had been willing to deal with the Greek debt early on—the one economy, which is quite small, that actually did have something of a public debt problem—and to use quantitative easing as necessary to keep borrowing costs in the weaker economies from rising, the prolonged financial crisis that followed the 2008–2009 recession in Europe could also have been avoided (as it was in the US).

Of course there are other ways to deal with the productivity imbalances that the eurozone started out with initially. The countries with lower productivity could have industrial policies that promote a higher rate of investment and productivity growth. This "upward harmonization" could be an explicit and planned goal of the monetary union, just as the prior integration through trade included funds for the poorer countries in order to prevent a "race to the bottom." Also, Germany could have a higher rate of inflation and/or wage growth than its lower-productivity trading partners—this would increase the relative competitiveness of the latter.

Whether it would have been politically feasible, or indeed worth the effort, to fix the eurozone in these ways is another question. The main point here is that these structural problems could have been addressed over the coming years, in a growing regional economy, if not for the macroeconomic policy blunders that followed the world recession. That is what so many of the "experts" and commentators seem to have missed. Some of the euroskeptics, who blame Europe's six years of crisis and recession on the structural imbalances in the eurozone, are missing the main point. Even if they are correct, it is somewhat like saying of someone who is shot and killed that he would have died eventually anyway. It's true, but not all that relevant to the murder investigation.

The same is true for the other much-discussed structural flaw in the eurozone—the lack of a mechanism for a common fiscal policy. Of course fiscal policy was not the cause of the crisis; as we have seen, it was not brought on by over-borrowing in the public sector. But the public sector debts of the weaker economies expanded as a result of crisis and recession (as they did in the US). Therefore something had to be done to prevent the vicious spiral of rising borrowing costs and explosive sovereign debt. And so the problem was constructed as one in which the richer countries did not want to backstop the debts of the weaker economies. But as we have seen, this problem was also resolvable with the appropriate monetary policy, which—if used—would have allowed the eurozone countries to grow their way out of their debt problems, instead of exacerbating them (see Chapter 2). That macroeconomic policy itself was much more important than any lack of coordination was driven home again in December 2011, when the European governments met and agreed—with the exception of the United Kingdom—to move toward a common fiscal policy. The measures that they approved, if they are actually implemented, would only worsen the long-term problems of the eurozone. Better to have no coordination of fiscal policy, than to coordinate and enforce austerity, as the fiscal pact of March 2012 committed these governments to doing.

Perhaps one of the biggest structural problems in the eurozone is the one that has been the least noticed: the neoliberal bias—in some cases quite extreme—that is built into its framework. The ECB is the most glaring example. Unlike the US Federal Reserve, which is at least legally supposed to be concerned about employment as well as inflation, the ECB has "price stability" as its dominant mandate.

Jean-Claude Trichet, the former president of the ECB, made this clear on September 8, 2011. A question about Germany leaving the euro provoked an uncharacteristically angry response from him at a press conference:

> We were called to deliver price stability! . . . We have delivered price stability over the first 12–13 years of the euro! Impeccably! I would like very much to hear some congratulations for this institution, which has delivered price stability in Germany over almost 13 years, at [an annual inflation rate of] approximately 1.55%. . . . This figure is better than any ever obtained in this country over a period of 13 years in the past 50 years.
>
> Our independence is inflexible . . . let me remind you that we are in the worst crisis since the Second World War. We are doing our job and it is not an easy one![49]

It indeed isn't an easy job, but the more important question is whether this is the job that a central bank should do. Is it really worth mass unemployment and prolonging "the worst crisis since the Second World War" in order to keep inflation at 2 percent or less?

The 2 percent inflation target also made it more difficult to resolve the imbalance of competitiveness between the member

---

49. European Central Bank, "Introductory Statement to the Press Conference (with Q&A)," September 8, 2011, http://www.ecb.europa.eu/press/pressconf/2011/html/is110908.en.html.

countries. As noted above, one way to resolve this imbalance would involve Germany running a higher rate of inflation than Spain and the less competitive eurozone economies. But if Germany's inflation is at 2 percent or less, this is extremely difficult—it may even require deflation in the weaker economies. This is not only difficult and painful to achieve, but in a situation of over-indebtedness, reducing inflation means increasing the real burden of the debt, both public and private. So Trichet really didn't have much to brag about.

The ECB's neoliberal bias was built into the structure of the monetary union. Unlike the Federal Reserve, which is able to backstop and even finance the United States' sovereign debt, the rules of the ECB were written to prevent such "lender of last resort" capacity for the euro governments. As the sovereign debt problems began to mount in early 2010, the ECB—after it created a crisis by refusing to do so—began to interpret these rules as allowing it to buy sovereign debt on the secondary market. The idea here is that the Central Bank would not be "monetizing" the debt of the eurozone countries, that is, financing their debt issues by creating money. And as we have seen, it continued for years to maintain that saving countries from being driven into a vicious spiral of exponentially rising debt and interest rates was not its job. In taking such a position, the ECB could cite the rules that created the monetary union. These rules—which were increasingly stretched as crisis and recession unfolded—were part of what can now be seen as a terribly destructive, even wantonly extremist, neoliberal bias.

In addition to the ECB and its mandate, there were other neoliberal pillars built into the eurozone. The Maastricht Treaty of 1991 required member governments to keep their annual budget deficits below 3 percent of GDP, and their public debt below 60 percent. There is no economic rationale for such requirements. During the recession of 2009, the US budget deficit reached

10 percent of GDP, and remained at nearly 9 percent of GDP in 2011.[50] If the US government had been held to such requirements, it could have ended up like Europe or possibly worse. The eurozone economies mostly did not adhere to this requirement either, but it remained a goal and indeed has been the target—with varying years to meet it—in the austerity programs imposed on the weaker eurozone economies. The 60 percent of GDP debt limit was also honored mostly in the breach, with the average eurozone economy having a gross public debt of 70 percent of GDP in 2010. But why should such a limit be imposed in any case? It is not necessarily a meaningful measure; the United States, for example, had a gross federal public debt of about 104 percent of GDP for 2013,[51] but its net interest burden on the debt was just 1.3 percent of GDP. This latter measure is what matters, and it is about as low as it has been in the post–World-War II era—despite all the fanciful rhetoric about "unsustainable debt" that Americans hear from the deficit hawks.

These built-in biases of the monetary union are so severe that they raise serious questions about the nature of the eurozone project itself. Most of the European left, including its broad base of social democrats, supported the euro for the same reasons they supported the consolidation and expansion of the European Union itself. The two were seen as part of a progressive project of a "social Europe."

But economic and even political integration for its own sake is not necessarily good policy. If the economic principles and policymaking built into the structure of a multilateral institution are

50. White House Office of Management and Budget, "Historical Tables: Table 1.2—Summary of Receipts, Outlays, and Surpluses or Deficits (-) as Percentages of GDP: 1930–2019." Retrieved May 2014 from http://www.whitehouse.gov/sites/default/files/omb/budget/fy2015/assets/hist01z2.xls.

51. IMF, "World Economic Outlook April 2014," April 2014, http://www.imf.org/external/pubs/ft/weo/2014/01/weodata/index.aspx.

such that they reduce the living standards, democratic rights, and input of the vast majority of people, then they cannot truthfully be considered a step forward. The euro has turned out to be a tragic, costly mistake for the vast majority of Europeans, not only the tens of millions who have borne the pain of unemployment, but also those who have suffered and will continue to suffer from the regressive social and economic changes that the troika and its allies have been able to engineer.

2

This Time Could Be Different

The Aftermath of Financial Crises

In the previous chapter we looked at how incompetent and politically driven economic policymaking drove Europe into prolonged recession and high unemployment. The financial crises and fear of a meltdown slowed world economic growth considerably. In October 2010, the International Monetary Fund (IMF) projected 4.6 percent growth for the global economy in 2013;[1] it ended up being just 3 percent.[2] This difference may not seem like much, but in terms of lost output it is more than $800 billion, and it is not only in the rich countries. This meant that tens of millions of people worldwide were pushed into poverty and unemployment, including in developing countries—despite the fact that the big policy mistakes were being made in Europe. To most of the people who write about these issues, and most of the media, there was not much that could have been done differently, that would have assured a speedy and robust recovery. But they are wrong.

1. IMF, "World Economic Outlook, October 2010," October 2010. Retrieved November 27, 2013, from http://www.imf.org/external/pubs/ft/weo/2010/02/weodata/index.aspx.

2. IMF, "World Economic Outlook, April 2014," April 2014. Retrieved May 9, 2014, from http://www.imf.org/external/pubs/ft/weo/2014/01/weodata/index.aspx.

One of the more common justifications for the slow recovery and prolonged unemployment that has followed the Great Recession—to varying degrees in both the United States and Europe—is that this is an inevitable result of recessions brought about by financial crises. This argument seems to have been given added weight by economists Carmen Reinhart and Kenneth Rogoff.[3]

While there is some debate over whether recessions caused by financial crises really do have more prolonged recovery periods,[4] such a historical relationship—if it exists—does not necessarily determine our destiny. It may be, for example, that governments historically have pursued the wrong policies in the aftermath of such crises. When we consider the power of financial interests in policymaking, as well as the incompetence of many decision-makers and the mythology in which the public debate—such as it exists in democratic societies—is immersed, this is not so far-fetched an idea. Indeed, the eurozone from 2009 to 2015—as we have just seen—provides a stellar example of unnecessary stagnation in the aftermath of such a recession. To a lesser extent, so does the United States, where the federal government deployed a stimulus package that was—after subtracting the fiscal tightening of the state and local governments—about one-eighth of what was needed just to replace the private demand lost from the bursting of America's $8 trillion real estate bubble.[5]

3. See Carmen M. Reinhart and Kenneth Rogoff, "The Aftermath of Financial Crises," *American Economic Review* 99 (2009): 466–472. The idea is also present, although not emphasized, in Reinhart and Rogoff's book *This Time Is Different: Eight Centuries of Financial Folly* (Princeton, NJ: Princeton University Press, 2009).

4. See, e.g., Greg Howard, Robert Martin, and Beth Anne Wilson, *Are Recoveries from Banking and Financial Crises Really So Different?* (Washington, DC: Federal Reserve Board, 2011).

5. See Dean Baker, *The End of Loser Liberalism: Making Markets Progressive* (Washington, DC: Center for Economic and Policy Research, 2011), p. 20.

There is also a compelling counterexample that—if the actual events were widely known—would lay to rest this myth about the inevitability of prolonged punishment following financial crises. This is the example of Argentina in the aftermath of its severe financial crisis of 2001–2002. As we shall see, the Argentine case is quite relevant to the present situation of Greece and perhaps other over-indebted countries that are faced with prolonged recession, stagnation, unemployment, and intolerable conditions imposed by creditors.

If ever a country was devastated by a financial crisis, and indeed a "systemic banking crisis," Argentina fits that description. Yet its economic recovery was quite rapid and robust, with the economy growing by 63 percent in the six years following its recession—the fastest growth in the hemisphere. More than 11 million people (in a country of 38 million) were pulled out of poverty, and the economy reached its pre-recession level of GDP in less than three years.[6] How did this happen? The overwhelmingly most important ingredient was that the government, beginning in 2002, was committed to restoring growth and employment. This commitment turned out to be serious, and involved a willingness to do whatever was necessary in terms of economic policy—without regard to powerful interest groups—to make sure that it was fulfilled.

Of course Argentina needed a new government in order to do that, and it got one when all hell broke loose at the end of 2001. In fact, the country went through five presidents in two weeks. This was a serious economic crisis, much more severe than what afflicted Europe and the United States during the Great Recession and its aftermath.

---

6. ECLAC, CEPALSTAT Database, United Nations Economic Commission for Latin American and the Caribbean, n.d. Retrieved February 7, 2015, from http://estadisticas.cepal.org/cepalstat/WEB_CEPALSTAT/estadisticasIndicadores.asp?idioma=i.

Beginning in mid-1998, the Argentine economy had lapsed into a recession that would become the worst that the country had ever experienced, and one of the worst worldwide in the twentieth century. It lasted four years, and before it was over, the unemployment rate passed 22 percent, and the official poverty rate soared from 18.2 to 42.3 percent, in a country whose living standards had recently been ranked among the highest in Latin America. Millions of middle-class Argentines sank into poverty, and there were press reports of increasing hunger and malnutrition among children, with people hunting down cats, dogs, rats, and horses for food.[7]

As in the current downturn in the eurozone countries, Argentina's misery during the recession was greatly exacerbated by badly devised, pro-cyclical macroeconomic policies. Argentina's exchange rate had been pegged to the US dollar since 1991, and although the peg was initially successful in taming high inflation, it overstayed its welcome. The Argentine peso became increasingly overvalued over the next few years. In this sense it was similar to the weaker eurozone economies such as Greece, Spain, or Portugal, for whom the euro was (and remains) an overvalued currency. The overvalued peso took its toll on Argentina's manufacturing and trade, but beginning with the Mexican peso crisis of 1995–1996, there was a bigger problem: creditors began to worry about a devaluation. These fears multiplied rapidly with the Asian financial crisis, which began in 1997 and, prior to the Great Recession, was considered one of the worst financial crises of the post–World War II era. Currencies collapsed in Indonesia, South Korea, and other hard-hit Asian countries. And then financial contagion, often driven by little more than herd behavior in international financial

---

7. See, for example: Cristian Alarcón, "Caballo y perro, parte del menú habitual en una zona de Paraná," *Página/12*, May 16, 2002; Cristian Alarcón, "Los chicos del país del hambre," *Página/12*, May 20, 2002; Alejandra Dandan, "Quilmes, a pocos kilómetros de la Rosada," *Página/12*, June 6, 2002; Anthony Faiola, "Despair in Once Proud Argentina," *Washington Post*, August 6, 2002, A01.

markets, spread like a virus to other countries. The Russian ruble and Brazilian real, both pegged to the dollar, crashed in 1998.

Argentina clearly needed to devalue, but the authorities stuck to the peg and therefore committed to an "internal devaluation" of the type that is now being attempted in the weaker eurozone economies. This meant rising interest rates on the country's debt and, under the direction of the IMF, budget tightening as well. Through four years of devastating recession, the IMF stuck to the view that "[f]ailures in fiscal policy constitute the root cause of the current crisis."[8] That statement came from Anoop Singh, the IMF's director for Special Operations, in Buenos Aires, in April 2002, after Argentina had already lost 22 percent of its national income in a horribly failed experiment.

But the Fund was sticking to its fundamentals.

Sound familiar? How many times have we heard statements from the European authorities that "fiscal consolidation" was the key to resolving the crisis in the eurozone? But it was no truer in Argentina in 1998–2002 than it is in the eurozone today. The Argentine authorities cut spending, and inflation fell into negative territory, but the recession continued to deepen with no end in sight. The economy had become trapped in a downward spiral: rising interest rates increased foreign debt service and therefore the current account deficit, capital flight increased as investors feared devaluation, and both of these trends fed on each other. And the government piled up debt by borrowing from the IMF in order to maintain the fixed exchange rate. The tightening of fiscal and monetary policy deepened the recession and spurred the accumulation of an unsustainable debt burden.

It all collapsed in December 2001 as the government was forced into default on its debt. At the time it was the largest sovereign

---

8. IMF, "Introductory Remarks on the Role of the IMF Mission in Argentina," Press briefing, Buenos Aires, April 10, 2002. Retrieved December 9, 2013, from http://www.imf.org/external/np/tr/2002/tr020410.htm.

debt default in history, about $100 billion. A few weeks later, the pegged exchange rate was abandoned, and the peso—which for a decade had been worth one American dollar—fell to as low as 25 cents.[9]

The government had to freeze depositors' accounts while it figured out how to deal with all the people and businesses who had income in pesos but had borrowed in dollars that were now three to four times more expensive. The economy went into free fall, bankruptcies soared, and unemployment and poverty rose sharply from already high levels.

Here was a country that could not borrow from anywhere, not even the IMF or other multilateral lenders, and its economy was collapsing. Forecasts of doom and gloom and hell on earth dominated the business press. After nearly four years of recession, the consensus was that Argentina's troubles were just beginning. It was assumed that Argentina would be punished severely—and for a long time—for this massive default on its sovereign debt.

The *Washington Post*'s reporting summed up the prevailing view as of May 3, 2002:

> More frightening to many financial experts and citizens here is the growing sense that Argentina faces a convergence of problems that appears to defy solution. The greatest minds in international economics disagree on what medicine to prescribe. . . .
>
> "I don't say this lightly: The situation in Argentina is hopeless," said Bruno Boccara, director of Latin America sovereign ratings at Standard & Poor's Corp. in New York. "We have never seen a financial crisis like this anywhere,

---

9. Banco Central de la República de Argentina, "Mercado de Cambio—Cotizaciones Cierre Vendedor: Peso," n.d. Retrieved September 27, 2013, from http://www.bcra.gov.ar/index.htm.

not where the problems were so complex and ran so deep. Argentina just seems to be falling apart."[10]

As it turns out, the prevailing assessment was wrong. In fact, as those paragraphs went to press, Argentina was just entering a remarkable economic recovery.

Figure 2.1 shows Argentina's real, seasonally adjusted, GDP. To be sure, the financial crisis resulting from the default and devaluation had taken a toll, with GDP falling by nearly 5 percent in the first quarter of 2002. But it was just one quarter; then the recovery began. The economy passed its pre-recession level of output in just three and a half years, and in 5 years it passed its trend level. Although Argentina had a brief downturn as the world economy slipped into recession in 2009, it recovered quickly, and its real growth over 11 years since recovery began in 2002 has been around 100 percent.[11] Poverty and extreme poverty fell by two-thirds over this period,[12] and employment hit record levels in 2010.[13] And it

10. Anthony Faiola, "Growing Crisis Leaves Argentines Feeling Helpless," *Washington Post*, May 3, 2002, A01.

11. In January 2014, the Argentine government announced a new consumer price index, replacing one that most economists believed had seriously underestimated inflation. In May 2014, the government revised downward its estimates of GDP growth for 2004–2013; the above numbers are based on the revised estimates. The chart was completed using the prior quarterly GDP series until 2003 and then imputing the rest of the series from the recently released quarterly growth rates for 2004–2013. There are some private estimates that would show somewhat lower cumulative growth, but they do not significantly change the overall picture.

12. This is based on independent estimates of inflation, not the official inflation rate. The official estimates, as of this writing, show considerably larger declines in poverty.

13. Mario Damill, Roberto Frenkel, and Roxana Maurizio, "Macroeconomic Policy for Full and Productive Employment and Decent Work for All," International Labour Organization, Employment Working Paper No. 109, 2011, p. 48. Retrieved December 2, 2013, from http://www.ilo.org/employment/Whatwedo/Publications/working-papers/WCMS_173147/lang--en/index.htm.

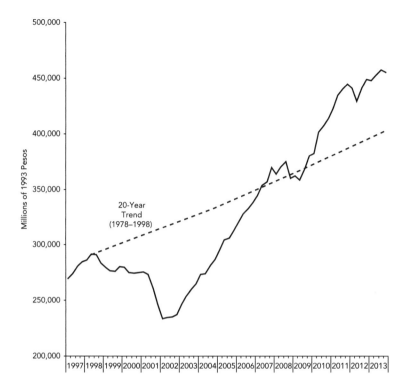

FIGURE 2.1 Argentina: Seasonally Adjusted Quarterly GDP

Source: International Monetary Fund, "International Financial Statistics." Online database; Instituto Nacional de Estadística y Censos, "Oferta y Demanda Globales: Series Desestacionalizadas," 2011. Ministerio de Economía y Finanzas Públicas: Online database, http://www.indec.gov. ar/nuevaweb/cuadros/17/cuadro12.xls; Instituto Nacional de Estadística y Censos, "Producto Interno Bruto a Precio de Mercado," Ministerio de Economía y Finanzas Públicas: Online database, http://200.51.91.244/cnarg/ agregados.php. Author's calculations.

was not only the quantity but the quality of jobs that increased. Formal sector jobs, those covered by social security, rose 37.6 percent between the fourth quarter of 2003 and the second quarter of 2012, while informal employment actually fell in absolute terms;

the percentage of workers underemployed dropped from 18.3 percent to 9.4 percent over the same time period.[14]

It took years of rapid growth before the international authorities and media would acknowledge that Argentina had engineered a very successful recovery—and many are still praying for the inevitable collapse that they have been predicting for the past decade.[15] In the fall of 2002, when the recovery was already well underway for half a year, the IMF projected 1 percent growth for the following year. It came in at 8 percent. The Fund would continue to make huge forecasting errors for the next three years.[16]

Eleven years is a long time to wait for an experiment you didn't like to disintegrate into failure. A more rational approach would be to think about what the authorities might have done correctly. But only a handful of economists or journalists have attempted that. Most have tried to dismiss Argentina's growth spurt as a "commodities boom," driven by rising prices for the countries' exports of primary products, especially soybeans. But the facts tell a different story. In Argentina's rapid economic recovery from 2002 to 2008, total exports account for just 12 percent of real GDP growth. And agricultural exports account for only about half of these exports.[17]

14. Ministerio de Trabajo, Empleo y Seguridad Social, "Mercado de Trabajo," 2014. Retrieved May 8, 2014, from http://www.trabajo.gob.ar/left/estadisticas/bel/index.asp. Informal employment is reported as "Empleo No Registrado" by the Ministry, defined as workers not covered by Social Security.

15. See, for example, Michael Boskin, "Why Does Chile Prosper While Neighbouring Argentina Flounders?" *The Guardian*, November 22, 2013. Retrieved December 9, 2013, from http://www.theguardian.com/business/economics-blog/2013/nov/22/chile-prosper-argentina-flounders.

16. David Rosnick and Mark Weisbrot, "Political Forecasting? The IMF's Flawed Growth Projections for Argentina and Venezuela," Center for Economic and Policy Research, 2007. Retrieved December 2, 2013, from http://www.cepr.net/index.php/publications/reports/political-forecasting-the-imfs-flawed-growth-projections-for-argentina-and-venezuela.

17. See Mark Weisbrot, Rebecca Ray, Juan Montecino, and Sara Kozameh, "The Argentine Success Story and Its Implications," Center for Economic and Policy

Of course, if prices for agricultural exports are rising, this can also boost growth. But even if we look at Argentina's agricultural exports in dollar terms, they clearly did not lead the country's growth during the expansion.[18] As a percentage of GDP, they did not even increase, instead dropping slightly from 5 percent to 4.7 percent.[19] So this was not a "commodities boom" in any meaningful sense. It was not even an export-led recovery by any stretch of the imagination. The devaluation did make imports more expensive, and thereby stimulated domestic production to substitute for imports, but this was not the major cause of the recovery, either.

The Argentine economy also got a boost from the return of billions of dollars that had fled the country during the recession and financial crisis, by those fearing devaluation. Now that assets were much cheaper in dollar terms, a lot of this money came back into the country.[20]

Unfortunately, most of the people who write about the Argentine recovery, especially in the context of the troubled eurozone economies, are too eager to dismiss Argentina's recovery as an export-led "commodities boom." This prevents the world from learning from a very positive example. No country would want to go through the harrowing experience that Argentina faced after its default and devaluation, if it had better options. But as we shall see, Argentina's rapid, sustained, and robust recovery compares quite

Research, 2011. Retrieved December 2, 2013, from http://www.cepr.net/documents/publications/argentina-success-2011-10.pdf.

18. This is true even if we were to include manufactured goods that are based on primary products, such as soybean oil, in this analysis. For more detail, see ibid., p. 6.

19. Ibid, p. 6.

20. See Roberto Frenkel and Martín Repetti, "Argentina's Monetary and Exchange Rate Policies after the Convertibility Regime Collapse," Center for Economic and Policy Research (CEPR) and Political Economy Research Institute (PERI), 2007. Retrieved April 25, 2014, from http://www.cepr.net/index.php?option=com_content&view=article&id=1121.

favorably with what the IMF is currently projecting for countries such as Greece or Spain.

The Argentines also faced enormous obstacles to their recovery. Most important, they didn't get any assistance from multilateral lenders—the IMF, World Bank, and Inter-American Development Bank. These institutions, led by the IMF, actually drained a net $4 billion out of Argentina during 2002, as the country was struggling to recover. This sum was quite large—it amounted to about 4 percent of Argentina's GDP at the time. As will be discussed in Chapter 4, these organizations, acting on behalf of international creditors, were trying to pressure the Argentine government to pay more of its defaulted debt to foreign lenders.

If it was not due to a "commodities boom," how did Argentina's economy recover so quickly and effectively? The recovery was led overwhelmingly by domestic consumption and investment. The biggest change in policy was that the government abandoned the pro-cyclical policies—fiscal tightening and high interest rates—that had kept the economy from recovering. In other words, the devaluation and default freed the Argentine government to abandon policies that were shrinking the economy, and to substitute pro-growth macroeconomic policies.

Of course, the devaluation itself did have some positive impact, as noted above. The overvalued exchange rate had previously hurt domestic production and exports, thereby making recovery even more difficult.

And the debt was a major obstacle to recovery. Argentina had to get rid of most of its debt burden if it were to ever to afford a fiscal policy that would allow it to grow. If the country were forced to run big primary budget surpluses[21] in order to satisfy its creditors, the federal government would have had to slow the economy for years,

---

21. A primary surplus is the surplus of the budget (revenues minus expenditures), not counting interest payments on the debt.

as is currently happening in the eurozone. Hence we observe the huge default and the hard line that Argentina took with its foreign creditors until they finally reached a debt-restructuring agreement with creditors that held 76 percent of the debt in 2005.[22]

Any country that does not have a "hard currency" as its own currency—as the United States has, for example—faces a foreign exchange constraint that is the ultimate limit on policy. A government can create domestic currency as necessary, and—so long as it does not feed an accelerating inflation—use it to pay its domestic obligations or finance its budget. But it must have enough foreign exchange to finance its imports. And in some cases, it must also have enough reserves to convince the public not to make a panicked rush for the exits, seeking to escape from a domestic currency that they believe might rapidly lose value. If foreign reserves run too low, there is the possibility of a serious balance of payments crisis. Argentina also needed enough dollars to intervene in the foreign exchange markets in order to stabilize its currency after the collapse of the fixed exchange rate.

For this reason, the foreign exchange controls implemented during the crisis and early recovery were very important. Exporters with revenues of more than $1 million had to turn these revenues over to the central bank. They were also taxed on their exports, so that the government was able to capture some of the windfall from the devaluation (since exporters' dollar earnings were now worth three times as many pesos). Together with a tax on financial transactions, something that many in Europe and the United States are fighting for today, these unorthodox sources of tax revenue added about 2.7 percentage points of GDP to government receipts.

This is why the devaluation was so important. The devaluation—combined with what economists call "heterodox"

---

22. A. Dhillon, J. García Fronti, S. Ghosal, and M. Miller, "Bargaining and Sustainability: The Argentine Debt Swap of 2005," CSGR Working Paper No. 189/06, 2005, p. 29.

government policies—helped the government avoid a balance of payments crisis at a time when Argentina was cut off from borrowing in international financial markets, and was also under unprecedented pressure to sacrifice growth for the benefit of foreign creditors.

The Central Bank, freed from outside interference, also adopted an unorthodox policy of targeting a "stable and competitive real exchange rate." The standard orthodoxy, in most of the world today, is for central banks to target a certain rate of inflation. By choosing instead to keep the real (inflation-adjusted) exchange rate stable and competitive—that is, not allowing the real value of the peso to rise too high or fluctuate too widely—Argentina's central bank allowed domestic industry to compete more effectively against imports and also in world markets.

Argentina did face rising inflation after 2007, which eventually reached levels of more than 30 percent. This was partly because the government was trying to avoid creating high levels of unemployment in order to reduce inflation, as most governments do when they consider inflation to be too high. Of course, it must be remembered that inflation itself does not determine what happens to the living standards of most people. If inflation is 20 percent but your income is growing at 28 percent, then you are much better off than if inflation is 2 percent but your income is growing by just 1 or 2 percent, or not at all. It is real—inflation-adjusted—income and, often more important, employment that matters to most people.

The Argentine economy has run into some trouble in recent years for a number of reasons, including the world financial crisis and recession of 2009. Inflation has also been a problem because it made the country's real exchange rate overvalued. These problems have led the business press to once again predict, some with long-awaited and hopeful anticipation, that economic collapse is near.

This outcome is unlikely. But however the government manages its current challenges, nothing can negate the remarkable success that Argentina had for years after it defaulted on its debt, left its fixed exchange rate, sent the IMF packing, and adopted the necessary policies for its recovery. That is the relevant experience for any government that is trapped in a macroeconomic policy regime that promises many years of intolerable unemployment and economic stagnation.

It should be said that it took some extraordinary courage and indeed some stubbornness on the part of Argentine officials to fight for the changes that were necessary to turn the country around. These leaders, including the late Néstor Kirchner (who was president from 2003 to 2007), had to struggle against prevailing conventional wisdom, including that of the economics profession—much as Franklin D. Roosevelt found himself doing during the United States' Great Depression (which had a comparable loss of output from 1929 to 1933). However, Kirchner had another layer of adversaries on top of that—the foreign creditors led by the IMF—who threatened to derail his efforts. The story of how Argentina prevailed against these odds is both fascinating and instructive, and it is unfortunate that it has gotten so little attention.

Is the Argentine Experience Relevant to Today's Crisis in Europe?

Greece has gone through six years of recession, with unemployment hitting a record 27 percent, and youth unemployment passing 57 percent in 2013.[23] Since many people have dropped out of the labor force or have left the country, and therefore would no longer be included among the unemployed, it is also useful to look at employment: there were fewer people employed in Greece in 2013

---

23. Eurostat, "Unemployment Rate by Sex and Age Groups—Annual Average, %." Retrieved April 25, 2014, from http://epp.eurostat.ec.europa.eu/portal/page/portal/employment_unemployment_lfs/data/database.

than there were 33 years earlier, in 1980, or any year between. This is in spite of population growth of about 17 percent over this period.[24]

By 2014 Greece had lost about 25 percent of its national income from its peak in the first quarter of 2008,[25] placing its losses among some of the worst financial crises (see Figure 2.2).

These numbers may seem abstract, but the human and social costs are not. There are press reports of hospitals running short of medicines and basic supplies,[26] as the government's real spending on health fell by about 40 percent from 2010 to 2013. These cuts have been made at a time when the recession was increasing the need for public healthcare; the Greek Health Ministry showed a 21.9 percent increase in the utilization of public primary care health services from 2010 to 2011.[27] Although there is a time lag in the reporting of health statistics, a number of grim effects of the recession had been documented by 2013. For example, the number of newly diagnosed HIV cases jumped by 57.2 percent from 2010 to 2011.[28] From 2008

24. IMF, World Economic Outlook Database, April 2014. Retrieved April 24, 2014, from http://www.imf.org/external/pubs/ft/weo/2014/01/weodata/index.aspx.

25. Hellenic Statistical Authority, "Gross Domestic Product—Timeseries," 2014. Retrieved May 15, 2014, from http://www.statistics.gr/portal/page/portal/ESYE/PAGE-themes?p_param=A0704&r_param=SEL84&y_param=TS&mytabs=0.

26. See, for instance, Karolina Tagaris, "Greek Health System Crumbles under Weight of Crisis," Reuters, June 15, 2013. Retrieved December 9, 2013, from http://www.reuters.com/article/2012/06/15/greece-health-idUSL5E8HF17O20120615; Zeinab Badawi and William Kremer, "Greece's Life-Saving Austerity Medics," July 10, 2013. Retrieved December 9, 2013, from http://www.bbc.co.uk/news/magazine-23247914.

27. Elias Kondilis, Stathis Giannakopoulos, Magda Gavana, Ioanna Ierodiakonou, Howard Waitzkin, and Alexis Benos, "Economic Crisis, Restrictive Policies, and the Population's Health and Health Care: The Greek Case," *American Journal of Public Health* 103, no. 6 (2013): 973.

28. Ibid., p. 976.

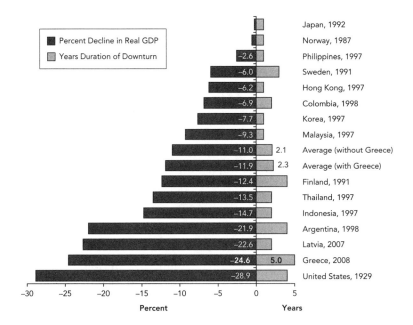

FIGURE 2.2 Greece: Comparison to Other Financial Crises

Source: Reinhart and Rogoff (2009) and author's calculations. Carmen Reinhart and Kenneth S. Rogoff, "The Aftermath of Financial Crises," National Bureau of Economic Research Working Paper No. 14656, 2009, http://www.nber.org/papers/w14656; and Latvijas Statisika, "Gross Domestic Product—Quarterly Data," 2009, http://www.csb.gov.lv/en/dati/statistics-database-30501.html; and also Hellenic Statistical Authority, "Gross Domestic Product—Timeseries," 2014, http://www.statistics.gr/portal/page/portal/ESYE/PAGE-themes?p_param=A0704&r_param=SEL84&y_param=TS&mytabs=0.

to 2010, the number of cases of problematic drug abuse (mostly through heroin) jumped by 11.6 percent.[29] Survey data show the proportion of people having attempted suicide nearly tripled from 2008 to 2011;[30] and suicide and homicide rates for men under the

29. Ibid., p. 976.

30. From 0.6 percent of the population attempting suicide in the month before the survey in 2008, to 1.5 percent in 2011. Ibid., p. 975.

age of 65 had already increased by 22.7 percent and 27.6 percent, respectively, from 2007 to 2009.[31]

Greece's downward spiral is a classic case of the medieval medicine of bleeding the patient who is already too weak to recover. From 2009 to 2013, the Greek government tightened its cyclically adjusted budget balance by 15 percent of GDP.[32] For those familiar with the United States, imagine a fiscal tightening of $2.25 trillion—one and a half times the peak US budget deficit of 2010, and doing this while the economy was shrinking, not growing. Of course nothing like this could happen in the United States, because the resulting depression would be political suicide for any government that caused it.

As could be expected, the massive spending cuts made it even more difficult for the Greek government to make its deficit targets, since revenue falls as the spending cuts shrink the economy further. Huge protests, riots, and public outrage made it more difficult for the authorities to pursue spending cuts in 2012, so most of the fiscal adjustment was switched to revenue increases. Since one of Greece's real structural problems is the failure of the government to collect taxes from high-income groups, the attempt to increase some of this tax collection was one of the few silver linings of the IMF/troika's dark storm clouds. But it was cold comfort. The IMF noted in December 2011 that the focus would have to shift back to spending cuts in 2013 and 2014,[33] and it did: primary (non-interest) spending was cut by 9 percent in the first eight months of 2013.[34]

31. Ibid., p. 975.

32. IMF, "Greece: Fourth Review under the Extended Arrangement under the Extended Fund Facility," July 2013, p. 4. Retrieved December 9, 2013, from http://www.imf.org/external/pubs/cat/longres.aspx?sk=40838.0.

33. IMF, "Greece Needs Deeper Reforms to Overcome Crisis," *IMF Survey Magazine*, December 16, 2011. Retrieved December 9, 2013, from http://www.imf.org/external/pubs/ft/survey/so/2011/car121611a.htm.

34. Last IMF review.

In February 2012, the troika had finally reached an agreement with the Greek government, providing a step that was obviously necessary, but which the European authorities had spent most of the previous four years denying they would do: the private bondholders agreed to take a haircut. It was sizable, with 53.5 percent of this part of the debt written off. But because much of the debt was still held by public entities (including the ECB), the write-off wasn't sufficient to leave Greece with a sustainable debt burden. Greece's interest payments on the public debt peaked at 7.2 percent of its national income in 2011—the highest in Europe, and one of the highest debt burdens in the world. The debt restructuring brought this down considerably, but by the time of the IMF's Fifth Review in mid-2014, the Fund was still projecting that the government would need to run very large primary budget surpluses—more than 4 percent of GDP for "many years to come," beginning in 2016. [35]

The ink was not even dry on the February 2012 agreement when a leaked IMF document, intended only for European finance ministers, revealed a more dismal forecast than the one that had been made public. Instead of Greece's debt stabilizing at 120 percent of GDP in 2020—of questionable sustainability in itself—this paper showed a debt of 129 percent of GDP in that year, or 160 percent under a less optimistic scenario.[36] If that was what Greece was facing, this agreement would lead to another restructuring—or outright, chaotic default—somewhere along the way.

35. See https://www.imf.org/external/pubs/cat/longres.aspx?sk=41614.0 and Weisbrot et al., "The Greek Economy: Which Way Forward?" Center for Economic and Policy Research, January 2015, http://www.cepr.net/index.php/publications/reports/the-greek-economy-which-way-forward.

36. Kate MacKenzie, "Greece: Preliminary Debt Sustainability Analysis," Alphaville (*Financial Times*), February 21, 2012, p. 1. Retrieved December 8, 2013, from http://ftalphaville.ft.com//2012/02/21/889521/that-greek-debt-sustainability-analysis-in-full/.

There was good reason to believe that the pessimistic scenario was the more likely one. For one thing, the IMF's projections had been terribly wrong in the run-up to this debt restructuring. In its Fifth Review (December 2011) of the fateful 2010 Stand-By Arrangement with Greece, the IMF projected GDP to be 6.9 percent lower than it had forecast a year earlier.[37] This is an enormous difference, with most of it coming in just the previous five months. Projections for unemployment during the same period were also revised sharply upward.

But just as in the United States' Great Depression, recovery has always been just around the corner: it was supposed to arrive in 2011,[38] 2012,[39] 2013,[40] and then—in the IMF review of July 2013—it was 2014.[41]

At the same time, the country has been paying a high price for keeping the European authorities at bay. The 2012 agreement with the troika required a 20 percent cut in the minimum wage, and a 30 percent wage cut for those under age 25. This is quite a hardship for workers earning the minimum wage, now reduced to 684 euros a month; but in Greece there are many workers earning

37. Projection of −6 for 2011 from IMF, "Greece: Fifth Review under the Stand-By Arrangement," December, 2011, p. 48. Retrieved December 9, 2013, from http://www.imf.org/external/pubs/cat/longres.aspx?sk=25429.0.

38. IMF, "Greece: 2009 Article IV Consultation," August 6, 2009, p. 11. Retrieved December 9, 2013, from http://www.imf.org/external/pubs/cat/longres.aspx?sk=23169.0.

39. IMF, "Greece: Fourth Review under the Stand-By Arrangement," July 13, 2011, p. 9. Retrieved December 9, 2013, from http://www.imf.org/external/pubs/cat/longres.aspx?sk=25038.0.

40. IMF, "Greece: Fifth Review under the Stand-By Arrangement," December 13, 2011, p. 64. Retrieved December 9, 2013, from http://www.imf.org/external/pubs/cat/longres.aspx?sk=25429.0.

41. IMF, "Greece: Fourth Review under the Extended Arrangement under the Extended Fund Facility," July 2013, p. 10. Retrieved December 9, 2013, from http://www.imf.org/external/pubs/cat/longres.aspx?sk=40838.0.

wages that are linked to the minimum wage, so the impacts are much more widely felt. So, too, is the reduction by 19 percent of the federal labor force. This was more than 4 percent of employed workers in 2013. The last IMF forecast (April 2015) forecasts unemployment still at 22.1 percent in 2016, but it will very likely be more than that.[42]

The end result, if the measures are implemented, will be a society with more poverty and inequality, and a smaller government—something closer to the United States and further from a European-style social democracy.

Did Greece have any alternative, if the IMF and European authorities insisted on continuing this reign of punishment and regressive social engineering? The example of Argentina suggests that they did. As noted above, the Argentine recovery after its default and devaluation was not a "commodities boom," or even an example of export-led growth. So the oft-heard claim that Greece could not "devalue and export its way out of the crisis, as Argentina did" is based on something that didn't happen in Argentina. A similar objection—that Greece doesn't have enough exports as compared to Argentina—is also wrong. In fact, Greece's exports of goods and services—including tourism—are about twice as large relative to GDP as were Argentina's exports before their devaluation. And once the economy was stabilized from the initial shock, Greece would—as Argentina did—very likely benefit from an inflow of foreign capital attracted to assets that would then be vastly cheaper to investors holding euros and dollars.

Greece would also be in a better position to borrow from alternative sources than Argentina was after the financial collapse that followed its default and devaluation in 2002. Argentina

---

42. IMF, *World Economic Outlook Database*, April 2015. Retrieved May 10, 2015, from http://www.imf.org/external/pubs/ft/weo/2015/01/weodata/weorept. aspx?pr.x=45&pr.y=12&sy=2013&ey=2020&scsm=1&ssd=1&sort=country& ds=.&br=1&c=174&s=LUR&grp=0&a=.

had nowhere to turn. Greece, however, might have other lenders if it ran short of foreign exchange. Unlike in 2002, there are now many countries—including China, Russia, the Gulf States, and others—who are collectively sitting on trillions of dollars of reserves. China itself has loaned Venezuela tens of billions of dollars, and has invested billions in Ecuador, Cuba, and other countries. It is not even clear whether Greece would need to borrow internationally once it defaulted on its international loans and devalued its currency—but if it did, we would be talking about a relatively small amount of money. Even if the European creditors were able to put together a united front to punish Greece—and it's not clear that this would be in their interests, since it could worsen the financial contagion—it is difficult to imagine that the rest of the world would join this effort and refuse to lend to the Greek government.

This addresses the objection raised by economists, from the IMF and elsewhere, that I have debated in forums and television and radio shows on the euro crisis. Greece cannot default, they argued, because the government was still running a primary budget deficit. In other words, even if all of its debt service is canceled through default, Greece still wouldn't be able to finance its general government operations. But by 2013 the government had already achieved a primary budget surplus. If the government were to leave the eurozone, it could also tax the windfall earnings of exporters, as Argentina did; they are already in the process of increasing tax collections on the high-income groups. Furthermore, with the return of the domestic currency, the government would not need euros to pay most of its bills. That is not to say that it could finance unlimited amounts of spending through money creation without having to worry about inflation, but the ultimate constraint on the government's budget would no longer be in euros.

For the economy as a whole, including the private sector, the main constraint facing Greece would be handling the balance of payments. In other words, the government would have to make sure that the economy did not run short of sufficient "hard currency"—for example, euros or dollars—to finance the imports that it needs. But the government could let the currency fall to a very competitive level, making its exports (and domestic assets) cheap and imports quite expensive. Foreign borrowing would only be necessary insofar as this was not enough to keep the country's foreign exchange reserves at a level that would be sufficient to stabilize the currency after it crashed. This seems unlikely—but if it were to happen, it seems probable that Greece would be able to borrow the relatively small sums that it would need.

It seems very likely that Greece would not have suffered the depth of damage, including lost output and employment, if it had abandoned the euro instead of agreeing to the troika's conditions beginning in 2010. We can see this just by looking at the worst financial crises of the past two decades that were associated with large devaluations. These are shown in Table 2.1. Although many of these economies, for example, in the Asian financial crisis of the late 1990s, took a serious hit at the beginning, Greece's 25 percent loss of GDP is already far larger than any of these countries suffered—more than two or three times as much, in most of these cases. Those countries' recoveries were much faster; three years after their devaluations, these countries had almost all recovered and were on average 5.7 percent above their pre-devaluation GDP levels.[43] Greece, by contrast, has had to endure six years of depression.

Former IMF economist Arvind Subramanian made a similar argument in a 2012 article in the *Financial Times*: "Expelled from the eurozone," he wrote, "Greece might prove more dangerous to the system than it ever was inside it—by providing a model of successful recovery."[44]

43. See Mark Weisbrot and Rebecca Ray, "Latvia's Internal Devaluation: A Success Story?" Center for Economic and Policy Research, 2011, http://www.cepr.net/index.php/publications/reports/latvias-internal-devaluation-a-success-story.

44. Arvind Subramanian, "Greece's Exit May Become the Euro's Envy," *The Financial Times*, May 14, 2012. Retrieved December 9, 2013, from http://www.ft.com/intl/cms/s/0/4bdda8a0-9dad-11e1-9a9e-00144feabdc0.html.

TABLE 2.1 Greece Compared With Major Devaluations and Ensuing GDP Loss

	Devaluation					GDP Decline		
			National Currency per US Dollar					Change in GDP 3 Years after Devaluation
	Date	Mos. until Trough	Before	Trough	Size of Devaluation	Quarters until Trough	Loss of GDP	
Argentina	Jan. 2001	5	1	3.6	−72.2%	2	−4.9%	17.2%
Finland	Sep. 1992	11	4.4	5.8	−23.9%	4	−2.4%	6.8%
Georgia	Dec. 1998	2	1.5	2.3	−36.8%	1	−1.6%	6.5%
Iceland	Oct. 2008	1	91.2	135.3	−32.6%	6	−10.4%	−5.7%[1]
Indonesia	Jul. 1997	12	2,446.6	13,962.5	−82.5%	5	−13.4%	−7.9%
Iran	Mar. 1993	2	67.3	1,635.7	−95.9%	4	−1.6%	10.6%
Italy	Aug. 1992	12	1,102.6	1,605.1	−31.3%	2	−1.7%	6.0%
Malaysia	Sep. 1997	4	2.7	4.4	−37.8%	5	−8.5%	6.7%
Mexico	Dec. 1994	3	3.4	6.7	−48.6%	4	−8.0%	5.9%
South Korea	Dec. 1997	1	1,025.6	1,701.5	−39.7%	2	−9.1%	14.0%
Sweden	Nov. 1992	9	6.2	8.1	−22.8%	2	−0.4%	8.9%
Thailand	Jul. 1997	6	25.8	53.8	−52.1%	5	−14.2%	−4.7%
UK	Aug. 1992	12	0.5	0.7	−23.1%	0	0.0%	9.7%
Greece	2008 Q1	92	0.64	0.7	−14.8%	23	−24.6%	−14.2%[2]

Notes:

1. For Iceland, this represents the change in GDP 2.75 years after devaluation.

2. As Greece did not devalue (as it was part of the euro), the three-year change measures GDP growth three years after peak GDP.

Source: Mark Weisbrot and Rebecca Ray, "Latvia's Internal Devaluation: A Success Story?" CEPR, 2011, p. 7, http://www.cepr.net/index.php/publications/reports/latvias-internal-devaluation-a-success-story.

This is certainly one possible scenario, and it is perhaps the main consideration that keeps the troika from inflicting even more punishment on Greece. But the point of this discussion is not to argue that Greece should leave the euro. There are political difficulties involved in such a decision, for Greece or any other country that is caught in this terrible recessionary trap and does not have sovereign control over its most important economic policies.

In Greece, for example, although it is clear that the vast majority of its citizens and residents would be much better off if they had left the euro rather than signing the first IMF agreement in 2010, the decision at each succeeding stage is more difficult. By 2014 the economy was finally showing positive growth for the year.

Yet, it will still take years for unemployment to reach normal levels. The country still faces a high risk of another debt crisis, since its debt was still 176 percent of GDP at the end of 2014, and it would face high interest rates if it returned to financial markets to borrow.

It is not surprising that even the left-wing Syriza party, which won elections on an anti-austerity program in January 2015, would not opt for leaving the euro but rather would put the burden on European officials to decide whether they were willing to compromise enough to allow a faster recovery, or to force Greece out of the euro. Leaving the euro—under any scenario—would at first impose unknown economic costs on most Greek voters. Any government that wanted to survive the initial crisis would want to convince the public that there was no choice, and that they had not been reckless but had done what they could to reach a compromise.

The election of Syriza is potentially a historic turning point in the slow-motion democratization of the eurozone that is necessary to accelerate its economic recovery. A government has been elected with a mandate to renegotiate its most important economic policies with the European officials who have been deciding it—with a result that is widely seen as a terrible failure—for nearly five years. It is a mandate that the new government, led by Prime Minister

Alexis Tsipras and Finance Minister Yanis Varoufakis, seems to have taken seriously. At this writing it remains to be seen whether there will be a compromise that European officials and the Syriza government can accept. This seems the most likely scenario, given that the European authorities, led by Germany, do not want Greece to leave the euro; and at the same time, the Syriza government does not want to leave the euro, nor does it have a mandate from the voters to do so. Given the initial pain that exit would entail—and the amount is uncertain—no government would want to make this move without the strong support of the population. However, if Greece is forced out of the euro, there are feasible alternative economic policies that can enable its recovery.

In many ways, the confrontation between the European authorities and the Syriza government in its first month was a repeat of the process described in the previous chapter, with European officials using—and in this case even exacerbating—a financial crisis in an attempt to force the new government to capitulate.[45] For example, on February 4, 2015, the ECB announced that it would no longer accept Greek government bonds and government-guaranteed debt as collateral.[46]

Although Greece would still be eligible for other, emergency lending from the Central Bank, the immediate impact of the announcement was to raise Greek borrowing costs, put pressure on its banks, sink the stock market, and encourage capital flight. The main difference between this pressure on the new Greek government and that exerted on the vulnerable eurozone countries in 2011 and 2012 is that—at least so far—the eurozone as a whole was not taken hostage, but only the Greek population. Yields on

45. For more detail on the confrontation between the Syriza government and European official, see http://www.cepr.net/issues/europe/greece/.

46. "ECB Raises Heat on Athens With Curb on Cash for Banks," *Financial Times*, February 4, 2015. http://www.ft.com/intl/cms/s/0/c3a1a602-acaf-11e4-beeb-00144feab7de.html?siteedition=intl#axzz3QjJojaYm.

Spanish and Italian 10-year sovereign bonds remained quite low, at around 1.5 percent—due to the commitment that the ECB had made back in July 2012 to do "whatever it takes" to preserve the euro.

But the main point of this chapter is that there is no economic basis for the idea that Greece has no alternative to following the austerity policies recommended by the troika, or that any alternative would likely cause more damage to the economy and population. There is no economic basis for the idea that recessions brought on by financial crises must last longer or have more persistent unemployment than other types of recessions. Obviously the ECB could, as the Federal Reserve has, use QE to buy up as much of the Greek sovereign debt as necessary to resolve its debt problems and engage in the kind of fiscal stimulus necessary to get back to full employment. But if the ECB is not willing to do its job—and clearly it hasn't been, up to this point—then the Greek government is fully capable of adopting the necessary policies on its own, even outside of the euro.

That is the economics of the situation; and if the economics were widely understood, the politics might be very different. It is true that public opinion polls in even the most victimized countries of the eurozone—Greece, Spain, and Portugal—have consistently found majorities in favor of keeping the euro, throughout years of recession. Of course the pollsters might have gotten a different answer if they had asked, "Do you want to stay in the euro if it means five more years of high unemployment, a stagnating economy, and more cuts to pensions, healthcare, and education?" There is also a class divide, with the more politically influential middle to upper classes more likely to be swayed by the cosmopolitan allure of the euro, and the working class that has borne the brunt of the troika's punishment likely to give more weight to employment, job security, and other basic needs that have been lost. Spain, Greece, and Portugal also lived under right-wing dictatorships for much of the post–World War II period; many people in these countries understandably appreciate the formal democratic guarantees of the European Union. As a Spanish economist told me, to many Spaniards having the euro is "like being a first class citizen of Europe."

Also, although it's not clear why any country couldn't leave the euro but remain in the European Union, many seem to conflate the two. Others argue that if the euro breaks up, European unity would suffer a terrible blow that would imperil the entire European project. But European unity is already taking a hard hit from the devastation caused by the prolonged economic malaise and unemployment, with the rise of nationalist frictions, as well as fascist parties and anti-immigrant agitation and even violence.

The main confusion remains in the economic realm; indeed it is arguable that even fascist parties like Golden Dawn in Greece and the National Front in France have grown mainly because the social democratic political parties have not offered people any alternative to prolonged suffering. Yet, real economic alternatives do exist and have been there since the beginning of the crisis.

3

Untold History, Unsolved Mystery

The Long-Term Economic Growth Failure

A middle-aged man in Mirebelais, in the Central Plateau of Haiti, raises a tattered T-shirt to show a group of *blans*—the Creole word for foreigners, or whites—his thin stomach, how long it has been since he has eaten. In the sprawling hillside *favela* of Jacarezinho, overlooking Rio de Janeiro, a 31-year-old single mother with two small children describes how she struggles to get by on $40 a month from childcare work. And in the capital of the richest country in the world, in Washington DC, a homeless man in his late fifties—who is good-natured and suffers from no drug addiction, or mental or physical disability—holds a cup to passersby each day for money.

When most people see these kinds of poverty—and there are many different levels and layers of poverty and deprivation throughout the world—they think first about the glaring inequalities of income and wealth, both within and between countries. But inequality is only part of the story, and depending on the place and the time period in question, it may not be the most important part of the story. It may be that other policies, in addition to redistributing income directly, have a vital role to play in reducing inequality.

In the past year, there has been something of a revival of the public policy debate on inequality of income and wealth, a welcome development in light of the alarming trends of the past few decades.

Thomas Piketty's brilliant work, *Capital in the Twenty-first Century*,[1] focusing primarily on the high-income countries, has succeeded in highlighting the problem. (It also helped that social movements such as Occupy Wall Street got major media and politicians to talk about the problem for the first time in decades.) Piketty's work has become one of the most influential books on economics in a long time, and for good reasons. His focus is on long-term trends, and most important, on the rate of return on capital (r) relative to economic growth (g). If $r > g$, he argues, it follows that income and wealth will tend to become increasingly concentrated because the owners of capital will see their incomes and wealth grow faster than the economy.[2] Much of Piketty's book is devoted to analyzing and explaining, in rich historical and data-driven detail, the economic, political, and demographic changes that have driven the long-term developments in the distribution of income and wealth. For him, the focus has been on trends such as population growth, cataclysmic events including the two world wars, and policy changes that directly affect the distribution of income—such as changes in the minimum wage, compensation of executives and professionals, and taxation.

But over some considerably long periods of time, macroeconomic policy and economic growth—in particular, the part of economic growth that is not driven by population growth—can also have a profound effect on the distribution of income and the living standards of the poor. As we will see in Chapter 5, the poverty rate in Latin America was constant or increasing for about two decades, then dropped from 44 to 28 percent from 2002 to 2013,[3]

---

1. Thomas Piketty, *Capital in the Twenty-first Century* (Cambridge, MA: Belknap Press, 2014).

2. More specifically it wouldbe $(r - c) > g$, where c is the share of returns to capital that is consumed.

3. Economic Commission on Latin America and the Caribbean, "Población en situación de indigencia y pobreza," 2014. Online database, consulted February 6, 2014, http://interwp.cepal.org/sisgen/ConsultaIntegrada.asp?idIndicador=182&idioma=e.

when economic growth picked up. The growth of income per person can also have a huge effect on poverty and living standards even if inequality is stagnant or worsening. To take the most important example, China has pulled hundreds of millions of people out of poverty over the past three decades; in fact, the world would not even have had a significant reduction in the number of poor people from 1981 to 2005 if not for China.[4] Yet China also had one of the biggest increases in inequality in the world during the same period. The Gini coefficient for income—a crude measure that, when based on household surveys as in this case, significantly understates inequality—increased from .30 in 1980 to .55 by 2012.[5] This increase in inequality far surpassed even the dramatic increase in the United States and moved China from a country with one of the more equal distributions of income in the world to one of the most unequal.

We have already seen in Chapters 1 and 2 how in the eurozone flawed macroeconomic policy, combined with a political and ideological agenda pursued by the architects of that policy, has reduced incomes and employment over many years and has contributed to what are likely to be higher rates of poverty and inequality into the indefinite future. But for developing countries, the impacts of bad policy are generally more destructive and long-lasting, and of course much worse in terms of their human costs.

---

4. World Bank, "New Data Show 1.4 Billion Live on Less Than US$1.25 a Day, But Progress Against Poverty Remains Strong," September 2008, http://www.worldbank.org/en/news/press-release/2008/09/16/new-data-show-14-billion-live-less-us125-day-progress-against-poverty-remains-strong. The World Bank reported in 2008 that the global population living on less than $1.25/day had fallen from 1.9 billion in 1981 to 1.4 billion in 2005. In the report, the Bank notes that China's population living on less than $1.25/day had fallen from 835 million to 207 million.

5. See Yu Xie and Xiang Zhou, "Income Inequality in Today's China," *Proceedings of the National Academy of Sciences*, February 20, 2014. http://www.pnas.org/content/111/19/6928.short.

In the poorer and even in the middle-income countries, economic growth will generally be much more important to achieving a decent standard of living than in higher income countries. In the US economy, which generates about $55,000 of income per person—that is, $220,000 for a family of four—there is enough income for everyone to have a good life. The real problems have to do with distribution, and at least as important, increasing the level of employment—which in turn also has a substantial impact on income distribution.[6]

But in Haiti, income per person is just $1,315 annually.[7] No matter how much income were to be redistributed in Haiti, as well in as many other poor countries, the size of the overall pie has to increase just to meet people's basic needs; and even more if they are to have the resources to increase the level of education so as to set the country on a path to sustained economic development. That requires rapid economic growth.

Even in middle-income countries, economic growth remains vital to reducing or eliminating poverty. In some countries it would not be economically possible to eliminate poverty through redistribution—there is not enough income at the top, even if governments could tax away everything that the upper income groups don't spend on food and housing. But even where redistribution could theoretically go a long way, as a political matter there are always limits. Even revolutions do not generally end up

6. See Dean Baker and Jared Bernstein, *Getting Back to Full Employment* (Washington, DC: Center for Economic and Policy Research, 2013).

7. IMF, "World Economic Outlook, 2014." This and other measures of income used for international comparisons in this book are expressed in purchasing power parity (PPP) dollars. This is a conversion from local currency to dollars that attempts to adjust for differences in the prices of goods and services between the different countries. By this method, one PPP dollar should have the same amount of purchasing power in the US as what that PPP dollar, converted into, e.g., UK pounds at the current exchange rate, would have in the UK.

diverting most of the income of the upper classes toward the poor or near-poor.

Most important, redistribution of income in middle-income countries tends to be much more feasible when national income is rising. It is then possible to steer a disproportionate share of the newly generated income toward the less well off—either through taxation and government spending, or through other mechanisms such as collective bargaining. This is difficult enough, even with robust growth, as the wealthy usually have sufficient political influence to block redistributive measures. But when the economy is not growing, gains at the bottom of the income ladder must generally come from real economic losses higher up. This has proven difficult to accomplish on a large scale, or for a sustained period, without violence and political repression.

When we look at economic growth here, we are looking at GDP per capita. If GDP grows only because of population growth, this does not raise average living standards. And of course the impact of per capita GDP growth can be negated by upward redistribution of income. This has happened in the United States over the past four decades, and it has propelled the return of inequality as a political issue. The median wage in the United States today is just $20.00 per hour, only 10.7 percent above its value, adjusted for inflation, in 1973; while productivity increased by 80.1 percent over the same period.[8]

But this is not the norm over long periods of time, in developing countries, in the past century at least. In general, over

8. Economic Policy Institute, *The State of Working America, 12th Edition* (Washington, DC: Economic Policy Institute, 2012). Retrieved July 14, 2014, from http://stateofworkingamerica.org/data/. Some of the productivity gains during this period are illusory, in the sense that they are a result of an increasing share of GDP going to depreciation; Baker (2007) has measured "usable productivity" for the period (2001–2006), and found it to have grown by 2.3 percent annually, as opposed to the standard measure of 3.2 percent. But by either measure, the median wage barely grew as compared to productivity.

long periods of time, the real income of the majority will tend to grow as the economy grows, even if the distribution of income is changing.[9]

The rise in GDP per capita is what has enabled people who live in the United States, for example, to enjoy a higher standard of living than their grandparents and great-grandparents. The United States was once a less developed country, and life was much tougher and shorter than it is today. At the beginning of the twentieth century, one out of six children would die before their first birthday. Today it is about one in 160. Life expectancy at birth was under 50 years; today it is 78.5.[10] Even as recently as 1965, less than 50 percent of Americans over 25 had graduated from high school, and fewer than 10 percent had finished college. The numbers today are 88 percent and 32 percent, respectively.[11]

Given the importance of economic growth, it is remarkable how often it is omitted from policy debates, especially in the major media. For example, there have been hundreds of articles in the media about the North American Free Trade Agreement (NAFTA) in the 20 years since Mexico, Canada, and the United States ratified it. Most have discussed Mexico's success in attracting foreign direct investment, or in increasing trade. But economic growth has often gone missing. This is like discussing a professional baseball player's performance without mentioning his batting average. He may be an excellent fielder and a good teammate, but if he bats .125, he's not going to make it in the major leagues. This has been

9. See Piketty, *Capital in the Twenty-first Century.*

10. US Centers for Disease Control and Prevention, "Life Expectancy," February 13, 2014. Retrieved July 14, 2014, from http://www.cdc.gov/nchs/fastats/life-expectancy.htm.

11. US Census, "CPS Historical Time Series Tables: Table A-2. Percent of People 25 Years and Over Who Have Completed High School or College, by Race, Hispanic Origin and Sex: Selected Years 1940 to 2013." Retrieved July 14, 2014, from http://www.census.gov/hhes/socdemo/education/data/cps/historical/.

the case with Mexico's growth since NAFTA's inception, which has ranked 18 in out of 20 Latin American economies over the past 20 years. Its average annual growth of GDP per capita has been just 0.9 percent over two decades, or one-fourth of what it was from 1960 to 1980.[12]

In fact, if Mexico had continued at its pre-1980 rates of growth, the country would be very close to European living standards today. Under these conditions, few Mexicans would have been interested in emigrating illegally to the United States, for jobs that did not pay that much more than what they could earn at home.

Figure 3.1 illustrates the difference that growth can make with a comparison between two countries: Brazil and South Korea. Brazil started out much better off than South Korea in 1960, with a per capita GDP of $3,040 as compared to just $1,765 for South Korea.[13] Both countries had rapid growth for the next two decades; by 1980 the gap had more than doubled in absolute terms, and was about the same in relative terms ($8,460 for Brazil and $5,470 for South Korea).

At this point, their growth paths diverged dramatically. Both countries were hit by the world recession and other external shocks in 1980, but while South Korea recovered and even surpassed its prior growth rate, Brazil stagnated. Twenty years later, Brazil had barely budged from its 1980 level of per capita GDP—a virtually zero increase over two decades. But per capita GDP in South Korea had grown by 259 percent. By 2010, South

12. Mark Weisbrot, Stephan Lefebvre, and Joseph Sammut, "Did NAFTA Help Mexico? An Assessment after 20 Years," Center for Economic and Policy Research, February 2014, http://www.cepr.net/index.php/publications/reports/nafta-20-years.

13. Figures are in constant 2005 dollars, on a purchasing power parity (PPP) basis. See Appendix 1 of "The Scorecard on Development, 1960–2010: Closing the Gap?" Center for Economic and Policy Research, April 2011, http://www.cepr.net/documents/publications/scorecard-2011-04.pdf for GDP measurement and comparison methodology.

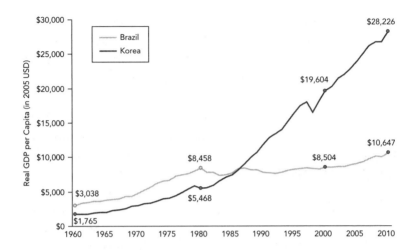

FIGURE 3.1 Per Capita GDP Growth in Brazil and South Korea

Source: Mark Weisbrot and Rebecca Ray. "The Scorecard on Development, 1960–2010: Closing the Gap?" Center for Economic and Policy Research, April 2011, p. 7, Figure 1, http://www.cepr.net/index.php/publications/reports/the-scorecard-on-development-1960-2010-closing-the-gap.

Korea had achieved the same level of living standards as Western Europe, with income per capita of $28,230. By contrast, Brazil in 2010 was still a developing country, with income per person of just $10,650.[14]

The differences between these two paths are huge, as measured by any number of other indicators. The United Nations Human Development Index (HDI), for example, attempts to measure progress in health and education as well as income. South Korea is now ranked 15th among all countries on the HDI,

14. Mark Weisbrot and Rebecca Ray, "The Scorecard on Development, 1960–2010: Closing the Gap?" Center for Economic and Policy Research, April 2011, p. 6, http://www.cepr.net/index.php/publications/reports/the-scorecard-on-development-1960-2010-closing-the-gap.

while Brazil is ranked 79th.[15] The average number of years of schooling in South Korea is 12, versus 7 for Brazil.[16] Poverty is still a widespread problem in Brazil: despite the progress over the past decade, some 10.8 percent of the population (about 21 million people) are living on less than $2 per day.[17] South Korea is listed as having less than 2 percent of the population living below the $2 per day poverty line; the actual percentage is probably lower than that.[18] Brazil's infant mortality rate is nearly four times that of South Korea, at 12.9 versus 3.3 per 1,000 live births.[19]

This comparison also illustrates how important economic growth is, at least for developing countries, for achieving social progress. Of course, there is much more to economic and human well-being than income per capita. The whole purpose of the HDI, for example, is to provide a broader measure of human progress that captures the ability of people to live long, healthy lives, with improved education and related welfare opportunities. The UN's Human Development Report documents some sizable divergences between countries' per capita income levels and their achievements in health, education, gender equality, and other measures of

15. UNDP, "Human Development Report," 2014, http://hdr.undp.org/en/ 2014-report/download.

16. UNDP, "Human Development Report," 2010, http://hdr.undp.org/en/content/ human-development-report-2010.

17. World Bank, "World Databank: World Development Indicators," 2014. Online database, accessed July 14, 2014, http://databank.worldbank.org/ddp/home. do?Step=12&id=4&CNO=2.

18. UNDP, "Human Development Report," 2009, http://hdr.undp.org/en/content/ human-development-report-2009. The UN statistics count anything less than 2 percent on this measure as the same.

19. World Bank, "World Databank: World Development Indicators," 2014. Online database, accessed July 14, 2014, http://databank.worldbank.org/ddp/home. do?Step=12&id=4&CNO=2.

human development. But as we shall see, improvements in health and education, and other quality-of-life indicators, are for most low- and middle-income countries very difficult to achieve without increasing income levels.

Economists, of course, understand what economic growth is and why it is important. But even they were largely silent as the vast majority of countries passed through one of the most extraordinary long-term growth failures in the history of modern capitalism. It is to that economic failure that we now turn.

The Growth Failure

Beginning in the 1980s, and in some countries a bit earlier, a cluster of policy changes often characterized as "neoliberalism" were adopted by governments in the vast majority of low- and middle-income countries. Because these policies were advocated by institutions based in Washington, such as the IMF and World Bank, as well as the US government and its agencies, they were sometimes called "the Washington Consensus"; others, focusing on the deregulatory aspects of these "reforms," referred to them as "free market" capitalism, or even "market fundamentalism." All of these labels are inadequate in some way; the "Washington Consensus," for example, did not include free mobility of capital, at least according to its original proponents.[20]

"Free market" capitalism and "market fundamentalism," as a general description, are also off the mark because many of the policy changes included heavy protectionism and/or government

20. John Williamson, "The Strange History of the Washington Consensus," *Journal of Post Keynesian Economics* 27, no. 2 (Winter 2004–2005): 195. http://relooney.fatcow.com/00_New_3103.pdf.

intervention.[21] This is especially true in the area of intellectual property, where the extension and increased enforcement of patent and copyright monopolies are the very opposite of what would happen in a "free market." On the contrary, such policies involve heavy intervention by the state to prevent competition, and cause the same distortions, inefficiencies, and monopoly pricing that the "free traders" so disparage in other markets—only on a much larger scale.[22] Pharmaceuticals that cost a few dollars to produce can sell for thousands or even tens of thousands of dollars due to state-enforced monopolies. The ultimately disastrous fixed exchange rates of Argentina, Brazil, Russia, and others in the late 1990s, supported by the IMF and others concerned about the currency stability for foreign investors, are another example of state (and supra-national) intervention, this time in currency markets. So, too, are all the loans made by multilateral lenders such as the IMF to bail out private bankers and investors. Whatever one thinks of any of these policies, they did not promote the operation of "free markets."

For these reasons, I would choose the more appropriate, if lesser-known, label of "neoliberalism," which describes a set of policy changes that were implemented during this period. These changes include more "independence" for central banks, along with tighter monetary policy (including higher real interest rates); an (often indiscriminate) opening up to international trade and capital flows, while at the same time increasing protection for "intellectual property"; some measure of deregulation, including financial deregulation; privatization of state-owned enterprises; a

21. See Dean Baker, *The Conservative Nanny State: How the Wealthy Use the Government to Stay Rich and Get Richer* (Washington, DC: Center for Economic and Policy Research, 2006).

22. Dean Baker, "Issues in Trade and Protectionism" (Washington, DC: Center for Economic and Policy Research, November 2009). http://www.cepr.net/documents/publications/trade-and-protectionism-2009-11.pdf.

weakening of the bargaining power of labor, often through legal or institutional changes; tighter fiscal policy, even to the point of governments pursuing pro-cyclical policies that cut spending as economies slowed; and not least, the abandonment of industrial and development strategies that governments had pursued in prior decades of development.

Most people who follow policy debates in the United States, Europe, and indeed much of the rest of the world would think that these policy changes were at least successful in promoting growth. It would be a difficult and probably intractable exercise, econometrically, to try to measure the impact of each of these policy changes worldwide. However, since these policies were adopted by the vast majority of countries in the world, it is worth looking at how the world's countries did in terms of economic growth, as well as other important social and economic indicators, in the ensuing decades.

In order to make this comparison, we have to take into account that there may be what economists call "diminishing returns" associated with economic growth—that is, as an economy reaches a higher level of per capita income, its rate of growth will slow. Although we do not observe much of this phenomenon in the example of South Korea above, there are reasons to expect that it is generally a constraint. Perhaps more obviously, we would expect diminishing returns in social indicators such as life expectancy and infant mortality. It should be much easier to raise life expectancy from 45 to 60 years, for example, than from 65 to 80.

To get around the problem of diminishing returns in comparing economic and social progress, we can divide countries into groups based on their starting level of the variable that we want to compare. In other words, instead of simply looking at what a country or group of countries achieved from 1960 to 1980—as we did in the above example of Brazil and South Korea—and comparing that to the same country's progress from 1980 to 2000, we can make a different comparison. We can look at all of the countries that start out at a given level of, for example, per capita GDP in 1960, and compare their progress to countries that start out at the same level in 1980. In this way we can compare the progress of countries that are poor, middle income, or high income in one period with how similarly situated countries did in the next period, thus avoiding the problem of diminishing returns.

If anything, this method of comparison should show a bias in favor of the countries that start out at the designated level in the later period. A country that has a given level of per capita income or life expectancy in 1980 should have access to at least some knowledge and technology that was not available to countries starting out at the same level in 1960.

This comparison can be seen in Figure 3.2, where countries are divided into five quintiles. In quintile 1 are the poorest countries, which started out each period with a per capita income between $303 and $1,429.[23] At the bottom of this group in 1960 were Sub-Saharan African countries such as Tanzania, Mali, and Ghana, with countries such as Egypt and Thailand near the top. As can be seen in the graph, the rate of growth of GDP per person slowed sharply from the first period to the second: it was 2 percent annually from 1960 to 1980. Countries starting out at this level in 1980 grew just over half as fast, 1.1 percent from 1980 to 2000, however.

The same pattern can be seen across all of the quintiles of countries. Some of these are very large declines in growth. For example, the fourth quintile saw its per capita growth rate drop from 3.1 percent annually for the period 1960–1980 to just 1.1 percent

23. These numbers are in constant 2005 dollars, so they are adjusted for inflation. For a full explanation of the methodology used here, see Appendix in Mark Weisbrot and Rebecca Ray, "The Scorecard on Development, 1960–2010: Closing the Gap?" Center for Economic and Policy Research, April 2011, http://www.cepr.net/index.php/publications/reports/the-scorecard-on-development-1960-2010-closing-the-gap.

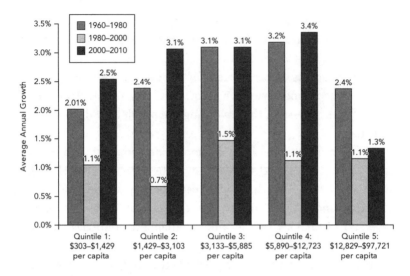

FIGURE 3.2 Average Annual GDP Growth, by Quintile

Source: Mark Weisbrot and Rebecca Ray, "The Scorecard on Development, 1960–2010: Closing the Gap?" Center for Economic and Policy Research, April 2011, p. 11, Figure 3, http://www.cepr.net/index.php/publications/reports/the-scorecard-on-development-1960-2010-closing-the-gap.

over the next 20 years. Measured cumulatively over a 20-year period, this is the difference between an average income growth of 88 percent, which is quite a large improvement in living standards, versus 22 percent.

It is amazing that such a huge, long-term growth failure in the vast majority of countries attracted so little attention among economists, and especially among journalists and professionals who write about economic issues.[24] Perhaps even more remarkable

24. One exception was a book by economist William Easterly, *The Elusive Quest for Growth* (Cambridge, MA: MIT Press, 2001). However, it did not consider whether neoliberal policy changes could have contributed to the slowdown. Easterly contends that he was fired by the World Bank for writing the book. See http://williameasterly.org/books/the-white-mans-burden/.

is that so many writers would assume, without looking at the data, that these neoliberal reforms coinciding with such a sharp slowdown in growth were actually a success.

Of course, the fact that this set of neoliberal policies coincided with, and was followed by, a long-term and large-scale economic failure does not prove that all of these policies were wrong, or that any of them were wrong for all the countries that adopted them. For any given policy—tightening fiscal or monetary policy, opening up to trade, privatization—there were undoubtedly times and places where these measures were appropriate and effective. But as an overall package of "reforms," implemented as they were across scores of countries, it does not appear that they worked. At the very least, the data should raise some questions about what went wrong.

The comparison between the two 20-year periods is a fair one. While the first decade of the base period, the 1960s, had favorable conditions for growth, the 1970s was a period of two major oil shocks—the first in 1973–1974, when oil prices more than tripled, and then another major shock toward the end of the decade. In the second period, the 1990s saw the longest-running economic expansion in US history; and with the United States having the largest economy in the world and increasing its imports substantially throughout the decade, this should have provided an important boost to growth in developing countries.

Some have pointed to the economic growth success stories of China and more recently India, and have argued that since this is nearly half of the developing world—about 2.6 billion people—the neoliberal reforms have been a success. As discussed below, there is scant evidence that these countries' years of rapid growth can be attributed to neoliberal policies. But equally important, if we are looking at an experiment that has been carried out in more than 100 countries, it has failed in the vast majority of them. This is at least *prima facie* evidence of bad policy. For these reasons, the appropriate unit of analysis here is the country: economic policy is decided at the level of the individual government, and so each country has the same weight in the comparison, regardless of population. It is worth noting, too, that of 83 low- and middle-income countries with data for both the 1960–1980 and 1980–2000 periods, only 21 grew at a faster rate in the second period.[25]

As would be expected given the slowdown in growth that occurred from 1980 to 2000, there was also a decline in progress for major health and social indicators such as life expectancy, and infant and child mortality.[26] Figure 3.3 shows the rate of progress in reducing child mortality over the last 50 years, with countries divided into quintiles from the highest child mortality (quintile 1) to the lowest (quintile 5). In the worst-off countries, we can see a huge decline in the rate of progress. Countries with the highest child mortality were reducing these deaths by a rate of 4.9 per thousand each year from 1960 to 1980; this fell to just 3.1 per thousand for 1980–2000. For the next-worst quintile, there was also a sharp drop, from an annual improvement of 3.7 per thousand down to 2.4 per thousand. This represents numerous unnecessary deaths of children that could have been avoided with more effective economic and social policies. As we move to the less poor countries in the figure, the decline in progress shrinks; but really we should be seeing an improvement in progress in an area where advances in medicine and public health have made it easier to reduce child mortality. Again, it should be emphasized that there is no impact of "diminishing returns" here, because we are not comparing the same countries over the two periods, but rather the countries that started out with a particular rate of child mortality at the beginning of the first period (1960) with those that started out

25. This is not including three countries that had zero or negative growth in both periods: Madagascar, The Gambia, and Senegal.

26. For more detail, Mark Weisbrot and Rebecca Ray, "The Scorecard on Development, 1960–2010: Closing the Gap?" Center for Economic and Policy Research, April 2011, http://www.cepr.net/index.php/publications/reports/the-scorecard-on-development-1960-2010-closing-the-gap.

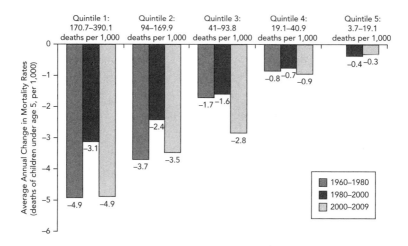

FIGURE 3.3 Average Annual Reduction in Child Mortality, by Quintile

Source: Mark Weisbrot and Rebecca Ray, "The Scorecard on Development, 1960–2010: Closing the Gap?" Center for Economic and Policy Research, April 2011, p. 25, Figure 9, http://www.cepr.net/index.php/publications/reports/the-scorecard-on-development-1960-2010-closing-the-gap.

at that level in the second period (1980). This decline in social progress is another illustration of the importance of economic growth to developing countries and the consequences of failed macroeconomic and development policies as these have occurred. Note that there is no bar for quintile 5 in 1960, because no country had yet achieved such a low level of child mortality. The quintile is empty in the first time period, but by 1980, 27 countries had achieved that level and by 2000 there were 67 countries at that level.

Recovery: Growth Rebounds, 2000–2010

The growth failure in the period 1980–2000, which extended into the first few years of the 2000s, went largely unnoticed in the scholarly and popular press. There was almost no inquiry by economists into whether any of the large-scale, widely adopted neoliberal policy changes implemented either just prior to or during this period might have had anything to do with it. The major media, especially the business press, pretended that such neoliberal reforms as more independent action by central banks, fiscal and monetary conservatism, liberalization of trade and financial flows, and getting the state out of development planning—among other changes—were sound policy and therefore must have been successful.

Thus it is not surprising that when this growth collapse was reversed, over the past decade, this tectonic shift also went unnoticed. If you don't see the disease, how can you recognize when the patient has begun to recover?

The rebound can be seen in Figure 3.2 earlier in this chapter. In every quintile except the highest-income group, the decade of 2000–2010 saw an annual per capita growth rate that was vastly higher than its performance in the prior 20 years and equaled or exceeded its annual per capita GDP growth in the 1960–1980 period. This result is despite the fact that the decade included the financial crisis and world recession of 2008–2009. How are we to explain this sharp turnaround after such a long period of growth failure?

A big part of the story of the last decade has been the role of China on the global stage. During this decade, China's imports helped lift the growth rate of most of the countries in the world that had stagnated for the prior 20 years. This can be seen in Figure 3.4, which shows China's imports from low- and middle-income countries—that is, countries that are not members of the mostly high-income club of the Organisation for Economic Co-operation and Development (OECD).[27] These imports are measured as a percent of these countries' total output.

27. The OECD has 34 member countries, 31 of which are high income (plus three middle-income countries: Mexico, Poland, and Turkey).

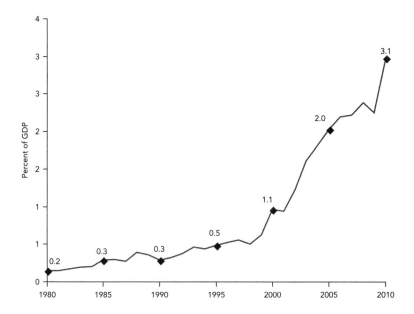

FIGURE 3.4 Non-OECD Exports to China, as Percent of Non-OECD GDP

Source: International Monetary Fund, "Direction of Trade Statistics," n.d. Online database, http://elibrary-data.imf.org/; and World Bank, "Quarterly Update," November 2010, http://siteresources.worldbank.

As the graph shows, China's imports from low- and middle-income countries shot up from 0.1 percent of these countries' output in 1980 to 3 percent in 2010. This trend contributed enormously to the growth rebound seen in the bottom four quintiles of countries over the last decade.

Of course China also increased its exports to these countries, and from a Keynesian perspective or national income accounting analysis, it would be the growth of net exports (exports minus imports) that would increase aggregate demand. But trade contributes to growth in other ways.[28] Even from a national income accounting

28. Some of these gains are real despite the fact that they are often exaggerated by economists supporting commercial agreements; e.g., see Gary Hufbauer and

perspective, if Chinese demand for many countries' exports had not grown so much, it is not likely that it would have been replaced by other sources; whereas on the import side, developing countries would likely have imported more from other countries in the absence of Chinese exports.

During this time China grew to be the largest economy in the world on a purchasing power parity basis, with per capita income multiplying 13 times over the last 30 years. Unfortunately for Europe, whose governments at the time of this writing have chosen to endure a prolonged period of stagnation, Chinese growth and its growing imports are not enough to power the world economy. But they can, and did, make a huge difference for countries in Africa, Latin America, Asia, and elsewhere.

It is important to highlight what happened over these 50 years since it runs so contrary to the conventional wisdom. The standard story that you usually hear or read about is that neoliberal "reforms" led to more successful growth for developing countries. But this appears to be the opposite of what actually happened: instead, initial reforms were followed by a long period—more than 20 years, actually—of economic failure in the vast majority of low- and middle-income countries.

But there was one country, China, the most populous country in the world, that did not adopt the neoliberal policies, and therefore was able to become the fastest-growing economy in world history. It grew to be an increasingly large part of the global economy *because* it grew so much more rapidly than did the economies with governments that participated, to various extents, in a failed neoliberal experiment. Only after this transformation of the Chinese and the world economy could China's imports help lift many developing countries to higher growth—for many countries to the norm

Jeffrey J. Schott, "Payoff from the World Trade Agenda," Peterson Institute for International Economics, June 2013, http://www.piie.com/publications/papers/hufbauerschott20130422.pdf.

of the pre-1980 years, before the widespread adaptation of neoliberal reforms.

What occurred in the high-income countries? Did they contribute anything to the rebound in growth that took place in low- and middle-income countries in the first decade of the twenty-first century? It turns out that they did, but unfortunately their contribution was negative. In the world's largest economy for nearly all of this period, the United States, growth in most of the decade was driven by a huge real estate bubble.[29] There was a brief recession toward the beginning of the decade caused by the bursting of the stock market bubble, but the downturn lasted only from March to November 2001. Its duration was relatively short and mild, although it didn't feel like that to many Americans since there was no net job creation between 2001 and 2004[30]—a hitherto unprecedented phenomenon since the Great Depression. But the reason that the first recession was not much deeper in terms of lost output is because the economy was rescued by a huge housing bubble that had already begun to balloon and was recognizable by 2002. Demand was driven not only by residential construction, which expanded from 4.8 percent of GDP in 2001 to 6.5 percent of GDP in 2005,[31] but also by bubble-driven consumption. Consumers borrowed against their homes, and spent furiously, since their wealth—in the form of home values—was increasing rapidly. The

29. For the most comprehensive analysis of the United States' bubble growth and its aftermath see Dean Baker, *Plunder and Blunder: The Rise and Fall of the Bubble Economy* (Sausalito, CA: PoliPointPress, 2009); *False Profits: Recovering from the Bubble Economy* (Sausalito, CA: PoliPointPress, 2010); and *The End of Loser Liberalism: Making Markets Progressive* (Washington DC: Center for Economic and Policy Research, 2011); as well as various papers cited therein.

30. Bureau of Labor Statistics, "Employment, Hours, and Earnings from the Current Employment Statistics survey (National)." Retrieved August 5, 2014, from http://www.bls.gov/ces/.

31. Bureau of Economic Analysis, "National Income and Product Accounts Tables: Table 1.1.5. Gross Domestic Product." Retrieved August 4, 2014, from http://www.bea.gov/iTable/index_nipa.cfm.

household savings rate fell to as low as 2 percent; it had averaged about 8 percent of disposable income from 1952 to 1998.[32]

There were also large real estate bubbles in Spain,[33] the United Kingdom, Ireland, and other countries. Bubble growth in the euro-zone in the 2000s expanded as well, partly because the presumed stability of the euro and much lower interest rates encouraged capital inflows, especially to the peripheral countries that were soon to pay an exorbitant price for their borrowing. Spain, for example, had—in addition to a real estate bubble that was bigger relative to its economy than that of the United States—a huge stock market bubble as well. Eastern Europe saw considerable bubble growth—even without the euro, in countries where the local currency was pegged to the euro or was seen as relatively stable (e.g., Latvia, Estonia, Lithuania, Bulgaria, Hungary, Poland), there were large capital inflows.

Of course the bubbles eventually burst. When this occurred—first and foremost the bursting of the US real estate bubble—it caused the Great Recession, which hit not only the United States but also many countries worldwide. The end result for the United States was that during the first decade of the 2000s, GDP grew at half the rate—not half the growth, but half the rate of growth—as it did from 1980 to 2000. The same is true if we look at the high-income economies as a group.[34] Thus the influence of the rich countries on the growth of low- and middle-income countries was decidedly negative. It is thus all the more remarkable that the

---

32. Bureau of Economic Analysis, "Comparison of Personal Saving in the NIPAs with Personal Saving in the FFAs," 2015. Retrieved February 12, 2015, from http://www.bea.gov/national/nipaweb/nipa-frb.asp.

33. Mark Weisbrot and Juan Montecino, "Alternatives to Fiscal Austerity in Spain," Center for Economic and Policy Research, July 2010, http://www.cepr.net/index.php/publications/reports/alternatives-to-fiscal-austerity-in-spain.

34. IMF WEO database, April 2014. We are looking at GDP, rather than per capita GDP growth here because that is what matters with regard to the rich countries' influence on the growth of low- and middle-income countries.

first decade of the twentieth century showed such a sharp rebound in per capita income growth for low- and middle-income countries after two decades of decline. It is no less remarkable that this rebound has attracted so little attention or attempts to explain it.

What else can account for this growth resurgence? There are policy changes that could have played an important role. Some of the worst mistakes made by neoliberal policymakers, which contributed to poor performance in the prior decade, were corrected, and were not repeated. These included the fixed exchange rates that ended in crisis and/or default at the end of the 1990s, for example in Argentina (see Chapter 4), Russia, and Brazil. The "shock therapy" that devastated Russia and the former Soviet states—most of which did not recover to their 1989 level of GDP for more than a decade—eventually ran its course.

As noted in Chapter 4, the middle-income countries of Asia piled up reserves after the Asian crisis of 1997–1999 so that they would never suffer the same kind of sudden reversal of capital flows that brought on that devastating crash. The reserve accumulations of the Asian countries also allowed them to avoid ever going back to the IMF, which damaged their economies during the regional crisis of the late 1990s. They were not the only ones to leave the IMF's orbit after its failures at the end of that decade: Russia and almost all of Latin America also opted out. Even though the IMF more than tripled its resources when the world financial crisis and recession (2008–2009) struck, it never regained its influence in the middle-income countries that it had lost (see Chapter 4). Since the Fund has often pressured governments to adopt pro-cyclical macroeconomic policies that have slowed growth, its loss of power over many middle-income countries may have contributed to the growth rebound. After all, the Fund's power over middle-income countries was not based solely on its own lending; until sometime in the past decade, it headed a "creditors' cartel" under which funding from the much-larger World Bank, regional lenders such as the Inter-American Development Bank, and sometimes even the private sector depended on IMF approval. This made the IMF the main avenue of influence in developing countries for the US government, which generally pushed a strong neoliberal policy agenda wherever it could. The collapse of this cartel widened the economic and financial policy space significantly in many middle-income countries.

The Fund's behavior during the 2008–2009 world downturn was also more moderate than in the past, especially compared to its actions during the Asian crisis of 1997–1999, or the crises of the 1980s. As noted previously, the majority of IMF loans to low- and middle-income countries as of October 2009 did contain pro-cyclical conditions, that is, either contractionary fiscal or monetary policy, or both, that could be expected to worsen a downturn or weaken recovery. But some of these policies were reversed as the Fund realized—somewhat belatedly for an organization that is charged with monitoring the world economy[35]—that the situation was worsening. The Fund made some efforts to stabilize the world economy, moreover; for example, although it is not clear how much impact the measure actually had, the Fund approved a $285 billion expansion of all countries' reserves held at the IMF.

Whatever the overall net effect of IMF policies during the period—and here one would have to consider its role in the prolonged economic failure of the eurozone, which had a significant negative impact on developing countries—it was clearly not as much of a drag on growth as it had been in the prior decades, in spite of many errors.

Finally, there were other important changes in macroeconomic policy as compared with prior world slowdowns. Leaving aside the debate over how much of these changes were a result of

35. Mark Weisbrot, et al., "IMF-Supported Macroeconomic Policies and the World Recession: A Look at Forty-One Borrowing Countries," Center for Economic and Policy Research, October 2009, http://www.cepr.net/documents/publications/imf-2009-10.pdf.

increased policy options due to the IMF's vastly reduced influence, there were an unprecedented number of developing countries that engaged in counter-cyclical policy, especially expansionary fiscal policy. Frankel, Végh, and Vuletin (2011) found that for the years 2000–2009, 35 percent of developing countries had counter-cyclical policies, as compared to only 8 percent for 1960–1999.[36] They attribute this shift to the increasing strength of institutions in developing countries. But whatever the cause, there is no doubt that there were major changes in macroeconomic policy that allowed many low- and middle-income countries to avoid the fate they had suffered at times when external demand collapsed during two prior decades.

China and India

As noted above, the growth rebound for many countries during the past decade was driven in large part by China. This is a country where the government controls the major banks and corporations—in contrast to the United States and many other countries, where effectively it's mostly the other way around. State-owned enterprises in China account for about 44 percent of the assets of major industrial enterprises.[37] The government owns the four largest banks. The currency is not freely convertible, although the government is currently moving in the direction of making it more convertible on international markets. The Chinese economy has been the most successful growth engine in history.

36. Jeffrey Frankel, Carlos Végh, and Guillermo Vuletin. "On Graduation from Procyclicality." NBER Working Paper 17619, 2011, p. 4.

37. World Bank, "Quarterly Update," June 2010, http://siteresources.worldbank.org/CHINAEXTN/Resources/318949-1268688634523/Quarterly_June_2010.pdf.

The importance of the state's role in the Chinese economy was on display during the 2009 world recession, when China was hit very hard by the results of incompetent economic policymaking in the West. A fall in net exports knocked 3.4 percentage points off China's GDP growth in 2009.[38] For most countries that would have been devastating, but China still managed to grow by more than 9 percent that year, again because of the state's control over the economy and especially investment. The Chinese, moreover, didn't just throw money at its banks, as in the United States; it required them to lend for projects that would stimulate growth and employment. The government is also responsible for the majority of investment, which in recent years has been around 47 percent of GDP[39]—thus the government's share of investment, relative to the economy, is larger than total investment in the US economy.[40] During 2009, China increased its fixed investment by a huge 22.6 percent,[41] thus negating the effect of the loss of demand from the world economy.

At the same time, China contributed enormously to world economic growth that year, because its exports were falling sharply while its imports grew. In fact, world economic growth would have been slightly negative in 2009 if China were not included; with China, it grew by 1.2 percent.[42] If China had been governed by more

38. IMF, "People's Republic of China: 2014 Article IV Consultation-Staff Report; Press Release; and Statement by the Executive Director for the People's Republic of China," July 30, 2014. Table 1, http://www.imf.org/external/pubs/cat/longres.aspx?sk=41799.0.

39. World Bank, "World Development Indicators: Gross Capital Formation (% of GDP)." Retrieved February 9, 2015, from http://data.worldbank.org/indicator/NE.GDI.TOTL.ZS.

40. Bureau of Economic Analysis, "National Income and Product Accounts Tables." Retrieved February 10, 2015, from http://www.bea.gov/iTable/iTable.cfm?ReqID=9&step=1#reqid=9&step=1&isuri=1.

41. Ibid., Table 1.

42. IMF WEO, April 2014.

neoliberal economic policy, as we have been seeing in the eurozone economies, the world recession would have been much worse. This is another illustration of how China—and its unorthodox, state-led economic policies—contributed to this striking rebound in the growth rate of most countries over the decade (2000–2010) that can be seen in Figure 3.2. If a similar crisis had occurred in 1980, when China represented just 2.2 percent of the world economy, many countries would have suffered much more.

Although China's "market-oriented" reforms are often touted as the key to its success, it is important to keep in mind that China's trajectory over the past 35 years is a story of state-led economic development, decidedly at odds with the neoliberal policy reforms of the era. As economists Nancy Birdsall, Dani Rodrik, and Arvind Subramanian noted with a rhetorical question a decade ago: "Would China have been better off implementing a garden-variety World Bank structural adjustment program in 1978 instead of its own brand of heterodox gradualism?"[43]

China's growth acceleration began in the late 1970s and 1980s, well before it opened up to trade or foreign investment. The government did not liberalize its trade in most goods until it could compete in those areas in world markets. As late as 1992, its average tariff was still over 40 percent, about three times the level of Latin America. Trade liberalization was able to contribute to China's growth because it was done carefully, so as not to disrupt existing production—unlike the indiscriminate opening up to imports that was adopted in many other countries.

In fact, China's transition to a mixed economy—with increasing use of markets—was carried out gradually and with caution.[44]

---

43. "How to Help Poor Countries," *Foreign Affairs* 84. no. 4 (Jul–Aug 2005): 136–152.

44. See Bell et al., "China at the Threshold of a Market Economy," International Monetary Fund Occasional Paper 103, 1993, Washington, DC, September 2014; Eswar Prasad, ed., "China's Growth and Integration into the World Economy," International Monetary Fund Occasional Paper 232, 2004, Washington, DC, September 2014, http://www.imf.org/external/pubs/ft/op/232/op232.pdf; and

The country undertook pilot projects, Special Economic Zones (in the 1980s) to experiment with foreign capital and technology, and gradual liberalization of prices. All this was deliberately designed to be able to correct mistakes and expand upon successes, a logical step to take when policymakers are entering uncharted territory. Nearly two decades into its transition, state-owned and collective enterprises still accounted for 75 percent of urban employment.

Compare this to what happened next door in Russia in the same period: "shock therapy," massive and rapid privatization, and rapid decontrol of prices that led to economic collapse, a prolonged depression in the 1990s, and an economy in which organized crime flourished.[45] This contrast illustrates that even when certain forms of liberalization can be beneficial, neoliberal prescriptions can still be disastrous, especially when they are overly simple and dogmatic in their lack of understanding of the particular conditions of an economy.

Although both foreign direct investment and exports did, in the 1990s, come to contribute substantially to China's growth, both were heavily managed and handled quite differently than in other developing countries. The government has played a major role in shaping investments that would fit in with the country's development goals. The government set certain priorities: producing for export markets; increasing the level of technology; transferring technology from foreign enterprises to the domestic economy; hiring local residents for managerial and technical jobs; and not allowing foreign investments to compete with certain domestic industries.

China's policy toward foreign investment has therefore been quite opposite to the major worldwide reforms of recent decades, including

Wanda Tseng et al., "Economic Reform in China: A New Phase," International Monetary Fund Occasional Paper 114, September 15, 1994, Washington, DC, November 2014. https://www.imf.org/external/pubs/cat/longres.cfm?sk=432.0.

45. See David M. Kotz and Fred Weir, *Revolution from Above: The Demise of the Soviet System* (New York: Routledge, 1997).

the rules of the World Trade Organization (WTO); the same is also true in the important area of intellectual property.

Even after China joined the WTO in 2001, for example, China imposed requirements that foreign investors use locally produced inputs in production in the wind turbine industry.[46] Such requirements are in principle forbidden by the WTO. These and other restrictions were successful in getting foreign investors to recruit and train local suppliers. As a result, China has become one of the largest producers of wind turbines in the world. Thus, even as China has become competitive in more and more areas, it continues to rely heavily on industrial policy to shift its comparative advantages to new, promising areas of higher value-added production. That is the history of successful economic development in the world,[47] and it is generally greatly at odds with neoliberal principles, which emphasize the pursuit of a country's current "comparative advantage."

The other big developing country that did not fit the pattern of the worldwide growth slowdown during the neoliberal era was India, which now has about 1.3 billion people and the world's third-largest economy.[48] Per capita GDP grew by just 1.7 percent annually in India from 1960 to 1980, but increased sharply to 3.4 percent from 1980 to 2000.[49] This is not a spectacular growth rate, for example, as compared to China's annual per capita growth of 8.5 percent during the same period. But it is a large increase, and such

46. Keith Bradsher, "To Conquer Wind Power, China Writes the Rules," *New York Times*, December 15, 2010. Retrieved December 14, 2014, from http://www.nytimes.com/2010/12/15/business/global/15chinawind.html.

47. Ha-Joon Chang, *Kicking Away the Ladder: Development Strategy in Historical Perspective* (London: Anthem Press, 2002).

48. IMF, "World Economic Outlook October 2014," October 2014. Retrieved February 6, 2015, from http://www.imf.org/external/pubs/ft/weo/2014/02/weodata/index.aspx.

49. Mark Weisbrot and Rebecca Ray. "The Scorecard on Development, 1960–2010: Closing the Gap?" Center for Economic and Policy Research, April 2011, p. 15, http://www.cepr.net/index.php/publications/reports/the-scorecard-on-development-1960-2010-closing-the-gap.

improvement was uncommon in the developing world during those decades. There were important liberalizing reforms in India in the early 1990s, and some analysts have credited these as having caused India's growth acceleration. The reforms included a sizable reduction in tariffs on imported goods; a loosening of the Monopolies and Restrictive Trade Practices Act, which had subjected many firms to investment licensing and other restrictions; ending most public sector monopolies; and some liberalization of foreign investment.[50]

However, these reforms are unlikely to be the main story, since India's growth for the 1980s, before the reforms, was the same as for the 1990s. India's biggest growth acceleration came in the years 2003–2010, when real GDP grew by an unprecedented rate averaging 8.4 percent annually.[51] Growth slowed in 2008 due to the world financial crisis and recession, but then rebounded sharply for another two or three years. Of course, there are some who would argue that India's record growth spurt for the decade 2000–2010 was a delayed result of the 1991 reforms, and that this growth acceleration, at least, is therefore a neoliberal success story after all.[52]

It is likely that some of the 1990s reforms contributed to the growth acceleration of the past decade. However, there were two macroeconomic policy changes that could have had a more important impact.[53] First was a change in central bank policy on interest rates, which in real terms fell by 4–5 percentage points

---

50. See, e.g., Arvind Panagariya, "India in the 1980s and 1990s: A Triumph of Reforms" (Washington, DC: International Monetary Fund, 2004).

51. IMF WEO, 2014.

52. For a review of the research and evidence on India's liberalization and growth, see Ashok Kotwal et al., "Economic Liberalization and Indian Economic Growth: What's the Evidence?" *Journal of Economic Literature* 49, no. 4 (2011): 1152–1199, http://mypage.siu.edu/lahiri/Econ429/kotwal%28JEL%29.pdf.

53. See, e.g., Surjit S. Bhalla, "Indian Economic Growth, 1950–2008: Facts and Beliefs, Puzzles and Policies," in *India's Economy: Performances and Challenges*, edited by Shankar Acharya and Rakesh Mohan (New York: Oxford University Press, 2010), 39–81.

from 1999 to 2003, just before the big growth acceleration began. Rodrik (2008) also argues that the exchange rate moved from a level that was slightly overvalued in 1960 to an undervaluation of as much as 60 percent in the 2000s, and that this contributed substantially to India's increase in economic growth in the post-1980 period.[54]

India's return to rapid growth after a dip in 2008 (growing by 8.5 and 10.3 percent, respectively, in 2009 and 2010)[55] is widely attributed to aggressive counter-cyclical fiscal and monetary policy.[56] The fiscal deficit widened by 5 percentage points of GDP in one year, and policy interest rates were lowered from 9 percent to 3.25 percent in just seven months, from September 2008 to April 2009. Monetary policy was further loosened with other measures, including a lowering of the cash reserve ratio from 9 to 5 percent during the same period.[57] India was therefore a prime example of the shift away from pro-cyclical toward counter-cyclical policy in developing countries in the first decade of the twenty-first century; and as one of the world's largest economies, it contributed to the growth rebound in that decade.

54. See Dani Rodrik, "The Real Exchange Rate and Economic Growth," *Brookings Papers on Economic Activity* 2 (Fall 2008): 365–412. The exchange rate (REER, or Real Effective Exchange Rate) did not move much during the growth spurt of 2003–2008. See Muneesh Kapur and Rakesh Mohan, "India's Recent Macroeconomic Performance: An Assessment and Way Forward," 2014, IMF Working Paper No. 14–68, http://www.imf.org/external/pubs/ft/wp/2014/wp1468.pdf.

55. IMF, "World Economic Outlook, October 2014," October 2014. Retrieved February 6, 2015, from http://www.imf.org/external/pubs/ft/weo/2014/02/weodata/index.aspx.

56. See, for instance, Muneesh Kapur and Rakesh Mohan, "India's Recent Macroeconomic Performance: An Assessment and Way Forward," IMF Working Paper No. 14–68, 2014, p. 8. Retrieved February 10, 2015, from https://www.imf.org/external/pubs/ft/wp/2014/wp1468.pdf.

57. Ibid.

Aside from the temporary counter-cyclical policies in response to the world recession, the trend in India toward lower real interest rates and a lower valued currency also represents a departure from the neoliberal orthodoxy, which had often led to higher interest rates and an overvalued exchange rate. The two are often related, since higher interest rates will tend to attract capital inflows and therefore push up the value of the domestic currency. These policies also argue against the idea of India's growth increase resulting from neoliberal policy changes.

Still, India's growth acceleration has some features that distinguish it from the experiences of other developing countries. The service sector, including export of services, has played an important role. The service sector share of GDP increased from about 38 percent in 1980 to 57 percent in 2008–2009.[58] The fastest-growing service sectors have included wholesale and retail trade, banking, communications, and business services (which include the call centers and data entry services that have been widely reported on). Whether this represents part of a new development model that other countries, or even India itself, can carry to higher levels remains to be seen.

Another aspect of India's growth acceleration that differs from previous late-developing countries is that it has run trade deficits each year for more than a decade. Fast-growing countries such as South Korea, China, and Taiwan all had export-led growth that produced trade surpluses. As a result, these countries exported capital to the rich countries. That is what happens when a country runs continual trade surpluses[59]—it is accumulating assets in

58. Barry Eichengreen and Poonam Gupta, "The Service Sector as India's Road to Economic Growth," National Bureau of Economic Research Working Paper, February 2011, http://www.nber.org/papers/w16757.pdf.

59. More specifically, it is the current account that is the more appropriate measure here. We are substituting trade for current account here for simplicity, since trade is generally the vast majority of the current account of the balance of payments.

foreign countries, and therefore investing in them or lending the money. This is somewhat at odds with the standard textbook understanding of how development should take place; capital should flow from the rich to the poor countries, seeking a higher return and also (hopefully) enabling the developing countries to increase their growth rates by having more resources available for investment. The Indian story fits the textbook model of development somewhat better in this sense, since by running trade (and current account) deficits it has been importing capital.

Although India has sharply increased its inflows of foreign capital over the decade, from 2.6 to 4.5 percent of GDP, this opening was done gradually and within an extensive regulatory framework of capital controls. Restrictions on the amount of foreign ownership were maintained in a number of important sectors, and foreign direct investment was limited. The result seems to be that Indian firms were able to tap into foreign capital markets, rather than being displaced by foreign firms.[60]

India's growth has fallen off sharply since 2011, and there is continuing debate over whether the growth surge of the 2000s represented a transition to a high-growth economy or was merely temporary. There are massive deficiencies, on one hand, in infrastructure and planning that would be needed for this kind of continued growth; on the other, the country's rate of capital formation—a foundation for economic growth—doubled from 15.6 percent in the 1970s to 31.2 percent for the years 2004–2009.[61]

60. Ajay Shah and Ila Patnaik, "India's Experience with Capital Flows: The Elusive Quest for a Sustainable Current Account Deficit," NBER Chapters, in *Capital Controls and Capital Flows in Emerging Economies: Policies, Practices and Consequences* (University of Chicago Press: National Bureau of Economic Research, 2007), 609–644.

61. Reserve Bank of India, Handbook of Statistics on the Indian Economy, http://www.rbi.org.in/scripts/annualPublications.aspx?head=Handbook+of+Statistics+on+Indian+Economy.

In any case, whether we are looking at 2000–2010, or the increase from the 1960–1980 period to that of 1980–2000, it is difficult to argue that neoliberal policy changes were the driving force in India's economic growth. And for the purposes of the analysis here, it is the 1980–2000 growth rate increase that was anomalous for the developing world. This was a period in which the vast majority of developing countries adopted neoliberal policy changes and, as we have seen, the growth of per capita GDP declined sharply. However large the economy and population of India, it is just one country out of scores in the data set. Even if it could be concluded that neoliberal reforms were successful there, it would not change the picture of the broad neoliberal experiment that failed in the overwhelming majority of cases, with only a few countries improving their economic growth.

Conclusion

In the last two decades of the twentieth century, and in a few countries a bit earlier, a set of policy changes that were—and still are—considered to be positive reforms were introduced in the vast majority of low- and middle-income countries in the world. The results strongly indicate that these reforms on the whole were a failure. This is evidenced by the sharp decline in economic growth in the great majority of low- and middle-income countries, which coincided with and then followed these changes for two decades, and the concomitant decline in progress on social indicators such as infant and child mortality, and life expectancy. Perhaps because it is difficult to come up with an alternative to policy failure as an explanation for this collapse of economic growth, and because there has been such a strong prejudice in favor of the neoliberal reforms implemented, this decline has gone largely unnoticed. Also remarkable is that the rebound had to wait for the most populous country to become large enough to pull other developing countries back toward more normal economic growth rates. It is likely not a coincidence that this country that broke all world-historical growth records—China—was one of the few important economies that did not adopt the neoliberal reforms during this period. China was of course very different from most developing countries in that it was transitioning from a planned economy, but neoliberal dogma was inappropriate in other countries for many and varied reasons. Unfortunately the failed experiment of neoliberalism is not merely of historical or academic interest, since it is ongoing. The prevailing orthodoxy in the economics profession, finance and economic ministries in low- and middle-income countries, and the global media from which many policymakers draw their inspiration and fears, remains much the same as it was 20 or even 30 years ago. The IMF, the World Bank, and the WTO are still largely pursuing policies in the same direction, and although they have met increasing resistance and have lost considerable clout in middle-income countries, they are still the most powerful and influential institutions of global governance.

While it was the norm in developing countries in the 1960s and into the 1970s to have national industrial policies and development planning, these practices were sharply curtailed in many countries during the neoliberal reform period, and have only begun to return in the past decade. Yet this occurs at a time when economic planning has become vastly more important in order to manage a transition to sustainable environmental and energy policies in order to avert global climate disaster. While it may be partly attributable to some movement away from certain neoliberal policies, including the pro-cyclical macroeconomic policies that have often been enforced by the IMF, the rebound in economic growth in the first decade of the twenty-first century does not mark the end of the neoliberal experiment—although it could be the beginning of the end. But just as an alcoholic is unlikely to be cured without recognizing that he has a drinking problem, a transition to more effective macroeconomic and development policies—wherever it takes place—will most likely require some recognition that neoliberal policies were involved in this long-term, large-scale, debilitating economic failure.

There are two objections that may be made to the overall significance of the neoliberal growth failure and its recovery, as well as the lack of recognition of both. The first has to do with flaws in GDP, and therefore also per capita GDP, as a measure of economic and social well-being. A number of valid criticisms have been raised for years:[62] GDP does not take into account the costs of environmental degradation, or conversely, the sustainability of any current growth path or its impact on the welfare of future generations. Various "bads" as well as goods can increase measured GDP, the classic example being cigarettes and the resultant medical treatment for lung and other cancers. In fact, any increase in disease can add to GDP so long as there is paid treatment for it. Non-market activities, including much of the care of children or household labor such as cooking, generally performed by women, are not included in GDP. A society's literacy and educational level are not measured by GDP. The United States has the most expensive healthcare in the world, yet it has worse health outcomes than other high-income countries that spend about half as much. How much of the 17.2 percent of GDP that the United States spends on healthcare[63] is really measuring the benefits of healthcare, rather than wasted resources due to the inefficiency of the healthcare system? GDP per capita does not

62. See, e.g., Joseph Stiglitz, Amartya Sen, and Jean-Paul Fitoussi. "Report by the Commission on the Measurement of Economic Performance and Social Progress," September 2009, http://www.stiglitz-sen-fitoussi.fr/documents/rapport_anglais.pdf.

63. Centers for Medicare & Medicaid Services, "National Health Expenditure Data," May 2014, http://www.cms.gov/Research-Statistics-Data-and-Systems/Statistics-Trends-and-Reports/NationalHealthExpendData/NationalHealthAccountsHistorical.html.

measure subjective well-being or happiness, moreover, although it is one important variable.[64]

While these criticisms represent genuine problems with GDP as a measure of human welfare, that does not detract from the importance of the growth failure and recovery described here. Measures of progress on social indicators declined considerably with the fall-off in GDP for reasons that include the fact that health and education generally depend on governments' ability to spend money in these areas, and that such expenditures generally increase with economic growth. A better overall measure of economic activity and human welfare, if such a unified measure existed for all of these countries, would show a similar huge drop-off, followed by a rebound.

The second, and perhaps more important, objection has to do with the environmental impact of economic growth.[65] This includes of course the most potentially catastrophic human-made environmental threat, climate change, but also other serious environmental problems, including freshwater scarcity, deforestation, species extinction, depletion of marine fisheries, and pollution.

Since greenhouse gas emissions increase with economic growth, it is possible to conclude that less economic growth is better. There is a strong case to be made that the residents of the rich countries and their citizens could make both themselves and the world better off by taking their productivity gains in the form of increased leisure, rather than increased consumption. Indeed, Western Europe has done that, in comparison with the United States, even before the Great Recession and the eurozone crisis. In the 1970s,

---

64. See, e.g., John F. Helliwell, Richard Layard, and Jeffrey D. Sachs, "World Happiness Report 2013," Sustainable Development Solutions Network, September 2013, http://unsdsn.org/wp-content/uploads/2014/02/WorldHappinessReport2013_online.pdf.

65. For a broad overview of the combined challenges of economic development and climate change, see Jeffrey D. Sachs, *Common Wealth: Economics for a Crowded Planet* (New York: The Penguin Press, 2008).

Americans and Western Europeans worked about the same amount of hours, but by 2005 Western Europe had about half the number of hours worked per person as the United States.[66] Partly as a result, Western Europe has also had about half the per capita energy consumption of the United States.[67] The importance of this difference should not be understated: a recent estimate showed that if work hours worldwide were reduced by an average of 0.5 hours per year annually through the end of the century, it would eliminate between one-quarter and one-half of the global warming that is not already locked in.[68]

The choice between increased consumption and more leisure time will also become important for the middle-income countries today that are on their way to becoming high-income countries some decades from now. Whether they choose to go the European route of shorter work hours, or the American way of increased consumption, will also have a significant impact on the rate of global warming.

But for most of the world, that result is quite a ways off. As a matter of politics and ethical claims, developing countries are not going to sacrifice their living standards—and for the poorer among them, basic human needs such as nutrition, health, and education—to save the planet from the effects of accumulated global greenhouse gases (GHG), about half of which were emitted into the atmosphere by the rich countries.[69]

66. Alberto Alesina, Edward Glaeser, and Bruce Sacerdote, "Work and Leisure in the U.S. and Europe: Why So Different?" National Bureau of Economic Research Macroeconomics Annual 2005, Vol. 20, http://www.nber.org/chapters/c0073.

67. See David Rosnick and Mark Weisbrot, "Are Shorter Work Hours Better for the Environment?" (Washington, DC: Center for Economic and Policy Research, 2006). http://www.cepr.net/documents/publications/energy_2006_12.pdf.

68. See David Rosnick, "Reduced Work Hours as a Means of Slowing Climate Change," Center for Economic and Policy Research, February 2013, http://www.cepr.net/index.php/publications/reports/reduced-work-hours-as-a-means-of-slowing-climate-change.

69. "Developing Countries' Contributions to Climate Change Approach 50%," PBL Netherlands Environmental Assessment Agency, October 31, 2013,

Of course, in the short run, a global depression would reduce the rate of GHG accumulation, while condemning hundreds of millions to unemployment and poverty. But that is not how the problem is going to be attacked, nor should it be.

Remember that the growth of GDP is a combination of population growth and growth of productivity—which we can define here as output per hour of labor.[70] Population growth has a straightforward negative impact on climate and the environment. But productivity growth is another story, and that is basically what we have been looking at above, since we have focused on *per capita* GDP growth. Productivity growth, depending on where it occurs and how it is achieved, can have a positive environmental impact. Productivity increases in the production of solar cells or wind turbines can speed the replacement of fossil fuels by lowering the price of these renewable sources of energy. Advances in good quality, reliable, and secure technology for video conferencing could keep billions of tons of carbon dioxide out of the atmosphere by reducing the need for travel. Productivity advances in agriculture in poor countries allow more people to be fed with use of less land. There are countless examples of technological change where productivity increases will be central to the feasibility of transitioning to sustainable resource use, whether of land, water, or the atmosphere. Productivity growth itself is not the problem; on the contrary, it is a necessary part of the solution. Its net impact on the environment, including climate change, will depend on where and how the investment in productivity growth takes place.

Then there is the other part of GDP growth—population growth—which must be reduced if the planet is to have a

---

http://www.pbl.nl/en/news/newsitems/2013/developing-countries%E2%80%99-contribution-to-climate-change-approach-50.

70. We can ignore here changes in the average number of hours worked per employee, as well as the labor force participation rate.

sustainable future. The difference between the United Nations' low and high projections for population growth show a difference between 16.6 billion versus 6.7 billion people in 2100. This translates into a difference of about 1.1 degrees Celsius in global average temperatures,[71] which is most of the warming anticipated under most of the scenarios projected by the Intergovernmental Panel on Climate Change in 2014.[72] Even lower population growth, and therefore less warming, is also possible. Most of the population growth will be in the poorer countries—for example, in the medium-growth projections Africa is forecast to rise from 1.1 billion today to 4.2 billion by the end of the century.[73] These population growth rates will drop sharply as various countries go through what is called the demographic transition.[74]

The demographic transition is a shift from one slow population growth equilibrium to another. The first equilibrium, which today's rich countries achieved when they were poor, is one of high birth rates (or fertility rates—the average number of children born to a woman in the country in her lifetime) and high death rates. Today, the rich countries once again have slow (or in some cases negative)

71. David Rosnick, "The Consequences of Increased Population Growth for Climate Change," Center for Economic and Policy Research, 2014, Table 6, http://www.cepr.net/documents/Climate-population-2014-12.pdf.

72. IPCC, "Fifth Assessment Report: Climate Change 2014: Synthesis Report," *Intergovernmental Panel on Climate Change*, 2014, Table 2.1, p. 63. Retrieved February 16, 2015, from http://www.ipcc.ch/pdf/assessment-report/ar5/syr/SYR_AR5_LONGERREPORT_Corr2.pdf.

73. Department of Economic and Social Affairs, Population Division, "World Population Prospects: The 2012 Revision, Volume I: Comprehensive Tables," United Nations Department of Economic and Social Affairs, 2013, p. 2. Retrieved February 13, 2015, from http://esa.un.org/wpp/documentation/pdf/WPP2012_Volume-I_Comprehensive-Tables.pdf.

74. David Rosnick, "The Consequences of Increased Population Growth for Climate Change," Center for Economic and Policy Research, 2014, p. 9, http://www.cepr.net/documents/Climate-population-2014-12.pdf.

population growth because they have low fertility rates and low death rates (e.g., Germany and Japan).[75]

But between the first and the second stage of low population growth equilibria, there is a big surge of population growth. This acceleration during the demographic transition is a result of the time lag between the lowering of mortality rates—due primarily to advances in sanitation, public health, and food production—and the drop in fertility rates. While the demographic transition is not fully understood, there is a fair amount of research on some of the most important economic and social changes that lower birth rates.[76] These include female education and the empowerment of women, who will tend to have fewer children as they have more economic and social choices; the availability of affordable birth control and family planning; urbanization since children are a source of labor for family farms; increasing economic security, especially in old age, since many people rely on their children for support when they can no longer work; and the infant and child mortality rate, since families will have fewer children—with a time lag—as the probability of survival for an individual child increases.

All of these changes—to reduce the population part of economic growth—will require increases in the productivity component of economic growth, which is of course the component that increases overall living standards. To increase education levels, it will be necessary to build schools and train teachers. Reducing infant and child mortality will require investments in public health. Increasing economic security in old age means public pensions and increased

---

75. For an overview of the historical demographic transition, see Timothy W. Guinane, "The Historical Fertility Transition: A Guide for Economists," *Journal of Economic Literature* 49, no. 3 (2011): 589–614.

76. For overviews, see Sachs, *Common Wealth*, Chapters 7 and 8; and David Lam, "How the World Survived the Population Bomb: Lessons from 50 Years of Extraordinary Demographic History," *Demography* 48, no. 4 (2011): 1231–1262.

private savings, which means rising incomes for the majority of the population.

The neoliberal policy failure that was evidenced in the last two decades of the twentieth century (and since the Great Recession in the rich countries) is a clear form of waste and inefficiency—the waste of the human potential of the unemployed and in many cases unused capital. It is waste that the world cannot afford. There are any number of economic alternatives that can lift people up from poverty while investing in technology that reduces GHG emissions and paves the way to a sustainable environmental path for the future. Those are the alternatives that must now be sought.

4

The Misunderstood Role of the International Monetary Fund

Over the last decade and a half, an epoch-making change took place in international economic relations. This change was so big that it was probably the most important development in the international financial system since the breakdown of the Bretton Woods system of fixed exchange rates in 1973. But hardly anyone noticed it.

What happened is that the International Monetary Fund (IMF) lost most of its influence in developing countries—in particular the middle-income countries. This has turned out to be important for a number of reasons. As noted in Chapter 3, it is most likely part of the explanation of why most developing countries have done better in the twenty-first century than they did during the prolonged economic growth failure during the last two decades of the twentieth century. The IMF often spearheaded big neoliberal policy reforms that coincided with the slowdown: tighter (and sometimes pro-cyclical) monetary and fiscal policies; the abandonment of development strategies and industrial policies; various forms of deregulation; and an often indiscriminate opening of international trade and capital flows.

While some of these reforms may have been helpful in some circumstances, as a package—and often applied as a one-size-fits-all package—they often brought awful results. We have seen, for example, how disastrous it has been for Europe to get its basic macroeconomic policies wrong in just the past few years. But these are high-income countries—even Spain, Greece, and Portugal are relatively well off compared to most developing countries. What has really made the eurozone a unique story is that for the first time in decades, it is high-income countries, rather than low- and middle-income countries, that have suffered from taking the prescribed medicine. But much of the rest of the world, unfortunately, had gotten this kind of treatment for decades; and for developing countries, the effects of bad policies are generally more harmful, and for a number of reasons the recovery time is usually longer.

Until quite recently, the IMF was Washington's most important avenue of influence over economic policy in developing countries. This was due to two institutional arrangements: first, the Fund was placed in the position of "gatekeeper" for funds flowing to developing countries. Borrowing countries who did not meet the IMF's conditions would not get money from the World Bank, regional lenders such as the Inter-American Development Bank, rich-country governments such as those belonging to the Paris Club of creditors, and sometimes even the private sector. This still holds true for many poor developing countries.

I witnessed the breakdown of this creditors' cartel when I went to Bolivia in February 2006, just a month after the country's first indigenous president, Evo Morales, took office. I met with the new economic ministers, and asked them whether Bolivia was going to renew its current Standby Arrangement with the IMF. At the time, Bolivia had been under IMF arrangements for 20 consecutive years, with the exception of a nine-month period. They had undertaken much of what the IMF had demanded of them, including the privatization of the country's vital hydrocarbons sector. Yet Bolivia's income per capita was still less than it had been 28 years earlier. One of the ministers replied that the IMF had been there and offered them a renewal, but the government had said no. Bolivia was still a low-income country, and the IMF asked if they were interested in borrowing through the Poverty Reduction and

Growth Facility. The government, they told me, said "no thanks." They told the IMF that they didn't need any loans.

I was glad to hear this, but then asked about other loans and even grants, for example from the European Union. They said that the IMF had informed them that other sources of funding would no longer be conditional on any IMF agreement. This was a new world for Bolivia—and part of a historic change that would give new freedom to many developing countries. (As we will see in Chapter 5, it would make a huge difference for Bolivia, as the government soon re-nationalized its hydrocarbons sector.)

The second institutional arrangement that made the IMF an instrument of US power was that the US Treasury Department, which represents the US government at the IMF, was not only given a direct veto over major decisions, but was also the predominant decision-making power at the Fund with regard to developing countries.

Although Europe could theoretically muster some allies and outvote the United States at the Fund, this almost never happened during more than 60 years of the Fund's operations. For example, in 1995, when some European governments, on one hand, were quite aggravated that the Fund would not allocate several billion dollars to help stabilize the Russian exchange rate and economy while it was melting down, with then unknown consequences for Europe, Washington, on the other, wanted $20 billion for the Mexican peso crisis.[1] Of course the crisis was a major concern for Wall Street, because of its investments in Mexican government bonds. The Europeans showed their displeasure by abstaining from the latter decision. That was about as contentious at it would get between US and European factions for most of the next two decades.

1. Paul Lewis, "Mexican Rescue Plan: Financial Markets; Wall Street and Its Latin Counterparts Respond with Relief and a Wave of Higher Prices," *New York Times*, February 1, 1995, A16.

In fact, the IMF's executive board rarely voted at all. This came to light in US congressional hearings in 1998, when the US Executive Director (i.e., the US representative) at the Fund, Karin Lissakers, was asked by a member of Congress how often the executive board actually voted. It took a few months to get an answer: of the last 2,000 funding decisions, she said, there had been just 12 formal votes.[2]

We will return to the governance of the IMF below. This is just to offer a glimpse of how the Fund's role in the world has been set by institutional inertia, gentlemen's agreements, and the tight solidarity of a handful of rich countries, led by Washington. The United States established its hegemonic role in the Fund from the institution's beginning, as the only standing industrial power after World War II. As Europe and Japan caught up with the United States economically, they never formally demanded a commensurate say in the Fund. To do so might open the way for developing countries—the ones most affected by IMF policy—also to demand a voice.[3] The IMF's special role as gatekeeper is nothing more than an informal arrangement—there is nothing in the World Bank's rules, for example, that says it must deny a loan to a government that does not meet IMF requirements. It is an agreement among the wealthy country governments in order to form a powerful creditors' cartel—one that can enforce debt collection, as well as impose conditions that US and/or European governments desire. It

2. "Review of the Operations of the International Monetary Fund, Before the Subcommittee on General Oversight and Investigations, Committee on Banking and Financial Services," April 21, 1998 (statement of Karin Lissakers, US Executive Director, International Monetary Fund), http://commdocs.house.gov/committees/bank/hba48110.000/hba48110_0f.htm.

3. This role of historical inertia in maintaining control over the Fund is similar to that of the Permanent Members of the UN Security Council, each with veto power: the US, Russia, France, the UK (the main Allied victors of WWII) plus China. As with the IMF, other rich countries would rather be excluded from this power than to open the way to more developing country representation.

has no more legitimacy than another gentlemen's agreement that has determined, since the institutions' founding, that the head of the IMF should be a European and the head of the World Bank should be an American.[4]

But the IMF's enormous loss of influence over the past decade has meant a serious reduction of US power in the world, and especially American influence over the economic policy of middle-income countries. For this reason, even those who did not understand the economic implications of these changes should have noticed the political implications, as the world moves toward a more multipolar system of international relations. They didn't, however.

Understanding these developments is important to understanding how the world has been transformed over the past decade, and where it may be headed.

The IMF Becomes Noticed in a Turn-of-Century Crisis

The Asian financial crisis, which began in 1997, was the first big blow to the IMF's credibility and power. It was the IMF's intervention in that crisis, and the affected countries' response, that set the stage for many of the changes that would take place in the 2000s—including some imbalances that still plague the global economy today. For example, the big trade imbalance between developing Asia and the United States[5] is to a large extent the result of these countries' decisions to export their way out of the crisis—as they had little other choice—and also a means to build

4. Martin A. Weiss, "International Monetary Fund: Selecting a Managing Director," Congressional Research Service, Library of Congress, R41828, May 20, 2011.

5. US Census Bureau, "Foreign Trade, U.S. Trade in Goods by Country," www.census.gov/foreign-trade/balance/.

up large foreign exchange reserves, so that they would never again have to return to the IMF and its creditors' cartel for funding.

The crisis was, in a number of ways, one of the formative events of the last years of the twentieth century. It popularized the concept of financial contagion, as the crisis spread from Asia to Russia, Brazil, Argentina, and other countries. For some time, many experts worried that it would spread to the United States. In September 1998, then Fed Chair Alan Greenspan said, "It is just not credible that the United States can remain an oasis of prosperity unaffected by a world that is experiencing greatly increased stress."[6] Greenspan's fears proved unfounded: it turned out that the oasis did indeed remain quite unaffected, so long as the US stock market bubble continued to swell. But the crisis was devastating to the region of its origin, and it was eye-opening to see how it spread to the financial markets of other non-rich countries with such apparent irrationality. It seemed that it took nothing more than the herd behavior of international investors looking around the globe to guess which country might be next, and pulling their money out, to spread the devastation.

This caused some of the relevant experts to reconsider the idea that opening up to international capital flows would automatically benefit developing economies, an idea that had taken root in policy circles despite the lack of empirical studies to back it up. These events led to a series of proposals for reform of what came to be known as "the international financial architecture." Some of these proposals were quite ambitious, although they were also sound and sensible. They included an international currency; a world central bank; an international bankruptcy court; an international

6. Alan Greenspan, "Remarks by Chairman Alan Greenspan at the Haas Annual Business Faculty Research Dialogue, University of California, Berkeley, California," Speeches of Federal Reserve Board Officers, September 4, 1998, http://www.federalreserve.gov/boarddocs/speeches/1998/19980904.htm.

regulatory body for the world financial system; and proposals for sweeping reform of the IMF.

I remember thinking that much of this was pie in the sky, and indeed more than 15 years later, there has been very, very little in the way of reform at the international level. But it was not cynicism or pessimism that led me to this conclusion; on the contrary, I was quite optimistic that change would come, and it has. In the debate that took place during those years about how this would happen, I argued that—while reform of IMF policy was something worth fighting for—the bigger changes in the foreseeable future would come not from within the IMF, but from the IMF and its creditors' cartel losing its influence over developing countries. That is what has happened.

The Asian crisis originated in a huge and relatively sudden reversal of international private capital flows in developing Asia. In 1996 there was a private net inflow of $9.3 billion to Thailand, Indonesia, South Korea, the Philippines, and Malaysia; the next year it was a private net outflow of $12.1 billion.[7] This was a change of about 11 percent of these countries' GDP. It is easy to see how this would, and did, cause a crisis: the domestic currency falls, and people want to move their money elsewhere. The foreign exchange reserves of the banking system fall, and then there are more panicked withdrawals. This downward spiral continues as firms go bankrupt. The companies that had borrowed in foreign currency, a practice that had increased substantially with the prior decade's liberalization, were particularly vulnerable. Financial instability increased, and the real economy weakened.

But it would have been relatively easy to stop and reverse the process, if the IMF had chosen to do so. The IMF is often thought of as a lender of last resort, but the Asian crisis made it plain to the

---

7. Steven Radelet and Jeffrey Sachs, "The Onset of the East Asian Financial Crisis," in *Currency Crises*, Paul Krugman, ed. (Chicago: University of Chicago Press, 2000), 105–153.

world that this was not the case. The Fund could have supplied the foreign exchange reserves necessary to stop the panicked capital flight, before it brought about a serious crisis and recession. But it chose not to do so.

The crisis was initiated with the devaluation of the Thai baht in July 1997, when the currency was allowed to float after being previously pegged to the US dollar. At this time it was still possible to avoid most of the damage that the region would suffer. There was even an effort to establish a $100 billion "Asian Monetary Fund" to stabilize the situation, proposed by Japan in September, and supported by China, Taiwan, Singapore, Hong Kong, and other countries. Although to the casual observer it might seem that it was none of Washington's business if these Asian countries chose to help their neighbors out of a financial jam, the proposal was nipped in the bud by the US Treasury Department. Larry Summers, then Deputy Secretary of the Treasury in the Clinton administration, was dispatched to the region to inform the locals that any "bailout" agreement had to go through the IMF.[8]

There was a reason for these dictates: like the European Central Bank (ECB) and its allies in today's eurozone, the US Treasury and the IMF saw the crisis again as an opportunity to win some very unpopular reforms that they wanted. Former US Trade Representative Mickey Kantor expressed this idea bluntly when he said—according to the *Times of London*—that "the troubles of the tiger economies offered a golden opportunity for the West to reassert its commercial interests. When countries seek help from the IMF, Europe and America should use the IMF as a battering ram to gain advantage."[9]

8. Edward A. Gargan, "Asian Nations Affirm I.M.F. As Primary Provider of Aid," *New York Times*, November 19, 1997, http://www.nytimes.com/1997/11/20/business/asian-nations-affirm-imf-as-primary-provider-of-aid.html.

9. "Fund Managers in a Surrey State," *The Times* (London), December 5, 1997, p. 31.

This they did, demanding such changes as South Korea's removal of remaining restrictions on international capital flows and controls on foreign exchange. This was despite the irony that it was the liberalization of capital flows that had caused the crisis in the first place. In a display of terrifically bad timing, just as the Asian crisis was getting underway, the IMF actually proposed changing its charter so as to take responsibility for getting countries to liberalize international capital flows.[10]

Indonesia during the crisis had perhaps a record number of conditions attached to its "bailout"—about 140, including reducing tariffs and removing some restrictions on foreign investment. Some of the conditions looked strange to the untrained eye, such as "allowing cement producers to export with only a general exporter's license."[11] One of the other initial conditions imposed by the IMF was that Indonesia give up its attempt to develop a national auto industry[12]—an effort that probably wouldn't have gotten anywhere, but why take a chance?

In the Western media we were told that it was all about fixing "crony capitalism," as though this were the cause of the crisis.

10. "It is time to add a new chapter to the Bretton Woods agreement," wrote the IMF's Interim Committee in 1997. "Private capital flows have become much more important to the international monetary system, and an increasingly open and liberal system has proved to be highly beneficial to the world economy." From IMF, "Statement of the Interim Committee on the Liberalization of Capital Movements Under an Amendment of the Articles," Report of the Managing Director to the Interim Committee on Strengthening the Architecture of the International Monetary System, October 1, 1998, http://www.imf.org/external/np/omd/100198.htm#attach.

11. Morris Goldstein, "IMF Structural Conditionality: How Much Is Too Much?" Peterson Institute for International Economics, Revision of Paper Presented at NBER Conference on "Economic and Financial Crises in Emerging Market Economies." Woodstock, Vermont, October 2000, http://www.petersoninstitute.org/publications/wp/01-4.pdf.

12. Seth Mydans, "Pressed By I.M.F., Indonesia Accepts Economic Reforms," *New York Times*, January 18, 1998, http://www.nytimes.com/1998/01/15/world/pressed-by-imf-indonesia-accepts-economic-reforms.html.

This made for good sound bites in the United States and Europe, and helped ensure that the Asian governments got the blame for not only the initial crisis but also the complications that followed. But the story was seen differently in the region, where the photograph of IMF Managing Director Michel Camdessus hovering over Indonesian President Suharto as he signed the hated agreement with the IMF became an iconic image. It hammered home what was happening. Despite large-scale corruption by Suharto and his family—his autocratic rule ended only after a wave of protests and riots that left more than 1,000 dead in 1998[13]—many millions throughout Asia still saw that image as symbolic of what the Western creditors' cartel was doing to them. It didn't help that Camdessus referred to the Asian crisis as a "blessing in disguise,"[14] at a time when some Indonesians in the countryside were reduced to eating tree bark, leaves, and insects to survive.[15]

Unfortunately for the hard-hit countries, the Western "battering ram" was not only used to gain advantage for US corporations and banks. The Fund and its allies also wanted to remold the stricken economies along more neoliberal lines. In the crucial first months of the crisis (August to December 1997), when foreign lending could have helped stop the capital outflows that devastated the region, the IMF concentrated on "structural" reforms, and argued that fundamental "structural weaknesses" were the cause of the

13. "Asia-Pacific Inquiry Blames Army for Jakarta Riots," BBC, November 3, 1998, http://news.bbc.co.uk/2/hi/asia-pacific/207067.stm.

14. Michel Camdessus, "The Asian Crisis and the International Response," Speech at the Institute of Advanced Business Studies, University of Navarra, November 28, 1997. Retrieved February 9, 2015, from https://www.imf.org/external/np/speeches/1997/mds9717.htm

15. Nicolas Kristoff, "Asia Feels Strain Most at Society's Margins," New York Times, June 8, 1998, p. 1.

crisis.[16] But these were countries with high savings rates, government budgets that were in balance or surplus, and relatively low debt burdens. They did have current account deficits[17]—and of course that was a problem when the capital inflows that covered these current account deficits came to a "sudden stop." But that is exactly the purpose—or should be—of providing foreign exchange to countries in a situation like this. A timely loan of foreign exchange reserves could have stopped the panic that caused the crisis, and would have given the countries time to lower their current account deficits gradually, including through devaluation.

But the IMF didn't do that until after these economies had sunk deep into recession, millions of jobs had been lost, and lives ruined. Worse, the Fund actually attached conditions to its lending that pushed these economies deeper into recession and exacerbated the crisis—much as the troika has done in the eurozone over the past several years. Budget tightening and increases in interest rates sent these economies spiraling downward.[18] The interest rate increases were more destructive than usual because companies in some of these countries—especially Korea and Thailand—had relatively high levels of debt financing.[19]

In their book *Thirteen Bankers*, former IMF Chief Economist Simon Johnson and James Kwak explain why global policymakers

16. IMF, "Korea—Memorandum on the Economic Program," December 3, 1997, http://www.imf.org/external/np/loi/120397.htm#memo.

17. The regional current account deficit peaked at 5.9 percent of GDP in 1996, with a range from 3.5 percent for Indonesia to 8 percent for Thailand.

18. See Mark Weisbrot, "Ten Years After: The Lasting Impact of the Asian Financial Crisis," Center for Economic and Policy Research, 2007. Retrieved February 11, 2015, from http://www.cepr.net/index.php/publications/reports/ten-years-af ter-the-lasting-impact-of-the-asian-financial-crisis.

19. Michael Pomerleano, Public Policy for the Private Sector, Note No. 155, "Corporate Finance Lessons from the East Asian Crisis," World Bank, October 1998, http://siteresources.worldbank.org/EXTFINANCIALSECTOR/Resources/ 282884-1303327122200/155pomer.pdf.

like the IMF (and more recently, the troika in Europe) see crises as an opportunity to restructure a stricken country's economy:

> [In the 1990s] the United States had urged emerging market countries to deal with the basic economic and political factors that had created devastating crises. This advice was often perceived as arrogant (especially when the United States also insisted that crisis-stricken countries open themselves up further to American banks), but the basic logic was sound: when an existing economic elite has led a country into a deep crisis, it is time for a change. And the crisis itself presents a unique, but short-lived, opportunity for change.[20]

This opportunistic attitude and Mickey Kantor's "battering ram" can help explain much of what the IMF did in Asia during the crisis. But pro-cyclical macroeconomic policies (shrinking the economy when it is already in recession) are a bit more difficult to understand, even from a creditors' or social engineering point of view. We must allow some room for incompetence as well, as part of the explanation. This can be seen, for example, in the closure of 16 banks in Indonesia, which the Fund had hoped would help restore confidence in the banking system. But the result was quite the opposite: there was a run on deposits at the banks that remained open, thus worsening the instability of the banking system.[21]

The IMF's failure in Indonesia was so blatant that even its own Internal Evaluation Office would later acknowledge that "in Indonesia .. the depth of the collapse makes it difficult to argue

---

20. Simon Johnson and James Kwak, *13 Bankers: The Wall Street Takeover and the Next Financial Meltdown* (New York: Random House, 2010), 56.

21. David E. Sanger, "IMF Reports Plan Backfired, Worsening Indonesia Woes," *New York Times*, January 14, 1998.

that things would have been worse without the IMF ... "[22] But it was also clear that the Fund had inflicted unnecessary harm on the entire region, not to mention the contagion that spread to other countries.

Of course some of the countries that were hit by the contagion were vulnerable in part because of IMF programs that had already been implemented or were still in effect. One of these was Russia, which lost about 26 percent of its national income under IMF programs and policies from 1992 to 1996,[23] and was barely recovering when the Asian crisis began in 1997. The decline from 1989 topped 42 percent, one of the worst economic collapses in modern history without a war or natural disaster. Interestingly, the Fund escaped blame for this unprecedented economic failure, in which tens of millions of people were thrown into poverty, and life expectancy for men plummeted from 65.5 years to 57. In fact, the magnitude of the economic failure was at the time barely recognized in the major media or policy circles. This is most likely because of Russia's prior status as a Cold War enemy and rival superpower in earlier decades. As a result of this legacy, failure was in some sense impossible, since Washington and its allies were not planning to establish a successful, prosperous Russia after the collapse of the Soviet Union.

Economist Jeffrey Sachs, who was advising the Russian government in 1992, later reflected on these motivations and his own misunderstanding of them. In that year, inflation in Russia was spiraling into the triple digits and the economy was collapsing. Sachs offered a plan to get inflation under control, which centered around stabilizing the exchange rate—a key element of a potentially successful anti-inflationary policy. For this to succeed it would have

---

22. "The IMF and Recent Capital Account Crises: Indonesia, Korea, Brazil," Evaluation Report, Independent Evaluation Office, 2003, p. 38.

23. IMF, "World Economic Outlook Database, October 2012," http://www.imf.org/external/pubs/ft/weo/2012/02/weodata/index.aspx.

been necessary to have a sufficient supply of foreign exchange reserves—in this case dollars—and Sachs thought he might get a commitment from the United States to provide these reserves. He was wrong. He didn't get the stabilization fund, or the immediate suspension of interest payments, debt cancellation, or other aid he was seeking from the G-7.

Looking back on those events, Sachs noted that "Richard Cheney, then the secretary of defense, and his deputy, Paul Wolfowitz, were drafting the controversial Defense Planning Guidance, which aimed to ensure long-term U.S. military dominance over all rivals, including Russia. . . .

"I had supposed in 1991 and 1992 that the United States would be rooting for Russia's success as it had been rooting for Poland's. With hindsight, I doubt that this was ever the case."[24]

Just as the colossal economic policy failure in Russia went largely unnoticed, so, too, did the economic boom that followed from 1998 to 2008, in which income per person grew by 100 percent.[25] Some of this increase was enabled by rising oil prices, but much was also due to replacing failed policies that marked earlier years. One of these changes was the abandonment of Russia's fixed, overvalued exchange rate, which made room for industrial recovery by allowing Russia's tradable goods to compete on a more level playing field. Russia also managed to vastly increase oil production during this decade, something that was not possible during the economic turmoil preceding these years. But it was difficult to find much open discussion of these factors. Even in 2012, when Vladimir Putin was elected president of Russia for the third time, a mysterious gap appeared in the most prominent discussions of the election. Putin

24. Jeffrey D. Sachs, *The End of Poverty: Economic Possibilities for Our Time* (New York: Penguin Books, 2005), 139–140.

25. IMF, "World Economic Outlook Database, October 2012," http://www.imf.org/external/pubs/ft/weo/2012/02/weodata/index.aspx.

had presided over almost the entire decade-long economic boom that had followed one of history's worst economic failures; a presidential candidate in almost any country would likely win under such circumstances. But news reports, pundits, and analysts seem to have missed this most obvious influence on the election.[26]

While the IMF's failure in Russia mostly escaped notice, the Fund's role in worsening the Asian economic crisis did not. Of course there was plenty of the usual whitewashing. *Time Magazine*'s famous cover photo of February 15, 1999, served up the official story with the perpetrators as heroes: "The Committee to Save the World: The inside story of how the Three Marketers have prevented a global meltdown—so far." The image could have made much of the world laugh, and cry: Treasury Secretary Robert Rubin, Fed Chairman Alan Greenspan, sagely smiling, along with a more somber-looking Larry Summers (Deputy Treasury Secretary).

But the IMF's reputation, authority, and legitimacy were damaged, and thenceforth challenged as never before, as a result of its policy failures in the Asian economic crisis. For the first time, the Fund received criticism from prominent economists, which stung. Joseph Stiglitz, the Chief Economist of the World Bank (who would subsequently receive a Nobel Prize in Economics), told the *Wall Street Journal*: "These are crises in confidence ... You don't want to push these countries into severe recession. One ought to focus .. on things that caused the crisis, not on things that make it more difficult to deal with."[27] The US Treasury Department was

---

26. See, e.g., Ellen Barry and Michael Schwirtz, "After Election, Putin Faces Challenges to Legitimacy," *New York Times*, March 5, 2012, http://www.nytimes.com/2012/03/06/world/europe/observers-detail-flaws-in-russian-election.html; Kathy Lally and Will Englund, "Putin Heads Toward Russia's Presidency," *Washington Post*, March 3, 2012, http://www.washingtonpost.com/pb/world/europe/putin-heads-toward-russias-presidency/2012/03/03/gIQArCC4oR_story.html.

27. Bob Davis and David Wessel, "World Bank, IMF at Odds over Asian Austerity," *Wall Street Journal*, January 8, 1998, A5. Accessed December 14, 2014, http://www.nytimes.com/2010/12/15/business/global/15chinawind.html.

not amused by his public criticism of the IMF; according to the *Financial Times*, there were rumors "for weeks" before Stiglitz's resignation—denied by the Treasury department—that Treasury Secretary Larry Summers had insisted on his removal.[28] Jeffrey Sachs, then at Harvard, was even more caustic than Stiglitz, calling the IMF "the Typhoid Mary of emerging markets, spreading recessions in country after country."[29]

Because of the crisis, the IMF sought a $90 billion increase in contributions from member states, which at that time was considered serious money. Washington's share was $18 billion, but an alliance of Republican conservatives and left-wing Democrats blocked the money on three consecutive votes in the US House of Representatives. The money was eventually approved because the Senate was in favor—but conditions were attached that created a commission of economists to examine the policies and conditions attached to IMF and World Bank lending. The report was highly critical of the IMF.[30]

The Asian economies eventually recovered, and the IMF made sure that the governments of the countries that were "bailed out" made good on many of the loans that the private sector had borrowed from foreign banks.[31] In that sense, at least, it was "mission accomplished" for the Fund and the US Treasury Department.

28. Nancy Dunne, "Knives Out in Washington for a Free Spirit. Joseph Stiglitz: He May Have Criticized the Institutional Consensus on Too Many Points," *Financial Times*, November 25, 1999 (London ed. 2).

29. Jeffrey Sachs, "With Friends Like IMF . . . ," *Cleveland Plain Dealer*, June 6, 1998, p. 8.

30. US Senate Banking, Housing, and Urban Affairs Committee, "Reform of the International Monetary Fund" (hearing before the Subcommittee on International Trade and Finance), 106th Congress, 2nd session (Washington, DC: Government Printing Office, April 27, 2000).

31. Jeffrey Sachs, "The IMF and the Asian Flu," *The American Prospect*, March/April 1998, p. 16. See also, "The IMF and Recent Capital Account Crises: Indonesia, Korea, Brazil," Evaluation Report, Independent Evaluation Office, 2003, pp. 17, 107.

The Argentine Crisis: A Government Says No, and Wins

The Argentine government collapsed in the face of widespread rioting and looting in December 2001, bringing about the end of an economic experiment that had been widely regarded as a proud example of successful reform just a few years earlier. Four presidents would take office over the next two weeks, and the government would default on about $100 billion of its public debt—the biggest sovereign debt default in history.

The IMF had a major role in the Argentine experiment, including its decline and collapse. Argentina suffered from bouts of extremely high inflation from the 1970s until 1991, when it brought inflation under control by means of what was called the Convertibility Plan. The Argentine peso was fixed at an exchange rate of one peso to the dollar, with the peso convertible to dollars upon demand.

This system brought inflation under control, but it subsequently created other problems that became more serious in the ensuing years. First, the currency was overvalued, and this put Argentine manufacturing and tradable goods (and service) industries at a disadvantage, since the country's exports became more expensive and its imports artificially cheap. As a result, part of the country's industry was wiped out, and Argentina began to run trade deficits beginning in 1992.

In February 1994, the US Federal Reserve began a series of interest rate hikes that would raise the short-term (federal funds) rate in the United States from 3 percent to 6 percent over the next year. This action drew capital out of emerging markets, where risks are much greater, and caused the "Tequila crisis" in Mexico in December 1995.

This action also worsened Argentina's problem: since Argentina's currency was tied to the dollar, its interest rates went up with the Fed rate hikes. The country's risk premium also increased as more investors began to worry that the Argentine peso's peg to the dollar could not be sustained. Capital fled Argentina, resulting in a steep recession. GDP fell by 8.1 percent from the last quarter of 1994 to the first quarter of 1996.[32]

Capital inflows resumed in the second half of 1996, but the recovery was short-lived: Argentina was hit again when the Asian financial crisis began in 1997. The country's interest rates on foreign borrowing continued to rise. The Argentine peso was also growing increasingly overvalued, as the US dollar, to which it was pegged, rose against other currencies. Argentina was stuck in a trap: the interest payments and overvalued currency swelled the country's current account deficit, which made investors fear devaluation. As their fears increased, so did interest rates and debt payments. These also added to the federal budget deficit, which added to the investors' fears and therefore the rising interest rates and debt. This constituted a vicious circle that could not be escaped without abandoning the fixed exchange rate.

In 1998, the Asian "contagion" spread to Russia, and then to Brazil. The ruble's fixed exchange rate collapsed in 1998[33] and the Brazilian *real* in 1999.[34] The fate of Argentina's fixed exchange rate was sealed, but its financial agony and depression would continue for nearly three more years as the government, with the help of the IMF, tried in vain to restart the economy without abandoning the peso's peg to the dollar.

32. ECLAC, CEPALSTAT Database, United Nations Economic Commission for Latin American and the Caribbean, n.d. Retrieved February 7, 2015, from http://estadisticas.cepal.org/cepalstat/WEB_CEPALSTAT/estadisticasIndicadores.asp?idioma=i.

33. William H. Cooper, "The Russian Financial Crisis of 1998: An Analysis of Trends, Causes, and Implications," Congressional Research Service, The Library of Congress, February 18, 1998, http://congressionalresearch.com/98-578/document.php?study=The+Russian+Financial+Crisis+of+1998+An+Analysis+of+Trends+Causes+and+Implications.

34. John McHale, "Brazil in the 1997–1999 Financial Turmoil," National Bureau of Economic Research, April 14–15,2000, http://www.nber.org/crisis/brazil_report.html.

The chronology and details of this story are important, because there has been considerable controversy over what went wrong and who is to blame for the worst depression in Argentina's history. The official story, promoted by the IMF and sympathetic economists, as well as many journalists, is that the disaster resulted from the Argentine government's alleged failure to rein in public spending.[35]

The facts and numbers tell a very different story. The combination of a fixed, overvalued exchange rate and completely free mobility of capital into and out of the country was a deadly one. As we have seen, Argentina got stuck in a situation in which rising interest rates added to its budget and current account deficits, creating more doubts about the country's ability to maintain the peso at parity with the dollar, thereby increasing its interest rates and borrowing, and so on, in an accelerating spiral toward devaluation and default. The government's fiscal policy had little or nothing to do with the problem.

This can be seen clearly from the official data alone. From 1993 to 2001, Argentina's national government saw its spending rise by 2 percent of GDP—but all of this increase was attributable to increasing interest payments. If we exclude interest payments, government spending, called primary spending, actually declined as a percentage of GDP during this period. The primary budget (i.e., not including interest payments) was in surplus throughout most of these years. And even if we look at the national budget as a whole, including interest, the deficits were fairly small, averaging only 1.3 percent of GDP for 1993–2001. During the last two years of the fixed exchange rate period, as the country approached economic collapse, the deficit rose to peaks of 2.4 and 3.2 percent of GDP. But even these deficits are relatively modest, in the context of the economic depression into which

---

35. Anoop Singh, "Introductory Remarks on the role of the IMF Mission in Argentina," Press Briefing, Buenos Aires, April 10, 2002, http://www.imf.org/external/np/tr/2002/tr020410.htm.

the country had fallen.[36] Most important, the deficits were caused by declining tax revenues as the economy shrank, not by government spending (other than the swelling interest burden described above). In other words, the deficits were a result, rather than a cause, of the country's economic crisis.

Equally important, the deficits that did accumulate between 1994 and 2001 can also be attributed to a factor that the IMF and its sister institution, the World Bank, had sponsored: the privatization of Argentina's social security system. Before privatization, Argentina had a "pay-as-you-go" system like that of the United States: beneficiaries receive payments from payroll taxes collected in the same year. But in order to create a system of individual accounts, the inflow of tax revenue that is currently paying benefits must be diverted to these accounts; and it takes some decades before the private accounts can be drawn upon for benefits. This means that the government must find a way to finance the "transition costs"—to pay current promised benefits while the individual accounts are built up.[37] In Argentina, privatization was implemented in 1994; nearly the entire federal budget deficit in 2001 can be attributed to the lost revenue, plus forgone interest, from the privatization of social security.[38]

Thus the idea that Argentina's fiscal profligacy was the "root cause" of the crisis is completely without foundation. Throughout

36. Some analysts have pointed to the fiscal deficits of the provinces as adding to the problem, but these totaled 1.1 percent of GDP in 2000 and peaked at 1.9 percent in 2001. Like the federal deficits, they were not large and were a result, rather than a cause, of the depression.

37. These transition costs were one of the major stumbling blocks in President George W. Bush's proposal to create individual accounts within the US Social Security system, with objections coming from fiscal conservatives.

38. See Dean Baker and Mark Weisbrot, "The Role of Social Security Privatization in Argentina's Economic Crisis," Center for Economic and Policy Research, Washington, DC, April 2002, http://www.cepr.net/publications/reports/the-role-of-social-security-privitization-in-argentinas-economic-crisis.

Argentina's troubles, the Fund recommended dealing with the series of external shocks from the global economy—over which Argentina had no control—by tightening the government's fiscal and monetary policies. As in the case of eurozone over the past few years, however, this just worsened the recession and the crisis.

The Fund kept pouring in more money, as private investors became increasingly reluctant to loan into an impending disaster. In January 2001 they arranged a $40 billion loan package—14 percent of Argentina's GDP—in a futile effort to maintain investor confidence, and foreign exchange reserves, within the doomed fixed exchange rate regime.[39]

After the default on the debt in December 2001, and the collapse of the peso, the IMF quickly moved to dissociate itself with the failed policies that had caused the worst economic disaster in the country's history. Fund officials and others maintained that all of these economic policies—including the pro-cyclical policies intended to maintain, against growing odds, the fixed exchange rate—were implemented at the insistence of the Argentine government, and often against the advice of the IMF. These arguments were widely accepted, and the most prominent criticisms of the IMF for the debacle have been that it was too lenient with Argentina—purportedly allowing lending despite the government's profligacy and unsound macroeconomic policies.

While it is true that the Argentine government "owned" most of the policies that led to disaster, including the convertibility system, it defies logic to claim that the Fund was merely guilty of throwing money at problems. The IMF would not lend $40 billion to Russia in order to finance the re-nationalization of Russian industry. The

39. IMF, "IMF Approves Augmentation of Argentina's Stand-By Credit to US$14 Billion and Completes Second Review," Press Release 01/3, January 12, 2001, http://www.imf.org/external/np/sec/pr/2001/pr0103.htm.

Fund cannot have it both ways: Argentina did not become the IMF's third-largest debtor during this period by defying the IMF's recommendations and pursuing its own course.

The idea that the IMF would lend Argentina money to support policies—including exchange rate polices—that it did not agree with was put to rest soon after Argentina had defaulted on its debt. "In the long term we do not believe a dual exchange rate system is sustainable,"[40] said Anne Krueger, then second in command at the IMF, when the government was considering a different exchange rate for exporters in order to capture some of the gains that they would get from the devaluation. Krueger added that until Argentina agreed on a "fairly coherent program that gives promise in the medium run" of improving Argentina's economy, "there is no point in our talking about a fund support program for them."[41] The Fund was very clear: no matter how desperate the situation, it would not lend money to a government that was implementing policies it did not like. This was just the start of Argentina's post-default troubles with the IMF.

Argentina in the beginning of 2002 needed real help, perhaps more than at any time in its modern history. The banking system had collapsed, bank accounts were frozen, and the country was facing an angry middle class that had been promised their peso deposits would always be matched by dollars at a one-to-one rate. The economy was at rock bottom, with first-quarter GDP down at a 16.3 percent annual rate. Official unemployment would peak at 21.5 percent, with underemployment at an additional 19 percent. The majority would fall below the poverty line in a country that

---

40. Anne O. Krueger, "Transcript of a Press Briefing on Argentina," International Monetary Fund, January 11, 2001, http://www.imf.org/external/np/tr/2002/tr020111.htm.

41. Anthony Faiola, "Argentina's Peso Is Freed to Float, and Quickly Sinks; Protests Against Economic Changes Become Violent in Buenos Aires," *Washington Post*, January 12, 2002, http://www.highbeam.com/doc/1P2-335669.html.

until recently had enjoyed among the highest living standards in Latin America.[42]

Yet the IMF was in no hurry to help. As it turned out, negotiations would drag on for the entire year of 2002, concluding only after it was clear that the Argentine economy was already recovering. The IMF still saw "failures in fiscal policy" as the "root cause" of the crisis, and was determined to attack the problem at its roots.

Under pressure from the IMF, the Argentine Congress passed a central government budget in the spring of 2002 that cut spending by about 15 percent, including salary and pension cuts of 13 percent for government employees. This was certainly a recipe for prolonging the depression.

But the Fund pushed not only for fiscal but monetary tightening as well. The IMF's Anoop Singh called for the central bank to "strictly limit the growth of its own credit" and to move toward establishing "a full-fledged inflation-targeting regime—such as that adopted by other countries, including Brazil after its own difficulties in 1999."[43] There's no telling how much further Argentina might have sunk if it had followed this advice.

In other words, the Fund continued to recommend the same contractionary policies that had helped the depression drag on for nearly four years. But perhaps equally remarkable in the depth of this economic crisis, when the country had such a desperate need to rescue a collapsed banking system and restart the economy, were the Fund's demands for a number of politically unpalatable changes that did not seem necessary for the recovery. For example, the IMF wanted Argentina to change its bankruptcy law. Mr. Singh

42. "Encuesta Permanente de Hogares, Incidencia de la Pobreza y de la Indigencia, Resultados del segundo semestre 2011," Instituto Nacional de Estadísticas y Censos, Republica de Argentina, Buenos Aires, April 25, 2012.

43. Anoop Singh, "Introductory Remarks on the Role of the IMF Mission in Argentina," Press Briefing, Buenos Aires, April 10, 2002, http://www.imf.org/external/np/tr/2002/tr020410.htm.

stated that "the international community could not be expected to support Argentina without the early adoption of a framework that provides an appropriate balance between creditor and debtor interests."[44]

But it seemed to be only creditors that the Fund was looking out for. IMF negotiators also demanded the repeal of an "economic subversion" law under which the government could investigate acts by firms, banks, or individuals that damage the economy or cause harm to large sectors of the population.[45] (This is something that would have been quite popular in the United States, and many other countries, after the 2008 financial collapse.) At the time, the law was being used to investigate capital flight that violated banking restrictions implemented during the crisis.

As the Argentine government conceded to more of the IMF's demands throughout 2002, it appeared that the goal posts were being moved, as new conditions were added. Some began to question whether the IMF really wanted an agreement, or whether its officials were concerned that an accord would appear to "reward" a country that had recently carried out the largest sovereign debt default in history.[46] Whatever the cause of the difficulties in negotiations, the episode certainly contradicts the notion that the Fund is set up to function as a lender of last resort.

If the IMF had acted as a lender of last resort, it could have prevented the collapse of the financial system as well as many bankruptcies, helped to arrange credit for export industries, and greatly

44. Anoop Singh, "Introductory Remarks on the Role of the IMF Mission in Argentina," April 10, 2012, http://www.imf.org/external/np/tr/2002/tr020410 .htm.

45. BBC, "Argentina Scraps Key Economic Law," May 30, 2002, http://news.bbc. co.uk/2/hi/business/2016410.stm.

46. Mark Weisbrot, "When Surrender Isn't Good Enough," Knight-Ridder/ Tribune Information Services, April 22, 2002, http://www.cepr.net/index.php/ op-eds-&-columns/op-eds-&-columns/when-surrender-isnt-good-enough.

reduced the loss of employment and output that Argentina suffered in the first quarter of 2002. But it did none of these things. Instead, it blocked credit in what appeared to be an effort to pressure the government into an agreement with its private foreign creditors on more favorable terms. This is pretty much a polar opposite of what a lender of last resort would do.

A $700 million loan that the World Bank had approved was not disbursed because the Bank was waiting for an agreement with the IMF.[47] Loans from private lenders, European governments, and apparently export credits were also held up.[48] Put another way, the IMF appeared to be playing its traditional role as head of a creditors' cartel, trying to win certain concessions from the debtor. Some of these concessions were idiosyncratic to the Fund and not necessarily of importance to the creditors, while others reflected the direct interests of the private creditors, with the Fund seeking to use its status as gatekeeper to increase the creditors' bargaining power.

This role as creditors' advocate would become more explicit after the IMF finally signed an agreement with Argentina in January 2003, a full year after the collapse of the Argentine financial system. By this time the economy was recovering on its own, and would grow by a healthy 8.8 percent in 2003. But the IMF agreement provided no new resources to Argentina, only allowing the country to roll over its debt to the international financial institutions. The new agreement only went up to August, and during this time the IMF would continue to press for Argentina to "negotiate

47. World Bank, "Press Release: World Bank Continues Support," July 19, 2002, http://web.worldbank.org/WBSITE/EXTERNAL/NEWS/0,,contentMDK:200551 57~menuPK:34466~pagePK:34370~piPK:34424~theSitePK:4607,00.html.

48. See Alan Cibils, Mark Weisbrot, and Debayani Kar, "Argentina Since Default: The IMF and the Depression," Center for Economic and Policy Research, Washington, DC, September 2002, http://www.cepr.net/publications/reports/ argentina-since-default-the-imf-and-the-depression.

in good faith" with private foreign creditors on its non-performing (defaulted) debt.

On May 25, 2003, Néstor Kirchner, a Peronist former governor of the sparsely populated province of Santa Cruz, was sworn in as president of Argentina. Although the scheduled second-round runoff election had not taken place, there was no question about Kirchner's mandate. He had a 30–40 percentage point lead in the polls against his opponent, Carlos Menem, who had been president from 1989–1999, and who was identified with what the majority of voters now saw as failed economic policies. Menem stood down, leaving Kirchner, who had campaigned against "neoliberalism," the presidency. Kirchner immediately pledged not to "return to paying the debt at the cost of the hunger and exclusion of Argentines, generating more poverty and social conflict."[49]

The government would offer about 25 cents on the dollar to the private holders of defaulted debt, and was in no mood to pay much more. This offer would still have left Argentina with a debt of about 90 percent of GDP. Given the low interest rates on most of the renegotiated debt, such a large debt load was potentially manageable for some years, at least until it had to be rolled over in the future at much higher interest rates.

Foreign creditors, especially from Europe and Japan, lobbied their governments to get the IMF to press for more. The Fund began to invoke a little-known internal policy which provides that the IMF should not "lend into arrears"—that is, lend to a government that has fallen behind on its debt payments unless "the member is pursuing appropriate policies and is making a good faith effort to reach a collaborative agreement with its creditors."[50] With only

---

49. Larry Rohter, "Argentina's Chief Is Sworn In and Comes Out Fighting," *New York Times*, May 26, 2003, http://www.nytimes.com/2003/05/26/world/argentina-s-chief-is-sworn-in-and-comes-out-fighting.html.

50. IMF, "IMF Policy on Lending into Arrears to Private Creditors," June 14, 1999, www.imf.org/external/pubs/ft/privcred/.

eight months of life for the January agreement, the pressure on Argentina to offer more was building.

As in 2002, the IMF had a number of politically troublesome demands for the government. According to press reports,[51] the Fund pressured the government to allow a rate increase for the utility companies, which were privatized and foreign-owned. This would have been a blow to most consumers, who were still suffering from the effects of the depression, and who resented the fact that these companies had made a windfall during previous years because their price increases were tied to the US consumer price index even while Argentina experienced deflation. It also seemed to many that this was none of the IMF's business, but rather another response to pressure from European governments whose companies had bought the privatized utilities: "The Fund has no reason to be lobbying for particular business groups," declared President Kirchner.[52] The Argentine government did not give in on this issue.

Perhaps the most difficult to comprehend of the IMF's demands was that the government get rid of the emergency mortgage foreclosure protection for homeowners. This is something that the millions of Americans who have lost their homes since the US housing bubble burst might relate to. Legislation passed in 2002 delayed foreclosures on mortgages for homes that were a family's "sole and permanent residence." According to Argentine government officials in 2003, the Fund insisted that this freeze on mortgage foreclosures had to go, if there was to be a new agreement with the IMF.[53] As a result of the economic collapse and the

51. Adam Thomson, "Argentina and IMF Lock Horns as Deal Expires," *Financial Times*, September 2, 2003.

52. Alan Beattie and Adam Thomson, "Argentina Loan Rollover Delayed by Wrangling IMF Deal," *Financial Times*, September 8, 2003.

53. Larry Rohter, "The Homes of Argentines Are at Risk in I.M.F. Talks," *New York Times*, June 23, 2003, http://www.nytimes.com/2003/06/23/international/americas/23ARGE.html.

devaluation—many homeowners had mortgages owed in dollars, but their bank accounts were converted to pesos, now worth about US$0.30—millions of Argentine homeowners were behind in their payments. Although it is not clear exactly how many would have been evicted if the freeze on foreclosures had been lifted, it could easily have been politically explosive. A leader of the Argentine Debtors Association summed up the general sentiment: "[I]t is not right that the same I.M.F. that remained silent when our savings were stolen from us is now pushing to have us thrown out of our homes."[54] What made the IMF's position on this issue—never publicly declared—so unusual is that even the domestic bankers' association appeared to be in favor of maintaining the freeze, for fear that too many repossessed homes hitting the market could further depress real estate prices.

On traditional IMF policy issues, there was the usual fiscal austerity, more than before: the Fund wanted the government to commit to a primary budget surplus (i.e., the surplus if interest payments are not included) of 4.5 percent of GDP for 2004, and even larger surpluses over the next two years. This was good for creditors but made the government and its various constituencies wary about choking off the country's hard-won, and presumably fragile, economic recovery.

The Fund also wanted to slow the growth of the money supply. This appeared even to conservative central bank and finance ministry officials in Argentina as another case of dangerous overkill. Like a general still fighting the last war, the IMF saw hyperinflation as a real danger, and that was a major reason for its support of the fixed exchange rate all the way to the abyss at the end of 2001.

To see how far off the mark the IMF economists' projections were, in January 2003 they forecast that Argentina would grow by

54. Ibid.

2.5 percent for the year, with inflation of 35 percent.[55] The actual results were in a different universe altogether: 8.8 percent growth and only 3.7 percent inflation.[56]

Alfonso Prat-Gay, who was appointed to head Argentina's Central Bank in December 2002, summed up the prevailing denial about the Argentine economic recovery that the Fund—and most of the business press—fell victim to:

> "People have gone from 'Argentina will hit hyperinflation tomorrow' to 'OK, it didn't happen, but it won't last long; this is an Indian summer,'" Mr. Prat-Gay said in an interview. Then it became "'OK, it might not be an Indian summer but there's no investment,'" he said, followed by "'OK, we can see some investment, but it's mostly construction, so it's not productive investment.' And now that they've seen investment in machinery and equipment, the story is [energy] bottlenecks."[57]

Much of this persistent pessimism was probably wishful thinking on the part of various experts who wanted to see Argentina pay a long-term price for defaulting on its debt. Editorials in the business press were quite bitter, all the way up to the settlement between Argentina and the creditors holding defaulted debt in

---

55. IMF, "Argentina, Memorandum of Economic Policies of the Government of Argentina for a Transitional Program in 2003," January 16, 2003, http://www.imf.org/external/np/loi/2003/arg/01/index.htm.

56. Ministerio de Economía y Producción, Republica Argentina. It is worth noting that IMF projections have generally been noticeably overoptimistic on growth. See Dean Baker and David Rosnick, "Too Sunny in Latin America? The IMF's Overly Optimistic Growth Projections and Their Consequences," Center for Economic and Policy Research, September 16, 2003, http://www.cepr.net/documents/publications/econ_growth_2003_09.pdf.

57. Michael Casey, "Does Argentine Recovery Have Legs?" Dow Jones Newswires, April 9, 2004, A7.

2005. But the IMF's errors on monetary policy were more part of a systematic bias endemic to the institution, and were repeats from previous crises in the late 1990s in Asia, Russia, and Brazil. In both Russia and Brazil, Fund economists had exaggerated the dangers of hyperinflation that could supposedly result from the collapse of fixed exchange rate systems. Fortunately in Argentina, the monetary targets that the government had agreed to for 2003 were soon abandoned, and that probably helped the country's recovery.

But there was one crucial, dramatic showdown between the Argentine government and the IMF in September 2003 that was perhaps a historic moment in the history of not only Argentina but also of the Fund and the region. The IMF was pushing hard for concessions on a number of issues, including the debt. The government refused to give in, but without a new loan from the Fund, Argentina would not be able to make payments due that month to the Fund itself. Now, this was much more serious than defaulting to private creditors. By international custom, the IMF was a special creditor, and nobody but "failed states" like Afghanistan or Sudan had defaulted to them. In such a case, essential credit in the private sector, such as letters of credit from banks that are necessary to carry on normal trade, can be cut off. Nobody knew if the IMF would use this "nuclear option" against Argentina; Brazil had indicated that it would help its neighbor in such an event. My own view at the time was that it would be too politically costly for the Fund to inflict this kind of punishment on a country that was not a "pariah" or "failed state," but it was a tense moment. The government of Néstor Kirchner was gutsy, and held firm; it technically went into default when the payment came due on September 9. Within a week, the IMF backed down and agreed to lend Argentina enough money to maintain its debt payments to the Fund.[58] Another crisis had

---

58. Tony Smith, "Argentina Defaults on $3 Billion I.M.F. Debt," *New York Times*, September 10, 2003, http://www.nytimes.com/2003/09/10/business/ argentina-defaults-on-3-billion-imf-debt.html.

passed, and the IMF's power as the leader of a creditors' cartel had taken another blow.[59]

Nonetheless, the IMF pushed hard for better terms for the private creditors,[60] including not only a better offer on the debt swap, but higher primary budget surpluses so that more of the national income could go to debt service. The Argentine government, under Kirchner, had to have another confrontation with the IMF in March 2004, going once again to the brink of default to the Fund itself. An agreement was signed, but by August the government suspended it, in another highly unusual, unilateral action.[61] It proved to be an important move: the government wisely avoided having to confront both the IMF and the private creditors at the same time. In other words, if not for the suspension of the IMF agreement, the Fund could have used its leverage in deciding whether Argentina was in compliance with agreed-upon benchmarks in order to exert more pressure on behalf of the private creditors.

The details of the Argentine case are important because they illustrate so starkly the most common misconceptions about the IMF, as well as some others about the global economy. Clearly the Fund did not act as a lender of last resort, as detailed above. To the contrary, it drained billions of dollars out of Argentina after the country's financial system collapsed. But it did try to use its considerable muscle as head of a creditors' cartel to win a better deal for the private creditors. As the Fund is widely viewed as a champion of "free markets," it is also worth noting that such intervention on behalf of creditors is the opposite of a market solution. The common description of the

59. Tony Smith, "Argentina Reaches Deal on 3-Year Aid Package," *New York Times*, September 11, 2003, http://www.nytimes.com/2003/09/11/business/argentina-reaches-deal-on-3-year-aid-package.html.

60. Adam Thomson, "Argentina Pays Dollars 3.1bn IMF Bill," *Financial Times*, March 10, 2004.

61. EIU, "Argentina: IMF Talks Suspended," Economist Intelligence Unit—Country Monitor, August 16, 2004.

IMF as an institution that promotes "free-market" policies is therefore also inaccurate.

A New IMF? The Fund since the Great Recession: Changing Slowly, Almost Glacially

We began this chapter with the observation that the collapse of the IMF's influence in most middle-income countries was a historic change, one of the most important changes in the international financial system in more than six decades. When Dominique Strauss-Kahn became managing director of the IMF in November 2007, the IMF's influence was at a low point. Total outstanding loans at that time were just $17 billion, down from $110 billion only four years earlier.[62] But by the time he resigned in May 2011, that number had bounced back to $125 billion,[63] with agreed-upon loans at least twice that much.[64] The IMF's resources available for lending tripled from a pre-crisis $250 billion to an unprecedented $750 billon by October 2009,[65] and would increase more in the ensuing years.[66]

---

62. IMF, "Total Fund Credit and Loans Outstanding," and "SDR/USD Exchange Rate," International Financial Statistics Database, n.d. Retrieved February 19, 2015, from https://stats.ukdataservice.ac.uk/index.aspx?r=662533&DataSetCode=IFS#.

63. Ibid.

64. IMF, "IMF Lending Arrangements as of April 30, 2011," 2011. Retrieved February 19, 2015, from http://www.imf.org/external/np/fin/tad/extarr11.aspx?memberKey1=ZZZZ&date1key=2011-04-30.

65. IMF, "IMF Standing Borrowing Arrangements," 2014. Retrieved February 19, 2015, from http://www.imf.org/external/np/exr/facts/gabnab.htm.

66. IMF, "IMF's Financial Resources and Liquidity Position, 2009—May 2011," n.d. Retrieved February 19, 2015, from http://www.imf.org/external/np/tre/liquid/2011/0511.htm.

Despite being vastly bigger than ever before, however, the Fund did not recover the influence that it had lost in middle-income countries. And since the IMF had been the most important avenue of influence for Washington on economic policy in developing countries, US influence had not rebounded, either. By 2012, most of the IMF's lending—even as measured just by outstanding loans—was in Europe. But it had commitments to the eurozone that were several times bigger than the approximately $90 billion in outstanding loans. So this was where the overwhelming majority of IMF lending was now concentrated. The middle-income countries of Asia, Latin America, and also Russia, which had broken away from the IMF after the Asian crisis, never came back. Now the IMF had a new role, in the implementation of austerity policies in high-income countries in the eurozone, as well as some middle-income countries in Eastern Europe and the former Soviet Union.

As has been noted in Chapter 2, the Fund's lending in the eurozone, which has overwhelmingly become its largest commitment, was different—here it was the junior partner in the troika, with the European Commission and the ECB. In matters of European economic policy, the United States would defer to the European authorities and their directors and governors within the IMF. This is much different from the IMF's traditional role either as an institution with its own decision-making, or in its historical role with the US Treasury Department mainly calling the shots, as was previously the case in its decisions regarding developing countries. Nonetheless, the Fund has something of its own identity and policy direction as an institution, and it is worth examining how much it has changed in its ideas and practices since the Great Recession.

The IMF's Independent Evaluation Office (IEO) took it to task for its errors and omissions in the run-up to the Great Recession, in a critical report published in 2011. Looking at the IMF's performance in the years 2004–2007, the report noted that the IMF "fell short" in its "most important purpose" of "warning member countries about risks to the global economy and the buildup of vulnerabilities in their own economies," and that this failure was due to such factors as "a high degree of groupthink; intellectual capture," and "an institutional culture that discourages contrarian views," . . . "while political constraints may have also had some impact."[67]

While the report was hardly loved in IMF circles, in reality it was probably too generous. The IMF produces the World Economic Outlook every six months, as well as the Global Financial Stability Report and the Fiscal Monitor, as part of its duty of surveillance of the world economy. It missed the two biggest asset bubbles in the history of the world: the US stock market bubble (which burst in 2000–2002), and the US housing bubble (which began to collapse in late 2006). Both of these bubbles caused recessions when they exploded, with the bursting of the US housing bubble directly causing the Great Recession. These bubbles were not only easy to recognize in hindsight; they were quite plain and obvious for years before they burst. Dean Baker took the time to explain the basic arithmetic underlying both of them, well in advance of their collapse.[68] As Baker demonstrated, the prices of stocks in the United States (not just technology companies or the NASDAQ, but the broad indices) in the late 1990s were not compatible with any plausible growth projections for the economy.[69] Similarly, during the housing bubble he pointed out that US house prices grew 50 percent more than inflation from 1997 to 2006, after just keeping pace with inflation

---

67. Independent Evaluation Office, "IMF Performance in the Run-Up to the Financial and Economic Crisis: IMF Surveillance in 2004–07," Evaluation Report, 2011, pp. vii, 1, http://www.ieo-imf.org/ieo/pages/CompletedEvaluation107.aspx.

68. See, e.g., Baker's 2002 paper, "The Run-Up in Home Prices: Is it Real or Is it Another Bubble?" Center for Economic and Policy Research, August 2002. Retrieved February 12, 2015, from http://www.cepr.net/index.php/reports/the-run-up-in-home-prices-is-it-real-or-is-it-another-bubble/.

69. Dean Baker, *Plunder and Blunder: The Rise and Fall of the Bubble Economy* (Sausalito, CA: PoliPointPress, 2009), 58.

for the prior half-century.[70] By looking at rents, demographics, and the various "this time is different" explanations for the run-up in home prices, he was able to show very clearly that there was no believable explanation other than that of a bubble.

It is no excuse to say, as defenders of the Fund will do, that most other economists and investment fund managers also missed these bubbles. Most of these actors had conflicting interests. For example, money managers are often rewarded or punished for their performance relative to their peers. A mutual fund manager who saw the stock market bubble in 1999 is faced with a dilemma: if, on the one hand, he pulls out of the stock market, and—before its bursting—it provides double-digit returns for another year to those who stay in, he may very well be punished. On the other hand, if he stays in, the bubble bursts, and his fund loses 20 percent along with everyone else, that could be much less threatening to his job or career. There were also financial giants like Goldman Sachs who clearly understood the housing bubble before it burst and were able to profit from "The Big Short."[71,72]

The IMF, by contrast, was spending hundreds of millions of dollars annually on research and was entrusted with monitoring the global economy, not simply managing a university endowment or a hedge fund. Members of the Fund's research department should have been able to check obvious sources and detect the magnitude of an asset bubble in real estate of more than $8 trillion. The IMF produced recommendations for improvement in its 2011 Triennial

70. Dean Baker, "Recession Looms for the U.S. Economy in 2007," Center for Economic and Policy Research, November 2006, http://www.cepr.net/index.php/publications/reports/recession-looms-for-the-us-economy-in-2007.

71. See Charles H. Ferguson, *Predator Nation: Corporate Criminals, Political Corruption, and the Hijacking of America* (New York: Random House, 2012).

72. Michael Lewis, *The Big Short: Inside the Doomsday Machine* (New York: W. W. Norton, 2010).

Surveillance Review.[73] There has been some improvement in the IMF's multilateral surveillance and risk assessment in the past few years, but it remains to be seen whether the Fund will do better in the run-up to the next global financial crisis. Overall, it has not done very well in its recommended policies since the Great Recession began.

A look at 41 countries[74] that had IMF agreements as of October 2009 found that 31 of them had been subjected to pro-cyclical macroeconomic policies—either fiscal or monetary policies (or in 15 cases, both)—that would be expected to worsen an economic downturn in the borrowing countries. In some cases, the IMF relaxed its targets and recommendations as the world economy and these particular countries' economies worsened. Sometimes (as in the cases of Hungary, Latvia, the Republic of Congo, and Haiti) the policy changes appeared to be the result of social unrest or other pressures on the borrowing government. But the original errors, made after the US economy had begun its Great Recession and the world recession was well under way, were often very costly; they were also somewhat inexcusable. No matter how one looks at it, IMF program lending during the Great Recession had harmful conditions attached for the majority of borrowing countries. This was not yet a "new IMF."

As late as April 2014, when the Fund approved a two-year, $17 billion Standby Arrangement with Ukraine,[75] it was *déjà vu* all over

73. IMF, "2011 Triennial Surveillance Review," October 2011, https://www.imf.org/external/np/spr/triennial/.

74. Weisbrot et al., "IMF-Supported Macroeconomic Policies and the World Recession: A Look at Forty-One Borrowing Countries," Center for Economic and Policy Research, October 2009, http://www.cepr.net/index.php/publications/reports/imf-supported-macroeconomic-policies-and-the-world-recession/.

75. IMF, "IMF Country Report: Ukraine: Request for a Stand-by Arrangement—Staff Report; Supplement; Staff Statement; Press Release; and Statement by the Executive Director for Ukraine," USA, 2014, https://www.imf.org/external/pubs/cat/longres.aspx?sk=41516.0.

again. After two years of almost no economic growth, the IMF was projecting a 5 percent decline in GDP for 2014. Yet the Fund insisted on austerity amounting to about 3 percent of GDP over the next two years—the equivalent for Ukraine of cutting out the annual $500 billion base budget of the Pentagon in the United States. Such a move had a very good chance of prolonging and/or deepening the recession, and indeed after a 6.8 percent contraction in GDP in 2014, the IMF is projecting another 5.5 percent decline for 2015.[76] Once again, the Standby Arrangement suggests that the IMF sees the crisis as an opportunity to reshape Ukraine's economy, rather than tending to the needs of economic recovery first.

Ukraine at this time was facing a number of downside risks that made austerity particularly inappropriate. The country's exports are about 50 percent of GDP, and half go to the European Union and Russia, two economies that were still weak at that moment. Investment in Ukraine was also weak (about half its pre–Great Recession peak) and the uncertainty surrounding the possibility of further civil conflict weighed upon investors. And the banking system was unstable, in large part due to the effects of the falling domestic currency on loans that had been contracted in foreign currencies. It remains to be seen if—assuming there are no unforeseen political calamities—the directors of the Fund will take into account the strategic interests of the US and EU governments, which presumably want political stability in Ukraine now that a pro-Western government has been elected there. There was a lot of political resistance to the 2010 IMF agreement, and the Fund cut off disbursements for non-compliance. The United States and the European Union may want to reconsider how much pain can be inflicted on a restive and still somewhat divided population,

---

76. IMF, World Economic Outlook Database, April 2015, http://www.imf.org/external/pubs/ft/weo/2015/01/weodata/weorept.aspx?pr.x=69&pr.y=8&sy=2010&ey=2020&scsm=1&ssd=1&sort=country&ds=.&br=1&c=926&s=NGDP_RPCH&grp=0&a= .

especially after the civil war has added considerable economic damage. But the Fund's program for the country has been straight out of the traditional playbook.

To be fair, there were a couple of positive developments in IMF policy during this time. In 2009, the IMF made available some $283 billion worth of Special Drawing Rights to member countries without conditions. (SDRs are IMF reserve assets that can be exchanged for hard currency.) It is difficult to say if this had much impact in countering the global recession. Most of the funds were allocated to the high-income countries, which had no need for it. About $20 billion was allocated to low-income countries, but many of these did not believe they could afford to take on new debt. The Fund also made some limited credit available without conditions, but it only went to a few countries that happened to have right-wing governments allied with the United States: Poland, Colombia, and Mexico. Still, for those hoping that precedents would lead eventually to new policies at the IMF, these were unprecedented policies.

Perhaps the biggest changes were in the Fund's research department, where there seemed to be more tolerance for open debate on some important policy issues. For example, there has been new IMF research that acknowledged that developing countries could benefit from capital controls in some situations.[77] Other research questioned whether central banks were targeting too low of an inflation rate, which could unnecessarily reduce growth and employment.[78] The IMF's research director, Olivier Blanchard, also produced a

---

77. José Antonio Cordero and Juan Antonio Montecino, "Capital Controls and Monetary Policy in Developing Countries," Center for Economic and Policy Research, April 2010, http://www.cepr.net/documents/publications/capital-controls-2010-04.pdf.

78. Olivier Blanchard, Giovanni Dell'Ariccia, and Paolo Mauro, "Rethinking Macroeconomic Policy," International Monetary Fund Staff Position Note 10/03, February 12, 2010, https://www.imf.org/external/pubs/ft/spn/2010/spn1003.pdf.

short piece in the October 2012 "World Economic Outlook" that caused a bit of a stir. It showed that IMF economists had significantly underestimated the fiscal multipliers in making their growth forecasts for countries during the world recession. In other words, the losses in output and employment were significantly worse than expected because of the error in measuring the impact of government spending and taxation on growth. Blanchard and Daniel Leigh followed up with a longer paper that confirmed this result.[79] It would be welcome news if this and other good research at the Fund had some impact on policy, but if it did, it is not yet noticeable. Blanchard himself has made any number of statements to the press against stimulus policies or against even beginning to reverse the austerity. In October 2012, in spite of his research and with Europe in the second phase of its "double-dip" recession, he told the German press that "now is not the time for fiscal stimulus." He had made similar statements regarding the United States: in October 2010, with unemployment stuck at 9.5 percent and amid talk of the need for more fiscal stimulus, Blanchard weighed in against any new stimulus measures.[80] A year later, when asked about his 2010 paper that advocated central banks targeting inflation as high as 4 percent, he walked back from this, too, saying that such a policy was meant "for normal times," and not for the weak economies that the high-income countries currently faced.[81] But this conclusion makes no sense, since a higher inflation target is much more urgently needed, and the risks associated with it much

79. Olivier Blanchard and Daniel Leigh, "Growth Forecast Errors and Fiscal Multipliers," International Monetary Fund Working Paper 13/1, January 2013, https://www.imf.org/external/pubs/ft/wp/2013/wp1301.pdf.

80. "IMF's Blanchard Says No Need for More U.S. Stimulus," Reuters, October 8, 2010, http://www.reuters.com/article/2010/10/08/us-imf-blanchard-idUST-RE6974AZ20101008.

81. "Blanchard Says Global Economy Faces 'Enormous Risks'," Bloomberg TV, http://www.washingtonpost.com/business/blanchard-says-global-economy-faces-enormous-risks/2011/09/23/gIQAUCcyqK_video.html.

smaller in the environment of weak demand and low inflation that prevailed at the time.

In other words, the glimpses of light in IMF research didn't seem to illuminate even high-level policy statements, much less actual policies. And these policies appear to be pretty well entrenched in the high-income countries as well. As explained in Chapter 1, an examination of 67 Article IV consultations—the reports produced by required regular meetings between the IMF and member governments—for the EU governments during the four years 2008–2011 revealed a consistent and disturbing pattern. Fiscal tightening, pension cuts, reductions in healthcare spending, increasing labor supply, and reducing the size of the state constituted the vast majority of the Fund's recommendations.

To be fair to the IMF under Strauss-Kahn (2007–2011) and his successor, Christine Lagarde, neither the managing director nor the Fund's top economists are ultimately in charge of policy. This is especially true when we are talking about policies for countries that are important to the people who actually run the institution. The IMF's governors and executive directors have the ultimate authority over decision making. In practice, this means that the US Treasury department has the overwhelmingly dominant voice, with some input from other rich countries— although Washington generally defers to the European governments on policy in Europe, such as that concerning the eurozone. In general, there are rarely substantive differences between the policymakers of these two huge economies.

So there would probably need to be a big shift in the structure of power at the IMF before there would be major changes in policy. This is true regardless of who is Managing Director. When Dominique Strauss-Kahn was at the helm, he seemed to be aware that the austerity in Greece was counterproductive not only for Greece but for the eurozone. However there was not much that he could do about it, despite the fact that he had a strong personal stake in the outcome: prior to the scandal that toppled him in

2011, he was planning to run for president of France, and certainly did not want to risk having the IMF involved in a major economic failure while he was running the organization.

The vast majority of the world has little or no say at all in the Fund, and there has been a movement to change that for more than two decades. In the last five years, there has finally been some change in voting shares within the Fund. The shift has been marginal, however; the share of "emerging market and developing countries"—with the vast majority of the world's population—has gone from 39.4 to 42.1 percent, while the G-7 countries have 43.1 percent, including 16.75 percent for the United States, down from 17 percent for the pre-reform period. China, the world's largest economy,[82] with about one-sixth of the world's population, has just 3.8 percent of the voting shares; the United Kingdom, with one-twentieth of China's population and about one-seventh of China's GDP, has more, with 4.3 percent. Further changes were proposed in 2010, but these have yet to be implemented and are also somewhat marginal. However, at this point the voting and governance structure is not the main obstacle to changing IMF policy. At present, the developing countries—and we should add in the victimized countries of the eurozone—are not using their potential influence within the Fund. Their representatives are mainly concurring with the decisions of the G-7. If any sizable bloc or blocs of these countries were to band together for change within the Fund, there could be some real reforms in the institution.

The World Trade Organization provides a compelling counter-example that shows what developing countries can do when they act together within a multilateral organization. For more than a

---

82. By the best measures of China's purchasing power parity (PPP) exchange rate, China's GDP has already passed that of the United States. See Robert C. Feenstra, Hong Ma, J. Peter Neary, D. S. Prasada Rao, "Who Shrunk China? Puzzles in the Measurement of Real GDP," National Bureau of Economic Research, January 2012, http://www.nber.org/papers/w17729.

decade and a half, they have formed blocs and opposed Washington and its allies on a number of issues—ranging from policies on patent monopolies for pharmaceuticals to policy space for development and food security. These efforts have succeeded in preventing and changing numerous initiatives from the rich countries that would have harmed developing countries, despite the fact that the WTO's founding rules have been very much rigged against their interests. The WTO formally has a consensus process, unlike the weighted voting-share system of the IMF that gives Washington and its allies a majority of the votes. But that is not what has made the difference between who has a voice in these two organizations; the main difference is the often active role taken by developing countries and their representatives in the WTO, versus the mostly passive role that they have at the IMF. Institutional inertia can be a powerful force, and it can persist for decades.

Of course, it is entirely possible that Washington and its allies would scuttle the IMF and World Bank entirely, if they could no longer control them in the manner to which they have been accustomed. That remains to be seen. In the meantime, the Fund will continue to lose influence as more and more countries become free to avoid its policy choices and recommendations. There is progress in history, if not so much within the IMF.

5

The Latin American Spring

President Richard Nixon was swearing—as he would later become known for doing—as his then National Security Adviser Henry Kissinger and Ambassador to Chile Edward Korry walked into the Oval Office for a meeting at 12:54 p.m. on October 15, 1970. "That son of a bitch, that son of a bitch," Korry recalled him saying. Nixon explained: "It's that son of bitch Allende—we're going to smash him."[1]

He was referring to the democratically elected president of Chile, Salvador Allende Gossens, a leftist. Some weeks later, Nixon would offer some reasons for his animosity, recorded in a memo that would be kept secret for thirty years: "Our main concern in Chile is the prospect that he [Allende] can consolidate himself, and the picture projected to the world will be his success. . . . If we let the potential leaders in South America think they can move like Chile and have it both ways, we will be in trouble. . . . Latin America is not gone, and we want to keep it. . . . No impression should be permitted in Latin America that they can get away with this, that it's safe to go this way."[2]

---

1. Peter Kornbluh, *The Pinochet File: A Declassified Dossier on Atrocity and Accountability* (New York: The New Press, 2013), pp. 24–25.

2. Ibid., p. 79; White House, Memorandum of Understanding, National Security Council Meeting—Chile, November 6, 1970. Retrieved February 12, 2015, from http://www.gwu.edu/~nsarchiv/news/20001113/701106.pdf.

Nixon and Kissinger were knee-deep in a losing war in Vietnam. But in those days, the United States had officials who could handle more than one crisis at a time, and by September 11, 1973, they succeeded in helping the Chilean armed forces overthrow President Allende in a military coup. A dictatorship led by General Augusto Pinochet was established, and proceeded to eliminate its political opposition. Thousands were murdered, and many more were imprisoned, tortured, and driven into exile. A Latin American experiment in social democracy was violently snuffed out.

It wouldn't be until 1975 that some of the details of Washington's involvement in the coup would be documented by the Church committee,[3] a Senate committee set up to investigate US covert operations. And it would take about a quarter-century before a left-wing government would again come to power through the ballot box in Latin America.

But when the election of leftist governments started at the turn of the millennium, it spread quickly. In the past 15 years, this shift was one of the most important geopolitical changes in the world. It has received relatively little attention in journalistic and academic circles, and what light it has received has mostly been filtered through a distorted lens. As late as April 2013, US Secretary of State John Kerry offended the region by referring to Latin America as the United States' "backyard,"[4] but he was at least a decade behind the curve. Latin America today, and especially South America, is more independent of the United States than Europe is. Beginning in 1998, left-wing governments were elected and re-elected until they had governed a majority of the

3. "Covert Action in Chile, 1963–1973," Staff Report of the Select Committee to Study Governmental Operations with Respect to Intelligence Activities, US Senate, 1975, http://fas.org/irp/ops/policy/church-chile.htm.

4. Committee on Foreign Affairs, "Securing U.S. Interests Abroad: The FY 2014 Foreign Affairs Budget," 113th Congress, 1st session, April 17, 2013, http://www.gpo.gov/fdsys/pkg/CHRG-113hhrg80463/html/CHRG-113hhrg80463.htm.

region: Venezuela, Brazil, Argentina, Bolivia, Ecuador, Chile, Uruguay, and Paraguay in South America; El Salvador, Nicaragua, and Honduras in Central America.

Although it could hardly be clearer, the reader may have a tough time finding much that is written about the main impetus for this seismic political shift. For more than 20 years during the neoliberal era, Latin America suffered a collapse of economic growth that was unprecedented in the region for at least a century, and indeed uncommon in the history of modern capitalism (see Figure 5.1). The result of this long-term economic failure was a revolt at the ballot box; indeed, most of the South American presidents, including Brazil's Lula da Silva when he was first elected in 2002, ran explicitly against what they called "neoliberalism."

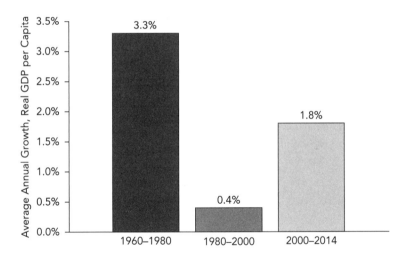

FIGURE 5.1 Per Capita GDP Growth in Latin America

Source: Mark Weisbrot and Rebecca Ray, "The Scorecard on Development, 1960–2010: Closing the Gap?" Center for Economic and Policy Research, April 2011, http://www.cepr.net/index.php/publications/reports/the-scorecard-on-development-1960-2010-closing-the-gap; and IMF, "World Economic Outlook, October 2014." Online database, http://www.imf.org/external/pubs/ft/weo/2014/02/weodata/index.aspx.

As we will see, these new governments implemented significant changes in economic policy. Depending on the country, there were changes in macroeconomic policy, including fiscal, monetary, and exchange rate policy, as well as social programs that included conditional cash transfers; increased access to housing credit or public housing; expansion of healthcare, public pensions, education, and credit; and increased public investment. The overall results have been quite positive, although one would not know it from most of the press, which has been overwhelmingly negative.

The political part of this story is also widely ignored or distorted, and it is inseparable from the economic changes. It also helps to explain why this geopolitical shift has been greeted with mostly silence or derision. Part of the reason that these Latin American electorates voted for the left and its anti-neoliberal agenda in the past decade and a half was because they could. In Latin America during most of the twentieth century, Washington—in collaboration with various local military and economic elites—effectively had a veto over electoral results that it did not like, from the gunboat diplomacy that led to Panama's break from Colombia in 1903, to the overthrow of Allende. These violent interventions and dictatorships convinced much of the Latin American left that an electoral route to social and economic change in their region was not possible.

That perception changed in 1998 and the first decade of the twentieth century, as the left won elections throughout most of the region, and ushered in the "second independence" of Latin America. This was an important part of the process in creating the policy space necessary to improve living standards that had stagnated for a generation. But the conflict with Washington was not over. Even as one country after another distanced itself from the International Monetary Fund (IMF)—which, as we have seen, had previously been the United States' primary instrument of influence over economic policy in developing countries—the US government pursued a Cold War strategy of "containment" and "rollback." This policy has failed in its objective to restore US influence to the status quo ante, with few exceptions—for example, Honduras (2009)[5] and Haiti (2004),[6] where US-backed coups succeeded in ousting leftist governments. Yet the United States continues to pursue this strategy to this day, and it remains part of the challenge that the region faces in pursuing a sustainable development path. We will return to this part of the changing dynamics below, after first looking at some of the economic and social changes that Latin America's "second independence" has brought.

Figure 5.1 shows the growth of per capita income in Latin America and the Caribbean over the past half-century, divided into three periods. The region provides a profound example of the growth collapse discussed in Chapter 3. From 1960 to 1980, per capita income nearly doubled, growing by 91.5 percent. This was not the fastest growth in the world, as compared, for example, to South Korea during this period, or the record-breaking growth that China would later accomplish. But it was enough to dramatically raise the living standards of the vast majority of people, including the poor in the poorest of countries.

From 1980 to 2000, the region had barely any per capita income growth at all, averaging just 0.3 percent annually for a cumulative total of 5.7 percent.[7] This is the worst long-term growth performance for the region in more than a century. The 1980s are often referred to

5. Mark Weisbrot, "Top Ten Ways You Can Tell Which Side the United States Government Is on with Regard to the Military Coup in Honduras," Center for Economic and Policy Research, December 16, 2009, http://www.cepr.net/op-eds-&-columns/op-eds-&-columns/top-ten-ways; and Mark Weisbrot, "Honduras Needs Help from the South," *The Guardian*, November 18, 2011, http://www.cepr.net/index.php/op-eds-&-columns/op-eds-&-columns/honduras-needs-help-from-the-south.

6. See Peter Hallward, *Damming the Flood: Haiti and the Politics of Containment* (New York: Verso Books, 2010).

7. Rebecca Ray and Mark Weisbrot, "The Scorecard on Development, 1960–2010: Closing the Gap?" Center for Economic and Policy Research, April 2011, http://www.cepr.net/documents/publications/scorecard-2011-04.pdf.

as "the lost decade," as per capita income actually fell for the decade. This prolonged depression and stagnation is sometimes blamed on the unsustainable borrowing during the prior years that led to a debt crisis. However, the debt crisis was really a result of the larger economic and financial crisis of the 1980s. It is true that the region was hit with a number of very serious shocks in the beginning of the decade: the US and world recession; a large increase in interest rates on foreign borrowing; declining prices of raw materials exported by some countries; and most important, a sudden cutoff of capital inflows, of the kind that precipitated the Asian crisis of the late 1990s.

But none of this should have led to such a prolonged and unprecedented slump. Recall that Argentina's economy contracted for just one quarter after its massive default and devaluation at the end of 2001, and then entered a period of six years of very rapid growth. Bértola and Ocampo (2012)[8] compare the 1980s with the defaults of the 1930s during the Great Depression, and note that the region's recovery during the Great Depression was much more robust.

Another illustrative comparison is the eurozone countries since the 2008 financial crisis and recession, particularly, Spain, Greece, Portugal, and Italy—a protracted slump that has resulted from bad policy. This is what happened in Latin America during the "lost decade" of the 1980s and into the 1990s. Although the results varied by country, the region was forced into a severe adjustment not only to pay off debt but, once the IMF was involved on behalf of the creditor countries, to institute structural reforms (as in today's eurozone) that the Fund and its sponsors in Washington desired.

The cause and effect here cannot be overemphasized, because it is so often misunderstood. It is also a major theme of this

8. L. Bértola and José Antonio Ocampo, "Latin America's Debt Crisis and Lost Decade," Institute for the Study of the Americas, February 20, 2012, http://www.ilas.sas.ac.uk/sites/default/files/files/filestore-documents/events/Papers/Bertola_and_Ocampo_paper.pdf.

book: there is *always* a feasible path to return to economic growth that does not involve suffering through a prolonged depression. External shocks can cause a recession, but it takes the wrong policies, sustained over a considerable period of time, to make that recession into a long-term economic tragedy. Latin America's depression and stagnation for the 15 years after 1980 was not a result of over-accumulation of debt, or for that matter anything that happened before 1980. In this case, it was because the feasible paths to recovery—which would have included, as in the 1930s, debt default—were blocked by powerful political actors who had other goals. These actors included the US government and its allies, among them the IMF and multilateral lenders, and the private banks for whom these official creditors and governments were trying to collect. Together they were able to squeeze out a massive transfer of resources, which averaged more than 6 percent of GDP over seven years, to outside the region.[9]

The results were devastating for Latin America, and included not only the long depression but increases in poverty (from 40.5 percent in 1980 to 48.4 percent in 1990;[10] see Figure 5.2) and inequality. Hyperinflation in several countries and high inflation in most were also a result of these awful policy choices. The most important underlying problem that led to these inflationary spirals was in balance of payments crises, brought on by unsustainable debt service that should have been erased through default and restructuring.

The region did considerably better in the twenty-first century, averaging 1.8 percent per capita GDP growth annually for 2000–2014. This can also be seen in Figure 5.1. It did not catch up

---

9. Ibid.

10. Economic Commission for Latin America and the Caribbean (ECLAC), "Social Panorama of Latin America 2013," United Nations, March 2014, http://repositorio. cepal.org/bitstream/handle/11362/36736/S2013869_en.pdf?sequence=1.

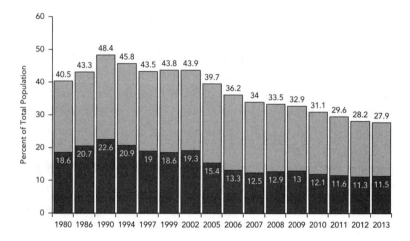

FIGURE 5.2 Latin America: Poverty and Extreme Poverty

Source: Economic Commission for Latin America and the Caribbean, "Población en situación de indigencia y pobreza," 2014. Online database, http://interwp. cepal.org/sisgen/ConsultaIntegrada.asp?idIndicador=182&idioma=e.

to the growth of the pre-1980 period, but it was nonetheless a huge improvement. And there were significant external shocks during this period, including the financial crisis and Great Recession of 2008–2009, and the general slowdown of the world economy, including China, in the years that followed, as well as the milder US recession of 2001 when the stock market bubble burst.

It also included a period of rising demand and prices for a number of commodity exports from Latin America, including hydrocarbons, other minerals, and agricultural products. It has become common to dismiss the rebound in the twenty-first century as a "commodities boom," but that is clearly not the main story. The idea of a "commodities boom" is that GDP growth can be boosted when there is a sizable increase in a country's export prices relative to import prices, or what is known as the country's "terms of trade." We have already seen (in Chapter 2) that this was not what propelled Argentina's upswing that began in 2002. The story is similar for the region as a whole, despite the fact that a few of the larger countries (Venezuela, Chile, Colombia, and Peru), as well as Bolivia and Ecuador, did experience a significant improvement in their terms of trade from 1999 to 2011. (Brazil, which is another country that is often seen as a major beneficiary of commodity price increases, actually did not.) But during this period, a statistical analysis of the data for 1999–2011 finds no correlation between GDP growth and improvements in the terms of trade.[11] Commodity prices were not the driving force of the growth rebound.

Of course, improvements in the terms of trade could have contributed to rising living standards, and therefore also to the reduction of poverty, in some countries, without increasing GDP growth. This is because imports are not calculated as part of domestic GDP, but if they become cheaper in terms of the value of a country's exports, that can lead to increases in domestic consumption.

But it is much more likely that the "commodities boom" contributed to regional growth indirectly in a different way. Prior to the twenty-first century, many Latin American countries were vulnerable to balance of payments problems—or even crises, as during the so-called lost decade. The increase in commodity prices during the first decade of the twenty-first century allowed exporters of these goods to increase their reserves and therefore avoid these difficulties. In the case of middle-income countries generally, the increase freed them from having to knock at the door of the IMF, and accepting its sometimes poisonous lending conditions during hard times.

As noted in the previous chapter, counter-cyclical macroeconomic policy was more prevalent in developing countries during and following the Great Recession, and this was certainly the case

11. See David Rosnick and Mark Weisbrot, "Latin American Growth in the 21st Century: The 'Commodities Boom' That Wasn't," Center for Economic and Policy Research, May 2014, http://www.cepr.net/documents/terms-of-trade-2014-05.pdf.

in most of Latin America. This contrasts with earlier decades, when pro-cyclical policy could lead to prolonged downturns and weak recoveries, as in the eurozone in recent years.

The balance of policy changes and other influences that led to Latin America's renewed economic and social progress was different in each country. In the following sections, we will look briefly at some of the highlights for four countries that underwent major changes in the twenty-first century: Brazil, Bolivia, Ecuador, and Venezuela.

Brazil

Tens of thousands of Brazilians poured into the streets of Sao Paulo and other cities when Lula da Silva was elected on October 27, 2002. It was Lula's (and his Workers' Party's [PT]) fourth attempt at the presidency. There was plenty of fear and animosity in high places this time, too, at home and to the north. "There is a real prospect that Castro, Chavez, and Lula da Siva could constitute an axis of evil in the Americas," wrote US Congressman Henry Hyde in a letter to President George W. Bush a few days before the election.[12] Hyde's rhetoric was extreme, but he was not an irrelevant party. At the time, he served as chair of the International Relations Committee in the US House of Representatives, a position in the US political system that can allow for significant influence over foreign policy.

The majority of Brazilians, who gave Lula (politicians are often referred to by their first name, or a nickname, in Brazil) his landslide victory of more than 61 percent, saw things differently. Here was a president from a different class of people entirely, not only in

---

12. Frank Gaffney, "Bush Is Asked to Prevent Hemispheric 'Axis of Evil' and Back Ouster of Venezuela's Chavez," Center for Security Policy, October 25, 2002, http://www.centerforsecuritypolicy.org/2002/10/25/bush-is-asked-to-prevent-hemispheric-axis-of-evil-and-back-ouster-of-venezuelas-chavez-2/.

his modest origins but in his career path as a labor union organizer and leftist political activist. He was the first Brazilian president ever who not only didn't attend college, but didn't go to high school, having begun working at the age of 12. Like millions of factory workers who use machinery, he had a lifetime reminder of this in the form of a missing finger. During the military dictatorship he was jailed, but came out fighting. He had spent his whole life organizing for working and poor people—an unusual resumé for a president of almost any country.

The Workers' Party had long called for land reform, a re-examination of the foreign debt (in prior years, a default), and redistributive policies in one of the most unequal economies on the planet. Lula also put forth a different vision of Brazil's place in the world: an end to "foreign domination" from the United States, whether through commercial agreements or the IMF. He campaigned against the proposed Free Trade Area of the Americas (FTAA), which he called "a policy of annexation of Latin America by the United States."[13] He promised an independent foreign policy that would look more seriously to South America, as well as to the rest of the world, and not just the United States and Europe.

Wall Street began to freak out as soon as Lula first pulled ahead in the polls. Goldman Sachs developed a "Lulameter," which purported to use currency fluctuations to help estimate Lula's probability of winning.[14] Their disapproval provoked a downgrading of Brazilian sovereign bonds by US financial firms and credit rating agencies. These actions, primarily foreign-led, helped spur a serious financial crisis that did not end until after the election. The

---

13. Marc Cooper, "Many Oppose Trade Deal," *The Nation*, February 11, 2002. Retrieved November 28, 2014, from http://www.thenation.com/article/many-oppose-trade-deal.

14. Goldman Sachs, "The 'Lulameter,'" *Emerging Markets Strategy: Bonds, Currencies, and Interest Rates*, June 6, 2002, GS Global Economics Website, http://moya.bus.miami.edu/~sandrade/Lulameter_GS.pdf.

Brazilian stock market and currency both crashed by about 40 percent between March and October 2002; dollar-denominated sovereign bonds took a similar tumble.

But Lula successfully reassured financial markets with the "right" cabinet appointments and a macroeconomic program that was, at least at first, continuous with that of the prior government. This consisted of three basic principles.[15] First, the Central Bank targeted inflation, within a certain band. (In recent years this has turned out to be a 4.5 percent target, with two percentage points in either direction.) Second, Brazil pursued a "managed" floating exchange rate regime, that is, the currency was allowed to float without any pre-announced target, but the government would intervene in the foreign exchange market when it deemed it necessary to move the currency in either direction. And third, the government targeted a sizable primary budget surplus—that is, a surplus if interest payments on the public debt are not included. Lula also pledged to make the Central Bank independent, a move that is always a crowd-pleaser in the financial sector, and agreed to meet the conditions of a new IMF loan negotiated at the height of the presidential campaign in 2002.

The Central Bank was able to meet its inflation target consistently after 2004, but this was done primarily by allowing the *real*, Brazil's currency, to appreciate. This in turn lowered import prices. In other words, when the Central Bank raised interest rates in Brazil, it could reduce inflation, but not in the way that the Federal Reserve does in the United States. There, when the Federal Reserve raises interest rates in order to lower inflation, it reduces demand for the important real estate and auto sectors and some other

15. See Franklin Serrano and Ricardo Summa, "Macroeconomic Policy, Growth and Income Distribution in the Brazilian Economy in the 2000s," Center for Economic and Policy Research, June 2011, http://www.cepr.net/publications/reports/macroeconomic-policy-growth-and-income-distribution-in-the-brazilian-economy-in-the-2000s.

borrowing, causing the economy to slow and unemployment to rise. Normally, the goal is to put downward pressure on wages and therefore prices. Most people don't know this; there would probably have been a lot more public concern with Fed policy, especially before the 2000s, if it were known that the Fed was actually trying to control inflation by throwing people out of work and thereby pushing wages down.

In Brazil, however, interest rate increases lower inflation by increasing net capital inflows and thereby appreciating the domestic currency (the *real*), which lowers import prices. One disadvantage of this kind of inflation-targeting policy, especially for a developing country, is that the exchange rate will move up and down as the Central Bank moves policy interest rates to keep inflation within the target range. This can add unpredictability to the exchange rate, and make it more difficult for businesses to plan investment. It also makes it much more difficult for the government to pursue an industrial policy, that is, the development of certain industries that can compete on international markets. In some cases, the domestic currency can become significantly overvalued for long periods of time and reduce the competitiveness of tradable goods and services.

At first glance, it might seem that the Workers' Party had abandoned its campaign promises to promote economic development and social justice, not to mention its leftist program of the decades prior to the election. But after 2004, external conditions became more favorable, and the government began a gradual transition that would have far-reaching consequences for tens of millions of Brazilians.

Partly because of increased export earnings, the government was able to greatly increase its foreign reserve holdings relative to short-term debt. Also, lower international interest rates allowed the Brazilian Central Bank to meet its inflation target with lower domestic interest rates since it is the difference between international and domestic rates that affects capital inflows and outflows.

There was another major change that did not receive the global attention it deserved: in 2005, Brazil paid off the IMF in full and was therefore able to avoid the IMF's further direct influence and conditionalities. The Fund had been a big player in economic policy decisions in Brazil, right up to and during Lula's election. In the summer and fall of 2002, as the prospect of Lula's victory as well as global financial instability hammered Brazilian markets and the economy, the IMF negotiated a $30 billion loan agreement. This was typical of IMF agreements in these circumstances: using a positive spin, it was billed as "reducing uncertainties on the external front," and "build[ing] a solid bridge to the new administration starting in 2003."[16] Another, less favorable way to look at it was that the loan agreement locked the next government into a set of policies that voters may not voluntarily choose. These included a commitment to a hefty primary budget surplus target of 3.75 percent not only for 2002, but also for 2003 and 2004.[17]

The post-2004 changes added up to some increase in policy space that allowed Brazil under the Workers' Party leadership to embark on a gradual transition to a different type of economy. Most important, the government loosened up enough on fiscal and, to a lesser extent, monetary policy to allow for sustained economic growth. This was responsible for the bulk of the poverty reduction that ensued.[18] From 2003 to 2014, GDP per capita grew by an average of 2.3 percent annually. This was more than three times as fast as during the prior eight years (1994–2002) of Fernando Henrique Cardoso's "Washington Consensus" policies; and there was negative per capita growth for the 14 years (1980–1994) before that.

16. IMF, "Brazil: Letter of Intent, Memorandum of Economic Policies, and Technical Memorandum of Understanding," August 29, 2002, http://www.imf.org/external/np/loi/2002/bra/04/index.htm.

17. Ibid.

18. Organisation for Economic Co-operation and Development, *OECD Economic Surveys: Brazil 2013*, http://dx.doi.org/10.1787/eco_surveys-bra-2013-en.

The Workers' Party government appeared to have broken away from the grip of nearly a quarter-century of economic stagnation.

The government also took advantage of the increased growth to put more resources into social spending, which increased from 13 percent of GDP in 2003 to more than 16 percent in 2014. One of the most successful programs that this spending funded won international recognition: the Bolsa Familia. This is a conditional cash transfer program that targets extremely poor families; they receive cash with the requirement that children attend schools and receive vaccinations. The program was initiated in 2003, and by 2012 real inflation-adjusted spending had more than quadrupled, from 4.8 billion to 20.7 billion *reais*. As a percentage of the economy, the program remained relatively modest, increasing from 0.2 to 0.5 percent of GDP. But coverage increased from 16.2 to 57.8 million people, or from 9 percent to a remarkable 29 percent of the population.[19]

After eight years of no progress in reducing poverty during the previous government, the poverty rate dropped by 55 percent, and extreme poverty by 65 percent, during the years 2003–2012. This meant that more than 31 million people were brought out of poverty, and 16 million from extreme poverty.

While economic growth was the largest contributor to this improvement in the lives of tens of millions of Brazilians, the Bolsa Familia program also played a major role. Table 5.1 shows some of the impact that the program had. For those in extreme poverty, Bolsa Familia comprised more than 60 percent of their income in 2011, as compared to 10.5 percent in 2003; for the poor, the increase went from 3.1 percent to 17.6 percent of their income.

19. For these and other statistics in this section, see Mark Weisbrot, Jake Johnston, and Stephan Lefebvre, "The Brazilian Economy in Transition: Macroeconomic Policy, Labor and Inequality," Center for Economic and Policy Research, September 2014, http://www.cepr.net/documents/brazil-2014-09.pdf.

TABLE 5.1 Brazil: Sources of Income, by Poverty Status

Source of Income	Extremely Poor		Poor		Vulnerable		Non-poor		Total	
	2003	2011	2003	2011	2003	2011	2003	2011	2003	2011
Labor Market	75.6	33.2	77.4	66.9	76	72.5	76	78	76.1	76.7
Social Security	5.8	1.2	13.8	9.3	19.1	19.9	18.3	17.6	18.3	18
BPC (Continuous Cash Benefit)	0.5	0.1	0.7	1.6	0.3	1.8	0	0.2	0.1	0.6
Bolsa Familia	10.5	60.9	3.1	17.6	0.4	2.5	0.1	0.1	0.3	0.9
Others	7.7	4.6	5.1	4.7	4.2	3.2	5.5	4.1	5.2	3.9

Source: Tereza Campello and Marcelo Cortes Neri, eds. "Bolsa Familia Program: A Decade of Social Inclusion in Brazil," Instituto de Pesquisa Econômica Aplicada (IPEA), 2014.

Another major boost for the poor was a very large increase in the minimum wage. From 2003 to 2014, the real (inflation-adjusted) minimum wage rose by more than 90 percent.[20] In Brazil, a minimum wage increase benefits many more workers than those who are earning below or near that level. This is because public pensions, unemployment insurance, welfare payments, and other government benefits are linked to the minimum wage; and the income of other wage-earners as well as self-employed workers is also affected by changes in the minimum wage.[21] Unemployment insurance coverage was also greatly expanded, doubling between 2000 and 2012.

There were other policy changes in Brazil under the PT that had positive economic impacts. There was a large expansion of credit, nearly doubling as a percent of GDP from 25 percent in 2002 to 49 percent in 2012.[22] Consumer credit jumped from 23 percent of all credit to 46 percent, helping to bring many previously excluded lower-income Brazilians into consumer markets.[23] And there were some significant moves toward rebuilding an industrial policy, with Brazil's large public development bank, the Brazilian Development Bank (BNDES), increasing its disbursements from 2.2 percent to 4 percent of GDP. Between 2006 and 2012, about 80 percent of these disbursements went to priority sectors for Brazil's industrial policy.[24]

20. "Salário mínimo real," IPEA Data. Retrieved November 28, 2014, from http://www.ipeadata.gov.br/.

21. Ricardo Summa, "Mercado de trabalho e a evolução dos salários no Brasil," Instituto de Economia, Universidade Federal do Rio de Janeiro, 2014, http://www.ie.ufrj.br/index.php/index-publicacoes/textos-para-discussao.

22. IMF, "Brazil: Technical Note on Consumer Credit Growth and Household Financial Stress, June 6, 2013, https://www.imf.org/external/pubs/cat/longres.aspx?sk=40591.0.

23. Ibid.

24. Mark Weisbrot, Jake Johnston, and Stephan Lefebvre, "The Brazilian Economy in Transition: Macroeconomic Policy, Labor and Inequality," Center for Economic and Policy Research, September 2014, http://www.cepr.net/documents/brazil-2014-09.pdf.

The rate of unemployment also underwent a steep decline under the Workers' Party government, falling to a record low level of 4.9 percent in 2013, from a peak of 13 percent in 2003.[25] Somewhat surprisingly, it continued falling and stayed at or near record lows, even as economic growth slowed sharply beginning in 2011. Some of this low unemployment undoubtedly resulted from people leaving the labor force as the economy slowed, and therefore not being counted among the unemployed. Another factor that may have contributed to lower unemployment was a shift in demand from industrial production to the service sector. Because services are more labor-intensive than manufacturing, this shift tends to increase employment. A cut in payroll taxes may also have helped firms to avoid layoffs during the slowdown. [26] So, while the sectoral shift toward services has disadvantages from the point of view of industrial policy and development, the secular decline in unemployment that appears to have taken place is one of the more important achievements of the past decade.

Not surprisingly, these policy changes and results also affected the distribution of income. Table 5.2 shows the how the gains from economic growth were distributed in 1993–2002, as compared with 2003–2012. Brazil's top 10 percent of households saw their share of the country's income gains fall considerably, from more than half (1993–2002), to about one-third (2003–2012). While a small piece of this was picked up by the bottom decile, most of it went to the 40 percent just above them, who nearly doubled their share of income gains from 11 percent to 21 percent.[27]

This is a sizable redistribution of the gains from economic growth, which—because growth was so much stronger in the past

25. Ibid.

26. Ibid.

27. Ibid.

TABLE 5.2 Brazil: Fraction of Total Income Gains Accrued, by Income Percentiles

Dates	Top 1%	Next 9%	Next 40%	Next 40%	Bottom 10%
1993–2002	14.10%	37.30%	36.10%	11.30%	1.20%
2003–2012	11.60%	21.80%	44.00%	21.10%	1.50%

Source: Instituto de Pesquisa Econômica Aplicada (IPEA), "Renda domiciliar per capita—média por décimo da população—1°–10°," 2014, http://www.ipeadata.gov.br/.

decade than during the prior two—allowed for such redistribution to take place while almost all deciles of households still had significant income growth. In fact, all except the top decile actually had more annual real income growth during the past decade than during the prior one. This is a good example of how growth makes it much easier for income redistribution to take place, as discussed in Chapter 3, since the gains for the majority do not have to cut into the current living standards of high-income households.

Nonetheless, even after more than a decade of significant income redistribution, Brazil's income inequality remained very high. The average household in the top 10 percent had monthly income nearly 35 times that of the bottom decile. These figures almost certainly understate the disparity, because much of the income at the top goes unreported in the household surveys that provide this data.

Brazil still has a long way to go, not only in terms of economic development, but also in reducing inequality and social exclusion. Anyone who has experienced the contrast between the wealthy playground of Rio's Zona Sul and the destitution of nearby favelas would have suspected as much. The question is, where is the country headed? Can the progress of the last decade be maintained? If we look at the labor market, there are signs of structural changes that have increased the bargaining power of labor and would therefore be expected to continue reducing inequality in the future. Certainly the sharp reduction in unemployment is part of this equation. So, too, is the incorporation of workers into the formal sector of the economy, where they can benefit from regulatory protection and social insurance. The percentage of workers stuck in the informal sector of the economy shrank from 22.5 percent to 13.3 percent in 2003–2014. In 2014, moreover, a law was passed requiring full-time domestic workers—who are numerous in Brazil, thanks to the crushing inequality—to be treated as formal employees,[28] thus providing desirable maximum work hours, minimum wages, and social security—much to the annoyance of many in the upper classes.

We can also look at the growth of average wages, shown in Figure 5.3. There has been a 35 percent real increase since 2003. It is interesting that the rate of growth continues, even after the economy began slowing in 2011. This is another indication that labor's bargaining power has undergone what could be a long-term increase.

Of course, macroeconomic policy is still crucial, and this appears to be what explains the post-2010 slowdown in Brazil's economy. There was a solid rebound from the Brazilian (and world) recession of 2009, driven by expansionary fiscal policy, with the economy growing by 7.5 percent in 2010. But in 2011, the economy began to slow, and the four years of Lula's successor, Dilma Rousseff, were not good, averaging just about 1.1 percent GDP growth per capita.[29] Why did this happen?

28. Jenny Barchfield, "Brazil Expands Labor Rights for Domestic Workers," Associated Press, August 21, 2014, http://bigstory.ap.org/article/brazil-expands-labor-rights-domestic-workers.

29. IMF, "World Economic Outlook: Legacies, Clouds, Uncertainties," October 2014, http://www.imf.org/external/pubs/ft/weo/2014/02/pdf/text.pdf.

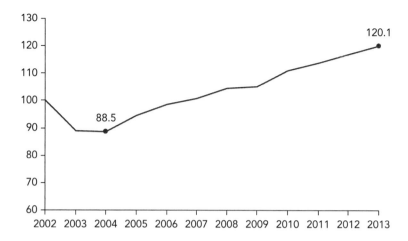

FIGURE 5.3 Brazil: Average Real Wages, Index

Source: Instituto Brasileiro de Geografia e Estatística (IBGE), "Sumário das tabelas disponíveis," 2014, http://ibge.gov.br/home/estatistica/indicadores/trabalhoerendimento/pme_nova/defaulttab_hist.shtm.

There was a slowdown in world economic growth from 2010 to 2011, and Brazil's exports suffered as a result. In real (inflation-adjusted) terms they had grown by 11.5 percent in 2010, but this growth fell to 4.5 percent in 2011 and just 0.5 percent in 2012. This external shock contributed to the slowdown of Brazil's economy, but it is not the whole story.[30]

Most important, the government took steps to slow the economy beginning in 2010. Policy (short-term) interest rates were increased from 8.75% in March 2010 to 12.50% in July 2011.

Credit growth was also curbed by "macroprudential measures." More importantly, the economy was also slowed by an increase

---

30. See Weisbrot, Johnston, and Lefebvre, "The Brazilian Economy in Transition," Center for Economic and Policy Research, September 2014, http://www.cepr.net/documents/brazil-2014-09.pdf.

in the structural primary budget surplus, which expanded from 1.9 percent of GDP in 2010 to 2.7 percent in 2011.

This combination of tightening monetary and fiscal policy, as well as credit, in the context of an economy that was already slowing, reduced GDP growth to just 2.3 percent for 2011. There was some attempt at reversing fiscal policy in 2012, but it proved to be too little and too late.

Another round of interest rate hikes began in April 2013, despite warnings from some government officials that "monetary policy as well as fiscal policies are being tightened despite the fact that growth recovery has only recently begun." By the third quarter of 2013, the economy was shrinking, and a recession began in the first half of 2014.

Thus began an election-year drama that once again illustrates the importance of public education on vital economic issues. A media narrative was created in which the slowing economy was the result of the Workers' Party government's "business-unfriendly" attitudes. Under Dilma, the narrative went, the government had allowed inflation to linger too much near to the top of its target range, and had not run large enough primary budget surpluses. It had alienated investors by the way it had treated Petrobras, the oil giant that is majority state-owned but still about 40 percent owned by private investors, who had grown used to having their way under previous governments. Locked into an inflation-targeting regime that mandated slowing the economy when (usually external) shocks raised the consumer price index, the government imposed price caps on domestic fuels. This cut into Petrobras's profits. Investors also chafed at the government's efforts to incorporate the national energy company into industrial policy: for example, by requiring the company to buy from local suppliers for such products as oil platforms and other heavy equipment. The government also required Petrobras to take the lead in new pre-salt oil development. All of this became part of the "too much big government interference" mantra that is a mainstay of right-wing politics in countries like the United States, but has even more widespread media support in Brazil.

Just give the most rich and powerful what they want, went the refrain, and investment will return and the economy will flourish. But investors rarely get excited about a sluggish economy, and the opposition's announced choice for finance minister, Arminio Fraga, had made it clear that he would engineer "a return to orthodoxy," as the *Financial Times* described it.[31]

There were other issues, too: Corruption in particular was a major emphasis of the media. And although it was never clear that the Workers' Party was worse than any other party in this regard, Lula did lose most of his cabinet in his first term to corruption scandals, and Dilma's presidency was plagued by investigations of funds diverted to her party from Petrobras, among other accusations and controversy. But Lula left office in 2010 with an approval rating over 80 percent, "the most popular politician in the world," as US President Barack Obama called him. Clearly it was the economy that was making the 2014 election too close to call.

The Brazilian media was overwhelmingly against the Workers' Party government. From a report in the *Los Angeles Times*:

> "It's an extremely unique situation now in Brazil to have such a popular government and no major media outlet that supports it or presents a left-of-center viewpoint," says Laurindo Leal Filho, a media specialist at the University of Sao Paulo. . . .
>
> "Brazilian society was based on slavery for over 300 years, and has almost always been run by the same social strata,"

---

31. Joe Leahy, "Arminio Fraga Offers Brazil an Orthodox Path," *Financial Times*, September 17, 2014, http://www.ft.com/cms/s/5982c43c-3e5e-11e4-b7fc-00144feabdc0,Authorised=false.html?_i_location= http%3A%2F%2Fwww.ft.co m%2Fcms%2Fs%2F0%2F5982c43c-3e5e-11e4-b7fc-00144feabdc0.html%3Fsite edition%3Duk&_i_referer=#axzz3KUNdpFVQ.

Leal Filho says. "Some parts of the upper class have learned to live with other parts of society that were previously excluded. . . but the media still reflect the values of the old-school elite, with very, very few exceptions.[32]

A similar problem challenged almost all of the new left governments in Latin America that were elected in the late 1990s and in the twenty-first century, although some created or expanded public media as a counterweight. In Brazil, media bias played a significant role in the 2014 election. For example, a project affiliated with the Instituto de Estudos Sociais e Políticos at the Universidade do Estado do Rio de Janeiro looked at hundreds of the major newspaper headlines during the campaign. For Dilma, only 1 percent was positive, while 43 percent were negative; for her conservative opponent Aécio Neves, it was 14 percent positive and 14 percent negative. Television and other media were at least as biased; just two days before the election, the influential weekly news magazine *Veja* alleged that Dilma and Lula personally knew about corruption at Petrobras. The allegations were unsubstantiated but were released just in time to provide fodder for Aécio's opening salvo in the last presidential campaign debate.

Fernando Henrique Cardoso, the Brazilian Social Democracy Party's most famous politician and still a darling in Washington circles, mused aloud during the campaign that it was the "less informed" voters who supported the Workers' Party. The irony went unnoticed. Yes, polls showed that the electorate was polarized along regional and class lines, with the poorer and less formally educated Northeast backing Dilma and the better off classes in Rio and Sao Paulo joining what *The Economist* aptly dubbed the opposition's "cashmere revolution." But who was less informed? The

32. Vincent Bevins, "Brazil's Dilma Rousseff Is Popular, But Not among News Media," *Los Angeles Times*, March 3, 2013, http://articles.latimes.com/2013/mar/03/world/la-fg-brazil-hostile-media-20130304.

opposition voters who believed that the PT administration's worst macroeconomic mistakes, magnified as promised, would revive the economy? Or the rural and urban workers who were smart enough to vote for their own interests?

When the votes were tallied, Dilma had won by 3 percentage points. The national and international media immediately pounced on the relatively tight margin to insist that she adopt the opposition's economic program to restore investor confidence.

Bolivia

When Evo Morales was elected in 2005 as the first indigenous president of Bolivia, he was inheriting the poorest country in South America. While scholars have written about the centuries of pillage and exploitation since the Spanish conquest, few have looked at the more recently imposed obstacles to the country's economic development. The country had been operating under IMF agreements continuously over the prior 20 years, except for a brief period of nine months. When the new president took office, Bolivia's per capita income was less than it had been more than 27 years earlier.

Morales clearly saw similarities between the Spanish colonial domination and the influence of Washington in the modern era, and independence was a major electoral theme and promise. In a 2010 interview, he tells the story of Túpac Katari, an indigenous leader who fought against the Spanish colonists in the eighteenth century. He recalls Túpac Katari's last words, before he was drawn and quartered by the Spanish: "I die as one, but I will come back as millions."

Evo then looks into the camera and says: "Now we are millions."[33]

Centuries after millions of indigenous forced laborers perished in the silver mines of Potosí, the gap in living standards—not to

33. Evo Morales, *South of the Border*, Documentary. Directed by Oliver Stone. Argentina: Cinema Libre, 2010. http://www.southoftheborderdoc.com/.

mention political participation—between Bolivia's indigenous majority and the rest of the population remained high. Indigenous Bolivians received less than half the labor income of their non-indigenous counterparts, and 40 percent less schooling.[34] But there were other statistics that told a more general story of what used to be called underdevelopment. The economy was divided between a relatively low-productivity sector, which accounted for 83 percent of employment but only about 25 percent of output, and a higher-productivity sector with only 9 percent of employment but 65 percent of GDP. Sixty percent of the population lived below the official poverty line in 2005. And Bolivia had nearly the most unequal distribution of land in the entire world, with less than 0.25 percent of all landholders controlling a majority of the land area.[35]

As noted in Chapter 4, one of the Morales administration's first decisions was to cut loose from the IMF, which had offered the new government a new loan agreement. The country's new autonomy would soon open up an array of possibilities. The Fund[36] had been opposed to any kind of re-nationalizing of Bolivia's hydrocarbon industry—mostly natural gas—that by 2006 already comprised about half of the country's exports.[37]

34. Mark Weisbrot and Luis Sandoval, "The Distribution of Bolivia's Most Important Natural Resources and the Autonomy Conflicts," Center for Economic and Policy Research, July 2008, http://www.cepr.net/index.php/publications/reports/the-distribution-of-bolivias-most-important-natural-resources-and-the-autonomy-conflicts.

35. Ibid.

36. IMF, "IMF Country Report: Bolivia: Fourth Review Under the Stand-By Arrangement and Request for Waiver of Nonobservance of Performance Criteria—Staff Report; Press Release; and Statement by the Executive Director for Bolivia," International Monetary Fund, Washington, DC, November 2004, http://www.imf.org/external/pubs/cat/longres.aspx?sk=17827.

37. Instituto Nacional de Estadística, "Exportaciones," 2014. Retrieved November 28, 2014, from http://www.ine.gob.bo/indice/general.aspx?codigo=50101.

In a surprise move on May 1, 2006, Morales's government sent troops to occupy the natural gas fields and took control of the gas industry that had been privatized in the 1990s. Over the next eight years under Morales's government, the revenue from hydrocarbons skyrocketed nearly sevenfold, from $731 million to $4.95 billion.[38] Some of this was the result of price increases, but most was due to the change in ownership of the country's most important mineral resource. Production in 2013 was twice as much as it was just before re-nationalization in 2006.[39]

This vast increase in revenue enabled the government to carry out a number of economic changes that would not otherwise have been possible, despite the fact that about half the revenues went to provincial and local governments.[40] Perhaps most important, government spending was able to boost the economy and give Bolivia its fastest economic growth in decades. From 2006 to 2014, Bolivia's real GDP per capita grew by 28 percent.[41]

The extra funds were particularly important in enabling Bolivia to counter the headwinds from the world financial crisis and

38. Ministerio de Hidrocarburos y Energía, Separata Nacional, May 2014, http://www2.hidrocarburos.gob.bo/index.php/prensa/separatas.html?download=38 8:separata-nacional-ministerio-de-hidrocarburos-y-energia-1ro-de-mayo-2014.

39. Andres Schipani, "Bolivia Facing Up to Lower Gas Export Prices," *Beyond-BRICS*, a blog in the *Financial Times*, October 23, 2014. Retrieved November 28, 2014, from http://blogs.ft.com/beyond-brics/2014/10/23/bolivia-facing-up-to-lower-gas-export-prices/?Authorised=false.

40. Mark Weisbrot and Luis Sandoval, "The Distribution of Bolivia's Most Important Natural Resources and the Autonomy Conflicts," Center for Economic and Policy Research, July 2008, http://www.cepr.net/index.php/publications/reports/the-distribution-of-bolivias-most-important-natural-resources-and-the-autonomy-conflicts.

41. IMF, "World Economic Outlook: Legacies, Clouds, Uncertainties," October 2014, http://www.imf.org/external/pubs/ft/weo/2014/02/pdf/text.pdf; and ECLAC, CEPALSTAT Database, United Nations Economic Commission for Latin American and the Caribbean, n.d. Retrieved February 7, 2015, from http://estadisticas.cepal.org/cepalstat/WEB_CEPALSTAT/estadisticasIndicadores.asp?idioma=i.

recession of 2008–2009. Within one year from the first quarter of 2008, a government budget surplus of 5.0 percent of GDP had shifted to a deficit of 0.7 percent of GDP, a very large expansion of nearly 6 percentage points of GDP. Public investment was a big part of this increase, about 2.6 percent of GDP. In 2009, while most of the hemisphere was in recession, Bolivia's economy grew by 3.4 percent, the highest rate in South America. This was an impressive achievement, given that Bolivia was hit hard by the world recession. Demand and prices fell for its hydrocarbon exports, which go mainly to Argentina and Brazil. Bolivia was also hit by a big falloff in remittances, which fell by 7.4 to 5 percent of GDP from 2007 to 2009, as well as declining foreign investment and a cutoff of trade preferences from the United States.[42]

Public investment more than doubled as a percent of the economy from 2005 to 2014, rising from 6.3 percent to 13.4 percent.[43] Private investment grew much slower, but still faster than the economy.[44] By 2013, in spite of a number of nationalizations carried out by the government (not only of hydrocarbons but of telecommunications, electricity, and national pensions), Bolivia also led the region in foreign direct investment, at 5.9 percent of GDP. It seems that foreign investors eventually began to appreciate the record economic growth as well as stability that the government had achieved. Prior to Morales's presidency, Bolivia had had

42. See Mark Weisbrot, Rebecca Ray, and Jake Johnston, "Bolivia: The Economy during the Morales Administration," Center for Economic and Policy Research, December 2009, http://www.cepr.net/documents/publications/bolivia-2009-12.pdf.

43. Jake Johnston and Stephan Lefebvre, "Bolivia's Economy under Evo in 10 Graphs," *The Americas Blog*, a blog on the Center for Economic and Policy Research site, October 8, 2014, http://www.cepr.net/index.php/blogs/the-americas-blog/bolivias-economy-under-evo-in-10-graphs.

44. Instituto Nacional de Estadística, "Crecimiento de la Formación Bruta Capital Fijo a Precios Constantes." Retrieved November 28, 2014, from http://www.ine.gob.bo/indice/general.aspx?codigo=40310.

80 governments since its independence in 1825, with at least 150 coups d'état or attempted coups.

Most of the government's windfall from hydrocarbons was saved: Bolivia's international reserves mushroomed from less than 20 percent of GDP when Morales took office to 48 percent of GDP in 2013—even higher than China, relative to the economy. This accumulation—although perhaps overly conservative from an economic and social development standpoint—had its advantages. With such huge foreign reserves, the government was able to maintain a stable currency, with the nominal exchange rate barely moving despite some spikes in inflation and episodes of serious political turmoil and instability. When the economy grew rapidly and imports surged, there was no question of a balance of payments constraint on growth. With a stable exchange rate and plentiful reserves, the government was also able to reduce the dollarization of the economy. In 2008, 53 percent of Bolivia's bank deposits were in dollars; by September 2012 this was reduced to 23 percent.[45] This is important for a number of reasons, including financial stability and increasing the effectiveness of monetary policy.

Morales confronted many obstacles in bringing about the reforms that the majority of people had voted for in 2005. In common with the other leftist governments, he faced an overwhelmingly hostile media—one of the most politically partisan in South America. I remember during a visit there in 2008 that the major media were promoting the idea that the country was on the edge of returning to the hyperinflation of the 1980s, when inflation hit 14 percent. In fact, the jump in inflation was almost all due to food price increases, and by 2009 it was back down to 3.4 percent. The government was wise to not to slow the economy in response to a

45. IMF, "Bolivia: Staff Report for the 2013 Article IV Consultation," February 2014, p. 5, http://www.imf.org/external/pubs/ft/scr/2014/cr1436.pdf.

temporary increase in inflation caused by an external shock; this provides another example of improved macroeconomic policy making a difference in Bolivia.

There were geographical and ethnic divisions that coincided with the distribution of the country's most important natural resources, in particular hydrocarbons and arable land. In the eastern half of the country are the "Media Luna" provinces—Santa Cruz, Beni, Pando, and Tarija—so-called because they form a half-moon shape. These provinces had 82 percent of the hydrocarbon production, and under the system in place when Morales was elected—unlike in any hydrocarbon-exporting country in the world—half of these energy revenues went to the provincial and local governments. At the same time, the indigenous population of these departments ranged from 16 to 38 percent, as compared to 66–84 percent in the five western departments. Not surprisingly, the Media Luna provinces also have a much higher income per capita. Santa Cruz, in particular, was dominated by large, export-oriented agricultural interests including soybean producers, and accounted for about a third of the country's land and 28 percent of its GDP.[46]

With more than three-quarters of rural Bolivians in poverty and 40 percent of the population working in agriculture, land reform was naturally an issue and a campaign promise of the Morales government. A more equitable distribution of the hydrocarbon revenue, which had grown rapidly since re-nationalization, was also an expected reform. But there was serious political opposition from powerful interests in the eastern lowlands, and it did not take long for a separatist movement to gather steam.

---

46. Mark Weisbrot and Luis Sandoval, "The Distribution of Bolivia's Most Important Natural Resources and the Autonomy Conflicts," Center for Economic and Policy Research, July 2008, http://www.cepr.net/index.php/publications/reports/the-distribution-of-bolivias-most-important-natural-resources-and-the-autonomy-conflicts.

The conflict came to a head in the summer and fall of 2008, when separatist protests turned increasingly violent and destabilizing, including the burning of the National Agrarian reform building in Santa Cruz and attacks on vital gas pipelines. On September 11, at least 19 pro-government protesters were killed in the province of Pando.[47] Bolivia's neighbors, having seen such scenarios lead to coups d'état (such as the one in Venezuela six years earlier), became concerned and convened an emergency summit in Santiago, Chile, on September 15. With almost all of the South American presidents meeting under the auspices of the recently created Union of South American Nations (UNASUR), they strongly backed the Morales government and made it clear that an extra-constitutional division or overthrow would not be tolerated.[48] UNASUR also launched an investigation into the killings in Pando.

The Santiago summit marked a turning point, partly because it sent a firm message to another very important force that appeared to be on the other side of the Bolivian conflict: the US government. Less than a week before the summit, the Morales government had ousted the US ambassador, accusing him and his government of intervening in Bolivia's internal affairs. The US embassy had previously been caught trying to use Peace Corps volunteers and a Fulbright scholar for spying,[49] and US ambassador Phillip Goldberg had met privately with opposition leaders at a bad time, when the opposition was engaged in

47. Amnesty International, "Bolivia: Victims of the Pando Massacre Still Await Justice," Press Release, September 9, 2009. Retrieved November 28, 2014, from http://www.amnesty.org/en/for-media/press-releases/bolivia-victims-pando-massacre-still-await-justice-20090909.

48. Al Jazeera English, "South American Leaders Back Morales," September 16, 2008. Retrieved November 29, 2014, from http://www.aljazeera.com/news/americas/2008/09/200891641749670258.html.

49. Jean Friedman-Rudovsky and Brian Ross, "Peace Corps, Fulbright Scholar Asked to 'Spy' on Cubans, Venezuelans," ABC News, February 8, 2014. Retrieved December 1, 2014, from http://abcnews.go.com/Blotter/Story?id=4262036&page=1.

violence.[50] Washington was also sending huge amounts of money to the country through the State Department's USAID program—about 1 percent of Bolivia's GDP at the time—and refused to disclose who the recipients were.[51] Since some of this money was clearly going to provincial and local governments and organizations, it was assumed that it was helping the opposition. Previous US documents had shown Washington's animosity toward Evo Morales and his party, the Movement Toward Socialism (MAS),[52] and the United States' bias was really no secret.

On September 26, 2008, Washington suspended Bolivia's trade preferences under the Andean Trade Promotion and Drug Eradication Act.[53] Then Bolivia ran into another problem with Washington over healthcare. Under Bolivia's new constitution, privatization of healthcare was prohibited. This was because the constitution established healthcare—like water and other necessities—as a basic human right. Because of this legal change, Bolivia requested that the prior government's commitment to allow foreign corporations to buy into its healthcare sector, including hospitals, be rescinded. WTO rules provided that if there were

50. Fran Chávez, "U.S. Ambassador Expelled for Allegedly Supporting Violent Opposition," Inter Press Service, September 11, 2008. Retrieved December 1, 2014, from http://www.ipsnews.net/2008/09/bolivia-us-ambassador-expelled-for-allegedly-supporting-violent-opposition/.

51. Center for Economic and Policy Research, "Press Release: U.S. Should Disclose Its Funding of Opposition Groups in Bolivia and Other Latin American Countries," September 12, 2008, http://www.cepr.net/index.php/press-releases/press-releases/us-should-disclose-its-funding-of-opposition-groups-in-bolivia-and-other-latin-american-countries/.

52. Jeremy Bigwood, "New Discoveries Reveal US Intervention in Bolivia," *Bolivia Matters*, October 11, 2008. Retrieved December 4, 2014, from https://boliviamatters.wordpress.com/2008/10/11/new-discoveries-reveal-us-intervention-in-bolivia/.

53. Abigal Poe, "President Bush Suspends Bolivia's Trade Preferences under ATPDEA," Security Assistance Monitor, October 6, 2008, http://justf.org/blog/president-bush-suspends-bolivias-trade-preferences-under-atpdea.

no objections to such a request within 45 days, it was approved. But Washington objected.[54] By 2014, these differences were still not resolved; the United States continued to refuse to disclose the recipients of its USAID grants, and Bolivia still did not have ambassadorial relations with the United States.

But in a historic departure from prior political realities, the success of Bolivia's government did not seem to be affected by the state of US-Bolivian relations. Evo Morales went on to win re-election in 2009 with a 37 percentage-point margin of victory. In 2014, he won again with 61.5 percent of the vote, this time getting a majority in eight of nine provinces—including Santa Cruz, the former bastion of right-wing opposition.[55]

It was clear that the government's economic policies were key to its political success. In addition to the 28 percent increase in per capita GDP mentioned above, poverty declined by 25 percent, from 60 percent to 45 percent, and extreme poverty by 43 percent—from 37 percent to 21 percent of households.[56] (Poverty data are for 2005–2011, the most recent available; given the economic performance of the past three years, it is likely that the poverty rate today is significantly lower.)

The minimum wage also grew quite fast, by 88 percent in real (inflation-adjusted) terms from 2005 to 2014.[57] And the government introduced and then expanded several programs targeted at poor

54. Mark Weisbrot, "The United States and Bolivia: A New Beginning?" *The Guardian*, February 25, 2009, http://www.cepr.net/index.php/op-eds-&-columns/op-eds-&-columns/the-united-states-and-bolivia-a-new-beginning/.

55. "Bolivia Elects Evo Morales as President for Third Term," Associated Press, October 13, 2014, http://www.theguardian.com/world/2014/oct/13/bolivia-evo-morales--president-third-term.

56. Jake Johnston and Stephan Lefebvre, "Bolivia's Economy under Evo in 10 Graphs," *The Americas Blog*, a blog on the Center for Economic and Policy Research site, October 8, 2014, http://www.cepr.net/index.php/blogs/the-americas-blog/bolivias-economy-under-evo-in-10-graphs.

57. Ibid.

families. One program provided a small cash stipend as an incentive for children to stay in school through the sixth grade. Another program, called *Renta Dignidad*, provides grants to low-income residents over 60; these currently stand at about $347 per year for those who receive social security payments, and $434 for those who do not. A third initiative, designed to reduce infant mortality, provides funding for prenatal, childbirth, and postnatal care.

The Bolivian government also bucked overwhelming global trends by lowering the retirement age. In 2010 the retirement age for men was lowered from 60 to 58 for men, and to 55 for most women (and 56 for miners). In a country with a male life expectancy of 65, this is more than reasonable. The public pension reforms, which included the re-nationalization of the previously privatized pension system, also allowed for informal sector workers—some 65 percent of the labor force in 2011[58]—to join the system. Thus Bolivia provided universal access and a guaranteed retirement benefit to many for the first time, and many will see significant increases in benefits. However, many workers will at present remain uncovered; hence the Renta Dignidad provides an additional safety net.

Since 2006, the government has redistributed more than 5 million hectares of land to peasant and indigenous communities, and promises to distribute millions more. It has also titled more than 60 million acres of land, the vast majority of all the land that has been titled since 1996; although the process of both titling and redistribution has slowed since 2010.[59]

58. Centro de Estudios para el Desarollo Laboral y Agrario, "El Sector Informal Urbano en Bolivia 2010–2011: Estadísticas del CEDLA," June 25, 2013, http://www.cedla.org/content/3467.

59. See Juan Carlos Rojas Calizaya (Director of the National Institute for Agrarian Reform (INRA), 2006–2011), "Agrarian Transformation in Bolivia at Risk," *Bolivia Information Forum Bulletin*, September 2012, for an overview; also *Resultados de la Reconducción Comunitaria de la Reforma Agraria en Bolivia II: la tierra vuelve a manos indígenas y campesinas* (La Paz: Instituto Nacional de Reforma Agraria [INRA], January 2010).

It is arguable that the Morales administration could have done more for the poor, although it was constrained by politics that limited how much of the increased hydrocarbon revenue would accrue to the central government. Although social spending increased by 45 percent in real terms, it fell slightly as a percent of GDP. In a country where in 2008 27 percent of children under five were malnourished enough to stunt their growth, the "fierce urgency of now" is louder than in most of South America. But there have been remarkable advances in the last eight years as compared to previous decades, and it is also likely that we will see much more as some of the lagged social indicators such as stunted growth catch up. Bolivia's transition to a stable, independent, and more representative government constitutes one of the most successful shifts in the hemisphere, toward greater economic and social progress.

Ecuador

Rafael Correa of Ecuador, who took office in January 2007, was the fifth of the leftist South American presidents elected in the twenty-first century. He was also the first to hold a PhD in economics. His training would prove valuable as he led the most far-reaching financial reforms in the hemisphere. He also knew when to ignore some of the profession's most wrong-headed dogmas. This combination of skills, and a combative but charismatic leadership that helped make him one of the most popular presidents in the region, were key to his government's political success.

This is not to say his presidency has been smooth sailing. When President Mel Zelaya of Honduras was overthrown by the military in 2009, Correa announced, "We have intelligence reports that say that after Zelaya, I'm next."[60] And a year later, he was held hostage

60. Associated Press, "Leftists Fear Domino Effect of Honduras Coup," August 19, 2009. Retrieved December 1, 2014, from http://www.nbcnews.com/id/32478307/ns/world_news-americas/#.VHvLock3KpE.

for more than 10 hours by a rebellion of police officers representing a serious attempt to overthrow the government, and Correa had to be rescued by 500 loyal troops from the military. At one dramatic moment before the shooting started, he appeared in the window of the police hospital where he was being held, loosened his tie and opened his shirt, and dared his opponents to kill him: "Gentlemen, if you want to kill the president, here he is! Kill me if you want to!"[61]

But at that moment nobody fired, and so Correa lived to pursue his "citizen's revolution" to a third election in February 2013, which he won with a 57 percent majority. By then, the country had lived for five years under a new constitution and other legal changes that allowed the government to play a new and dramatically different role in the economy.

In 2008, the government faced its toughest economic challenges when the world price of oil collapsed. Ecuador's oil export prices fell from $126 in July of that year to less than $30 in December.[62] At the time, Ecuador was depending on oil exports for 62 percent of its export earnings and 34 percent of government revenue.[63] It was also heavily dependent on remittances, which peaked at about $800 million in the first quarter of 2008, or more than 6 percent of GDP. These crashed following the collapse of the huge real estate bubbles of the United States and Spain, the biggest destinations for Ecuadorian workers who sent money back to their families. Relative to Ecuador's economy, the shock was comparable in magnitude to the collapse of the housing bubble that caused the Great Recession in the United States.

61. Robert Mackey, "Dramatic Video of a Standoff in Ecuador," *The Lede*, a blog in the *New York Times*, October 1, 2010. Retrieved December 1, 2014, from http://thelede.blogs.nytimes.com/2010/10/01/dramatic-video-of-a-stand-off-in-ecuador/. See also "Chaos in Ecuador as Police Protest in Streets." ITN News, http://www.dailymotion.com/video/xf0rc6_chaos-in-ecuador-as-police-protest_news.

62. Mark Weisbrot and Luis Sandoval, "Update on the Ecuadorian Economy," Center for Economic and Policy Research, June 2009, http://www.cepr.net/index.php/publications/reports/update-on-the-ecuadorian-economy.

63. Ibid.

Ecuador was further handicapped in confronting the crisis by not even having its own currency. In 2000, a prior government had adopted the US dollar as its national currency. This meant that the government was severely limited in its use of monetary policy, and could not use exchange rate policy in order to counter the downturn. The country's future looked potentially very bleak.

Despite these huge shocks and disadvantages, Ecuador suffered only a mild recession that lasted three quarters, with a total loss of 1.3 percent of GDP.[64] A year after the recession ended, the country had returned to its pre-recession level of GDP. Expansionary fiscal policy was part of the solution, with a stimulus that amounted to nearly 5 percent of GDP beginning in 2009.[65] There was a 50 percent increase in credit for housing, financed mainly through the Social Security Institute and including concessional mortgage lending, which targeted low-income groups that might otherwise not have been able to afford to buy a home. This continued to 2011, and while the world and regional economy slowed, a 21 percent increase in construction brought Ecuador 7.8 percent GDP growth for that year.[66]

But there was still the problem of regulating the financial system and maintaining adequate reserves, not only to avoid balance of payments constraints, but also because Ecuador's national currency remained the US dollar, which the Central Bank could not create. This is where the financial reforms of the new government were especially important.[67]

64. Ibid.

65. Ibid.

66. See Rebecca Ray and Sara Kozameh, "Ecuador's Economy since 2007," Center for Economic and Policy Research, May 2012, http://www.cepr.net/index.php/publications/reports/ecuadors-economy-since-2007.

67. See Mark Weisbrot, Jake Johnston, and Stephan Lefebvre, "Ecuador's New Deal: Reforming and Regulating the Financial Sector," Center for Economic and Policy Research, February 2013, http://www.cepr.net/index.php/publications/reports/ecuadors-new-deal-reforming-and-regulating-the-financial-sector.

When Correa took office, the Central Bank was officially "independent"—that is, not answerable to the executive or legislative branch of government. Making Central Banks independent has been one of the central goals of the neoliberal reform agenda. There are a number of arguments for doing so—for example, the Central Bank has to take a longer-term perspective and therefore shouldn't be subject to short-term political pressures. But these arguments could be applied to other institutions of government that make decisions on taxes, spending, public investment, etc. The argument for Central Bank independence rests on an elitist foundation, that is, that monetary policy must be insulated from the desires of the electorate—otherwise the wrong decisions will be made, and inflation will be too high. But the empirical evidence that independent Central Banks do better is mixed at best;[68] and historically they have played an important role in economic development when they have been more integrated into the government's economic team.[69]

The new 2008 constitution got rid of the 1998 constitution's requirement that the Central Bank be independent and primarily concerned with price stability. A 2009 law changed the rules for selecting the Bank's board of directors: it would now be made up of representatives from the various economic ministries (finance, economic policy, etc.), including a new economic planning ministry

68. See, e.g., Alberto Alesina and Lawrence Summers, "Central Bank Independence and Macroeconomic Performance: Some Comparative Evidence," *Journal of Money, Credit and Banking* 25, no. 2. (May 1993): 151–162, http://www.econ.ucdenver.edu/smith/econ4110/Alesina%20Summers%20-%20Central%20Bank%20Independence%20and%20Macro%20Performance.pdf; and P. S. Pollard, "Central Bank Independence and Economic Performance," *Federal Reserve Bank of St. Louis Review*, July 1993, pp. 21–36, http://research.stlouisfed.org/publications/review/93/07/Bank_Jul_Aug1993.pdf.

69. Gerald Epstein, "Central Banks as Agents of Economic Development," United Nations University World Institute for Development Economics Research (UNU-WIDER), May 2006. Retrieved February 11, 2013, from http://www.wider.unu.edu/stc/repec/pdfs/rp2006/rp2006-54.pdf.

created in 2007 to coordinate economic policy. These were major structural changes in economic decision-making that were essential to the government's financial and economic reform program.

One of the first steps that the government wanted the Central Bank to take was to regulate interest rates; Correa had made a campaign promise to bring down lending rates, and the Central Bank concurred by setting maximum rates for housing, commercial, consumer, and other types of loans. From 2007 to 2013, average real (inflation-adjusted) lending rates came down from 8.3 percent to 3.8 percent.[70]

In May 2009, with the economy still in recession, banks were required to hold 45 percent of their liquid assets in the country; this increased to 60 percent in 2012. The government also instituted a tax on capital flight. This became an important source of tax revenue, increasing from less than 1 percent of revenue in 2008 to 10 percent in 2012.[71] The Central Bank itself was required to repatriate $1 billion in assets held abroad, rising to $2 billion by 2012. The proportion of banks' assets held domestically increased from 33.4 percent in 2009 to 69.7 percent in 2012.[72] All of these measures were essential to Ecuador's remarkably effective counter-cyclical monetary and fiscal policy and recovery.

The country had survived a traumatic experience with the collapse of its banking system in 1999.[73] The new government wanted to prevent such future crises, and prevention was all the more important since the adoption of the dollar limited the Central

70. Weisbrot, Johnston, and Lefebvre. "Ecuador's New Deal: Reforming and Regulating the Financial Sector."

71. Ibid.

72. Ibid.

73. For an overview, see Luis Ignacio Jácome, "The Late 1990s Financial Crisis in Ecuador: Institutional Weaknesses, Fiscal Rigidities, and Financial Dollarization at Work," IMF, January 1, 2004, https://www.imf.org/external/pubs/cat/longres.aspx?sk=17127.0.

Bank's capacity to create money as a lender of last resort in the event of a financial crisis. It also did not want taxpayers to be stuck paying the bill for any bailouts that might be needed to ensure the solvency of the banking system, as had occurred in the 1999 crisis. The government thus created a liquidity fund to make sure that the banks themselves would fund any necessary bailouts, as the new constitution mandated. The size of the fund rose quickly to $1.2 billion in 2012. It was funded by a tax on banks' deposits.

The government also had to confront the political power of the banks, as they were major players who could block reform and worse. Think of Wall Street in the United States, but more powerful relative to other political actors, even controlling the most important media. When Correa took office, banks owned most of the major TV media.[74] This was soon prohibited, and by 2011, private media companies were also precluded from holding shares in companies outside the media industry. Bankers, of course, remained powerful on the political scene; Correa's principal opponent in the 2013 election was Guillermo Lasso, who headed the Banco de Guayaquil, the country's second-largest bank. However, due to Correa's reforms, banks do not have the overwhelming power they held previously.

A new regulatory body was also set up in 2011 to enforce anti-trust legislation, and considerable effort was undertaken on Correa's campaign promise to expand what was defined in the 2008 constitution as the "popular and solidarity sector" of the financial system. This sector, which includes member-based organizations such as credit unions, cooperatives, and savings and loan associations, was targeted in a 2008 government program for help in increasing their lending to small businesses. From 2007 to 2012,

74. A. Checa-Godoy, "The Banking Sector and Media Ownership: The Case of Ecuador," *Revista Latina de Comunicación Social* 67 (2012): 125–147. La Laguna (Tenerife, Canary Islands): La Laguna University. Retrieved December 4, 2014, from http://www.revistalatinacs.org/067/art/950_Sevilla/06_ChecaEN.html.

co-op loans nearly doubled as a percentage of private bank lending, from 11.1 to 19.6 percent.[75]

Correa made another campaign promise that did not win him friends in the international financial press: he said he would set up a commission of international experts to examine the country's foreign debt, and promised not to pay any debt that was found to be illegally or illegitimately contracted. In November 2008, the commission found that $3.2 billion—about one-third of the country's foreign debt—belonged to that category.[76] The government stopped payment on the debt the next month and then defaulted, buying up the defaulted bonds for about 35 cents on the dollar. Even unsympathetic observers were impressed with how the default was executed. One analyst from Greylock Capital called it "one of the most elegant restructurings that I've seen."[77] The country had little to lose since it could hardly borrow on international markets at the time. Still, it was unusual and perhaps unprecedented to see such a "default of choice," as the government's interest payments on the debt at the time were just 1.5 percent of GDP.[78] Its debt service remained at a low 1.3 percent of GDP in 2013.[79]

Despite the unfortunate timing of Correa's ascension to the presidency less than a year before the US Great Recession began, and the

75. Weisbrot, Johnston, and Lefebvre, "Ecuador's New Deal: Reforming and Regulating the Financial Sector."

76. Comisión Para la Auditoría Integral Del Crédito Público, "Informe Final de la Auditoría Integral de la Deuda Ecuatoriana, 2007, http://www.auditoriadeuda. org.ec/images/stories/documentos/informe_final_CAIC.pdf.

77. See, e.g., Felix Salmon, "Lessons from Ecuador's Bond Default," Reuters, May 29, 2009. Retrieved December 1, 2014, from http://blogs.reuters.com/ felix-salmon/2009/05/29/lessons-from-ecuadors-bond-default/.

78. Ray and Kozameh, "Ecuador's Economy since 2007."

79. Banco Central del Ecuador, "Información Estadística Mensual." Online database, accessed December 2014, http://www.bce.fin.ec/index.php/publicaciones-de-banca-central3.

serious external shocks noted above, Ecuador has done quite well by a number of important economic and social measures. GDP growth per capita averaged 2.8 percent annually for 2007–2014,[80] and poverty was reduced by more than 30 percent (from 36.7 to 24.8 percent of the population).[81] Public investment increased from 4.6 percent of GDP to 14.8 percent,[82] boosted by increased tax revenues. Government revenues increased enormously from 24.1 percent of GDP in 2006 to 38.9 percent in 2014,[83] thanks to much faster economic growth, the new taxes on the financial sector, a bigger take from foreign oil companies, and better collection of taxes owed.

Inequality was also considerably reduced, with the ratio of the income of the richest decile and the poorest falling from 36 to 25.[84] The proportion of the urban labor force enrolled in the social security system increased from 26 to 67 percent.[85]

The Ecuadorian experience has implications for a host of widely held neoliberal beliefs about economic policy that may be wrong, or at least considerably exaggerated. It is commonly argued that the policy options of governments are severely constrained by the

80. IMF, "World Economic Outlook Database," October 2014, http://www.imf.org/external/pubs/ft/weo/2014/02/weodata/weorept.aspx?pr.x=40&pr.y=1&sy=2007&ey=2019&scsm=1&ssd=1&sort=country&ds=.&br=1&c=248&s=NGDPRPC&grp=0&a=.

81. El Instituto Nacional de Estadística y Censos (INEC), "Resultados principales," September 2014, http://www.ecuadorencifras.gob.ec/pobreza/.

82. Banco Central de Ecuador, "Operaciones del Sector Público no Financiero-SPNF-Porcentaje del PIB (mensual)," 2014, http://www.bce.fin.ec/index.php/component/k2/item/295-operaciones-del-sector-p%C3%BAblico-no-financiero.

83. IMF, "World Economic Outlook," 2014.

84. Socio-Economic Database for Latin America and the Caribbean (CEDLAS and The World Bank), "Incomes," February 2014. Accessed December 4, 2014. http://sedlac.econo.unlp.edu.ar/eng/statistics.php.

85. El Instituto Nacional de Estadística y Censos (INEC), "Reporte Laboral," June 2014, http://www.ecuadorencifras.gob.ec/documentos/web-inec/EMPLEO/Empleo_junio_2014/15Anios/Informe%20Econom%eda%20laboral%20-%20jun14%28rev%29.pdf.

dictates of the "global economy," including the mobility of capital across national boundaries. Among their most important goals should be to win the favor of foreign investors, according to this narrative. Ecuador, however—a relatively small, middle-income developing country that did not even have its own currency—was able to impose a coherent set of regulations on its financial sector in order to facilitate its economic recovery, avoid potentially serious balance of payments problems, and restructure its financial system to pursue a set of new social, economic, and development goals. At the same time, the government confronted powerful, entrenched political interests that opposed its program. It is an experience that not only developing countries, but also perhaps some high-income countries, may want to seriously examine.

Venezuela

At first glance, it might seem odd to include Venezuela in a discussion of how much better Latin America has done since its "second independence" was achieved in the twenty-first century. As this chapter is being written, Venezuelan consumer price inflation is over 60 percent and the economy is in recession. There are widespread shortages of consumer goods, which change from week to week, and have included such items as milk and toilet paper. In June 2015, the black market exchange rate passed 400 *Bolivares Fuertes* (Bf, the domestic currency), or more than 60 times the lowest official rate (6.3), at which most of the government's dollars are sold. The government also is in arrears on billions of dollars of payments to businesses and contractors. Its sovereign debt yield on the benchmark bond maturing in 2027 hit 19 percent,[86] the highest in the world.

---

86. Kejal Vyas, "Venezuela to Use Diamonds to Boost International Reserves," *Wall Street Journal*, December 4, 2014, http://online.wsj.com/articles/venezuela-to-use-diamonds-to-boost-international-reserves-1417735501.

Since the late President Hugo Chávez Frias was elected and took office in 1999, the government's detractors—who include most of those writing or producing for the Western mass media—have predicted economic collapse and ruin for the country. During most of the past 15 years, that predicted collapse has been just around the corner, although it never happened. Has the long-awaited apocalypse finally arrived? We will return to the country's recent economic problems in a moment, but first it is worth explaining how the current governing party—first led by Chávez and then, from 2013, by his successor, current President Nicolás Maduro, was able to win 13 out of 14 national elections and referenda during a decade and a half.

The explanation is not difficult if we look at the major economic and social indicators during this period. In Figure 5.4, we can see the annual per capita GDP growth for 2004–2014.[87] This averages 2.0 percent annually. The historical comparison is to a genuine economic disaster, also shown in Figure 5.4: Venezuela had one of the worst economic declines in Latin America during the two decades prior to the Chávez government, with real GDP per person actually falling at an annual rate of 1.2 percent. But during 2004–2013, despite an 18-month recession in 2009–2010, growth was quite healthy.

Why start with 2004 when Chávez took office in February of 1999? The fact is that the new government had little control over the economy from 1999 to 2003 because it did not control the national oil company (PDVSA). Actually it was much worse than that. During this time, PDVSA—which was the source of 90 percent of the country's foreign exchange and about half of the government budget—was controlled by the political opposition, which was openly using it to crash the economy in an attempt to

---

87. This is measured from the fourth quarter of 2003 to the third quarter of 2013 (the latest number available for quarterly GDP growth, seasonally adjusted). This is the same data used by the IMF for its annual data, but because the decline in GDP from the oil strike of December 2002–February 2003 and the recovery were so sharp, it is more accurate to use the quarterly data.

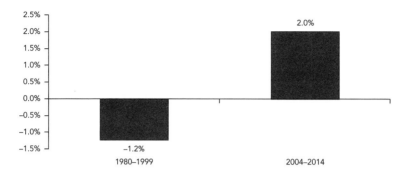

FIGURE 5.4 Venezuela: Average Annual per Capita GDP Growth

Source: IMF, "World Economic Outlook, October 2014," http://www.imf.org/external/pubs/ft/weo/2014/02/weodata/index.aspx.

overthrow the government. In December 2002, just seven months after a failed military coup, the management of PDVSA launched an oil strike that sent the economy into a deep recession. Opposition leader Teodoro Petkoff, who remains one of the more influential anti-government voices today, later wrote that from 1999 to 2003 the opposition had a "strategy that overtly sought a military take-over."[88] Because of this openly acknowledged and quite devastating economic sabotage, it does not make sense to attribute the economic performance of 1999–2003 to the policies of the new government.[89]

88. Teodoro Petkoff, "A Watershed Moment in Venezuela," *Inter-American Dialogue Working Paper*, July 2008, http://www.thedialogue.org/PublicationFiles/A%20Watershed%20Moment%20in%20Venezuela%20-%20Teodoro%20Petkoff%20(July%202008).pdf.

89. We could start with the second quarter of 2003, when the government gained control over the oil industry. However, this would bias the measurement in favor of the government, since the economy was still in deep recession. The last quarter of 2003 is when GDP caught up with its pre-strike level. Measuring from here is fair to both sides.

We can see the chronology of the major events that affected economic growth in Venezuela in Figure 5.5. For the first four years, there was much political and economic instability including business strikes, the military coup, and an oil strike. Then in February 2003 the oil strike ended and the economy began a rapid recovery. Oil production had dropped from 2.9 million to just 25,000 barrels per day because of the strike. It resumed fairly quickly after the strike, although due to the geology of oil extraction, the stoppage caused a large permanent decline in the output of light and medium crude oil in the following years from the country's eastern region.

The new 1999 constitution allowed for a referendum to recall the president halfway through his or her term. In May 2003, the opposition decided to pursue this route. Chávez won the recall referendum by a 59–41 percent margin in August 2004, but the opposition refused to accept the results, despite certification by international observers, including the Organization of American States (OAS). Nonetheless, political stability had returned and the economy grew very rapidly. For more than five years, from the third quarter of 2003 to the end of 2008, there was uninterrupted growth, averaging 9.5 percent annually, although the pace slowed in 2008 as the United States went into recession. The big shock came when world oil prices crashed, falling from a peak of $145 a barrel in July 2008 to less than $40 in December. Venezuela's first recession since the oil strike began in the first quarter of 2009 and lasted until mid-2010. Although most of the Americas went into recession during the 2008–2009 financial crisis and world recession, Venezuela's downturn was longer because the government's fiscal policies were pro-cyclical.[90]

---

90. See Mark Weisbrot, "Venezuela in the Chávez Years: Its Economy and Influence on the Region," in *The Revolution in Venezuela: Social and Political Change under Chávez*, Thomas Poniah and Jonathan Eastwood, eds. (Cambridge, MA: Harvard University Press, 2011).

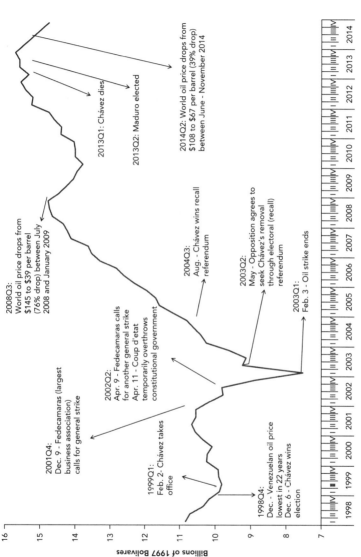

FIGURE 5.5 Venezuela: Quarterly GDP, Seasonally Adjusted

Source: Banco Central de Venezuela (2013), Table 5.2.4; IMF, WEO (2014), author's calculations. Quarterly data for 2014 estimated based on GDP projections from CEPAL, http://repositorio.cepal.org/handle/11362/37345.

In mid-2010, the economy began to recover, and then growth was led by a large government-sponsored housing program, which would bring more than 630,000 new homes to Venezuelans in 2011–2014—the equivalent of more than 6 million homes in the United States. By 2012, annual growth reached 5.7 percent. It is also interesting to look at what happened to inflation during this period. Despite the accelerating growth, inflation actually fell sharply over more than two years of expansion, from 31.3 percent in June 2010 to 17.9 percent in October 2012.[91] This indicates that inflation in Venezuela is not well understood by most analysts, who typically see it as driven by excess demand fueled by money creation.

What happened next was that a weakness in the government's macroeconomic policy became an Achilles heel. Venezuela's fixed exchange rate had long been overvalued, but it wasn't a huge problem since the country frequently ran current account surpluses and more than 90 percent of its exports were from oil. There had been four devaluations since 2004, but a year after each of them, inflation was actually lower or not significantly higher than before the devaluation. Then, in October 2012, the government suddenly cut the supply of dollars by half. The following February it was cut even more.[92]

We can see what followed, in Figure 5.6. There had been a black market for dollars for a number of years, but it had not been a major problem. Now the black market price took off from 10 Bf per dollar in October 2012 to 80 per dollar 16 months later. People were buying dollars as a store of value, thinking that they were a

91. Central Bank of Venezuela, CPI, http://www.bcv.org.ve/excel/4_5_2.xls?id=415.

92. Nathan Crooks and Corina Pons, "Chavez Mulls Revamping Currency Controls as Bolivar Plunges," Bloomberg, November 14, 2012, http://www.bloomberg.com/news/2012-11-14/chavez-mulls-revamping-currency-controls-as-bolivar-plunges.html.

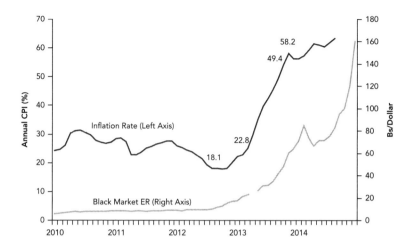

FIGURE 5.6 Venezuela: Annual Inflation and Black Market Exchange Rate

Source: Banco Central de Venezuela and Dolartoday BCV, "Indice nacional de precios al consumidor," Banco Central de Venezuela, n.d., http://bcv.org.ve/c2/indicadores.asp. Dolartoday, Black Market Exchange Rate Time Series, n.d., https://d1phdof6oyl82t.cloudfront.net/indicadores/.

one-way bet. Producers and importers who did not have access to enough cheap dollars would also buy them on the black market. Since prices are determined by the highest cost suppliers, even a relatively small black market as a percent of the market for dollars was able to drive up the consumer price index as the black market dollar rose.

Scarcities of goods were driven by the same dynamic—the shortage of dollars—and as can be seen in Figure 5.7, they followed the black market and inflation rate in this upward spiral. The economy was caught in a feedback loop in which the rising black market exchange rate fed inflation, and increasing inflation pushed more buyers into the black market for dollars. The huge black market differential also encourages a lot of corruption—it was more lucrative than cocaine if you could get access to official dollars and sell

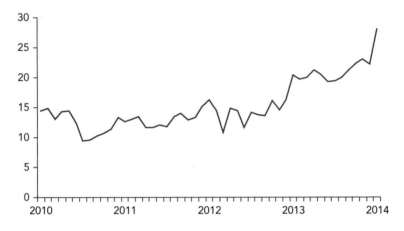

FIGURE 5.7 Venezuela: Scarcity Index

Source: Banco Central de Venezuela.

them at the black market, and you didn't have to risk dying in a hail of bullets. Capital flight cannot be accurately measured, but it was certainly large and increasing; private estimates put it at about $10 billion per year.

The government did succeed in temporarily stabilizing the black market rate from a high of 88 in February 2014 to a rate that fluctuated between 65 and 75 until July, by creating a new (now the third) legal exchange rate in March that was supposed to float. Perhaps more important, they announced that this was a step toward unifying the exchange rate system. With unification coming, it did not make sense to buy black market dollars as a store of value, since a unified rate would be nowhere near 80 Bf per dollar. Private estimates at that time put an equilibrium exchange rate in the 20s.

By July 2014, when it appeared that the unification of the exchange rate was not imminent, however, excess demand for the new, ostensibly floating exchange rate returned and the black market price of the dollar began to rise again. As the world price of oil fell by 35 percent between June and November 2014, the black market rate soared upward, reaching more than 170 by December 2014. People were again buying dollars on the bet that the government was facing a serious balance of payments crisis and the black market dollar would continue to soar until there was hyperinflation.

It is not clear when, or if, the government will take the necessary steps to fix its broken exchange rate system. But like other crises brought on by macroeconomic policy mistakes, it is fixable. In fact, by July 2014, Venezuela had already gone through the toughest part of the necessary adjustment, experiencing a 33 percent drop in imports over two years[93]—one of the biggest such adjustments in the world. (For comparison, Greece reduced its imports by 36 percent in six years of recession.)[94] This means that if the government were to let the currency float, there would be an adjustment of relative prices but not the overall decline in living standards that would usually result from such a large contraction of imports. The country is not facing a genuine balance of payments crisis—where it cannot earn enough dollars to pay for its imports. Rather, it is giving away the dollars that it earns much too cheaply.

On the positive side, by December 2014 the country still had at least $40 billion in reserves,[95] and it continues to get concessional lending from China, which considers Venezuela to be a "strategic ally." Since almost all of the dollars earned from oil exports accrue

93. The first six months of 2014 compared to the same period in 2012. National Institute for Statistics, 2014, http://www.ine.gov.ve/documentos/Economia/ComercioExteriorComentarios/html/CuadroComercioImport.php?cuadro=1&tipo=I.

94. See Mark Weisbrot, David Rosnick, and Stephan Lefebvre, "The Greek Economy: Which Way Forward?" Center for Economic and Policy Research, January 2015, http://www.cepr.net/index.php/publications/reports/the-greek-economy-which-way-forward.

95. This includes funds held outside the Central Bank reserves. One problem is that about 70 percent of the Central Bank reserves are in gold. These can be sold and are considered semi-liquid, but the markets do not seem to assume that the government would sell them rather than default on its debt.

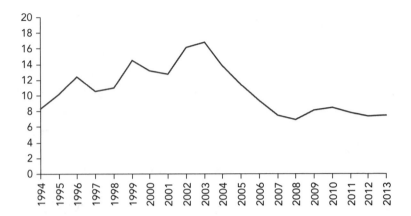

FIGURE 5.8 Venezuela: Unemployment Rate (Percent of Labor Force)

Source: INE (National Institute for Statistics, 2014, Venezuela), http://www.ine.gov.ve/index.php?option=com_content&view=category&id=103&Itemid=40.

to the government, they would be able to compensate people who lose from the switch to a "managed floating" exchange rate.

Whatever happens in the coming year, even including the current crisis, it is clear that so far there have been gains for Venezuela comparable to what the other leftist governments have achieved. Along with the growth of income per person, we can see that there has been a large, secular decline in the unemployment rate. This is shown in Figure 5.8. Despite the current crisis, unemployment stands at 7.5 percent, far below the 14.5 percent rate when Chávez took office.

Most important from a socioeconomic standpoint was the decline in the poverty rate, shown in Figure 5.9. For the period from 2004 to the first half of 2014, the percentage of households in poverty fell by 49 percent, and in extreme poverty by 63 percent. This graph includes only cash income; it does not include, for example, the impact for millions of people of gaining access to healthcare for the first time. These were provided through the *Misión Barrio Adentro*,

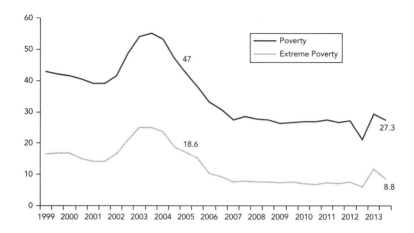

FIGURE 5.9 Venezuela: Poverty and Extreme Poverty (Percent of Households)

Source: INE (National Institute for Statistics, 2014, Venezuela), http://www.ine.gov.ve/index.php?option=com_content&view=category&id=104&Itemid=45.

which established thousands of neighborhood clinics staffed with Cuban doctors.[96]

There were other gains that help explain the re-election of the Chavistas. In addition to the *misiones* for healthcare and housing, there were others for literacy and continuing education.[97] College enrollment grew enormously, with the percentage of the college-age population enrolled in tertiary education nearly tripling, from 28.3 percent in 2000 to 78.11 percent in 2009, one of the highest

96. See, e.g., Carles Muntaner et al., "History Is Not Over: The Bolivarian Revolution, 'Barrio Adentro,' and Health Care in Venezuela," in *The Revolution in Venezuela: Social and Political Change under Chávez*, Thomas Poniah and Jonathan Eastwood, eds. (Cambridge, MA: Harvard University Press, 2011).

97. For an overview of Venezuela's education achievements in the Chávez years, see "Logros de la Educación venezolana en Revolución," VTV, December 25, 2013, http://www.vtv.gob.ve/articulos/2013/12/25/logros-de-la-educacion-venezolana-en-revolucion-8607.html.

rates in the world.[98] Public pensions also increased enormously: The percentage of the population over 60 receiving pensions nearly doubled, from 27.2 percent in 2004 to 52.8 percent in 2013. This was a near threefold increase of people receiving pensions, from 526,000 to more than 1.5 million.[99] Formal sector employment also increased from 55 percent to 62.1 percent of the labor force in the 1999–2013 period. And inequality, as measured by the Gini coefficient, had one of the sharpest declines in the Americas, from .469 to .398 for the same 1999–2013 period.[100] This is consistent with data from the UN Economic Commission for Latin America, which shows Venezuela with the second-smallest ratio of income of the top to bottom quintile, after Uruguay, of 18 countries.[101]

Even if we look at inflation, it is worth noting that it is much lower than it was during the pre-Chávez era, as can be seen in Figure 5.10. Of course this could still change if the government does not act to break the current inflation/depreciation cycle. But inflation has played a key role in bringing about the current crisis. As Venezuela's inflation has been continuously and substantially higher than that of its trading partners, it appreciates the (fixed) real exchange rate by a large percentage each year. This leads to periodic devaluations, as we have seen since 2004. But under certain conditions it can also slide into an inflation-depreciation spiral that has occurred in the past two years, along with increasing capital flight that pours more fuel on the fire. Any stabilization program—preferably with a managed floating exchange rate—will have to bring down inflation if it is to avoid recurring crises.

98. UNESCO, UNESCO Institute for Statistics Database, n.d., http://data.uis.unesco.org/.

99. Sistema de Indicadores Sociales de Venezuela, n.d., http://sisov.mppp.gob.ve/indicadores/SS0100300000000/.

100. INE (National Institute for Statistics).

101. ECLAC, "Social Panorama of Latin America 2013," p. 20.

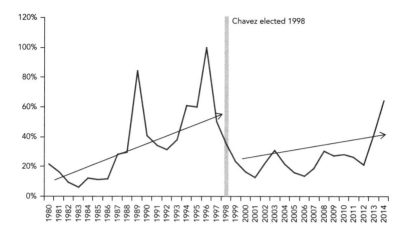

FIGURE 5.10 Venezuela: Consumer Price Index, Annual
Year-over-Year

Source: IMF, "World Economic Outlook, October 2014," http://www.imf.org/
external/pubs/ft/weo/2014/02/weodata/index.aspx.

The overall social and economic gains during the Chávez era
received scant attention in the mass media; of all the leftist governments elected in the past 15 years, the coverage of Venezuela has
been most relentlessly hostile. The treatment of Chávez himself,
among the most demonized democratically elected presidents in
world history, can perhaps best be summed up by Bertrand Russell's
description of the American revolutionary Thomas Paine: "He had his
faults, like other men, but it was for his virtues that he was hated
and successfully calumniated."[102] It has been governments allied with
the United States that have bought into the hatred or the calumny.
When Chávez died in March 2013, 55 countries were represented

102. It should be noted that Chávez was successfully calumniated in the Western
Hemisphere, in that the mass media coverage ensured that he was viewed nega-
tively outside of Venezuela. It was the governments, and of course some special-
ists outside government who followed events more closely, that had a different
view of him.

at his funeral, and 33 heads of state, including all of Latin America. Fourteen Latin American countries decreed official days of mourning, including the right-wing government of Chile. In contrast to the emotional outpourings and praise that came from Latin American leaders, the White House issued a cold and unfriendly statement that, to the horror of many Latin Americans, didn't even offer condolences.

It was not difficult to explain the enormous chasm between the views of Washington (and the Western media), and the world's governments. Chávez played a huge role in bringing about Latin America's second independence. To the world outside Washington, this was a historic achievement. In Washington, depending on who was talking, it was either a tragedy or a crime. "Perhaps his ideas will come to inspire young people in the future, much as the life of Simón Bolívar, the great liberator of Latin America, inspired Mr. Chávez himself," wrote Brazil's most popular president, Lula Da Silva. Lula had campaigned for Chávez in his 2006 and 2012 elections, and noted that he played a crucial role in the formation of the Union of South American Nations (UNASUR), the Community of Latin American and Caribbean States (CELAC), and other efforts at regional integration.

Concluding Thoughts: Abiding US Hostility, National Sovereignty, and Economic Progress

What can we learn from the lessons of Latin America's transition over the past 15 years? From looking at the details of these four countries' experiences (and Argentina's transition, which was examined in previous chapters), it is clear that the region's winning its "second independence"—especially in South America—was essential to opening up the policy space that enabled its success. Whether it was regaining control over hydrocarbon resources (in Bolivia, Venezuela, and Ecuador), or getting rid of IMF influence on economic policy, all of these new governments had to free themselves from Washington's giant shadow in order to try to deliver on their electoral promises, and in some cases merely to survive.

It would require an entire book or more to describe Washington's substantial resistance to this new independence. It would probably have been even worse had the United States not been bogged down in wars in Afghanistan and Iraq for most of this period. Venezuela became the primary target in the region (and after the invasion of Iraq, probably in the world, excepting Iran) for "regime change." It was not, as many believed, because of Chávez's blunt statements about the United States. After Chávez made his famous speech at the United Nations referring to President George W. Bush as "the devil," then Ecuadorean presidential candidate Rafael Correa was asked at a press conference what he thought of the remarks. "I think it is unfair to the devil," he responded, "because although the devil is evil, he is at least intelligent. Bush is an incredibly dim-witted president, who has caused much harm to his own country and the world."[103] Correa was elected two months later, and Bush called to congratulate him. Bush was focused on Venezuela, and he was keeping his eyes on the prize. That was Venezuela's 500 billion barrels of oil reserves—the largest in the world.

Correa kicked out the US military base at Manta, saying that the United States could keep it if Ecuador could have a military base in Florida; he would later also have his run-ins with the United States, as did Bolivia, Argentina, and most of the left governments. Even Brazil, with which Washington was trying to maintain friendlier relations, was the target of a covert US State Department effort in 2005 within the country to promote legislation that would weaken

---

103. "El diablo será malvado, pero aunque sea es inteligente. Bush es un presidente tremendamente torpe que ha hecho mucho daño a su país y al mundo." Agencies, "El izquierdista Correa, favorito para ser el nuevo presidente de Ecuador según una encuesta," *El País*, September 28, 2006, http://internacional.elpais.com/internacional/2006/09/28/actualidad/1159394401_850215.html.

the Workers' Party.[104] But Venezuela was special. In 2002 the US government aided a short-lived coup in which President Chávez was kidnapped by the military for 48 hours. The US State Department later admitted that the Bush administration "provided training, institution building, and other support to individuals and organizations understood to be actively involved in the military coup" of 2002. CIA documents later showed that the Bush administration also had advance knowledge of the coup; but when it occurred, the White House tried to convince the world that it was not a coup at all, but that Chávez had resigned. There is also evidence that Washington tried to convince other governments to support the coup.[105] Former *Washington Post* foreign editor Scott Wilson, who covered Venezuela at this time, would acknowledge years later what his newspaper would never print: "There was U.S. involvement [in the coup], yes," he said in an interview, in which he described this involvement.[106] In the years that followed, the major media would continually portray Chávez as the aggressor, despite the fact that Washington stepped up funding to anti-government groups after the coup[107] and contributed to numerous efforts to destabilize the government.

104. Sérgio Dávila, "EUA tentaram influenciar reforma política do Brasil," *Folha de São Paulo*, July 22, 2005, http://www1.folha.uol.com.br/fsp/brasil/fc2207200820.htm. See also Mark Weisbrot, "The US Game in Latin America," *The Guardian*, January 29, 2010, http://www.theguardian.com/commentisfree/cifamerica/2010/jan/29/us-latin-america-haiti-honduras.

105. For links to the relevant documents, including those from the State Department and CIA, see Mark Weisbrot, "Venezuela's Election Provides Opportunity for Washington to Change Course," McClatchy Tribune Information Services, December 6, 2006, at http://www.cepr.net/index.php/op-eds-&-columns/op-eds-&-columns/venezuelas-election-provides-opportunity-for-washington-to-change-course/.

106. See "Scott Wilson on US involvement in Venezuela Coup," YouTube, uploaded July 30, 2010, https://www.youtube.com/watch?v=KzSnH4_p0PY.

107. Bart Jones, "U.S. Funds Aid Chávez Opposition," *National Catholic Reporter*, April 2, 2004, http://natcath.org/NCR_Online/archives2/2004b/040204/040204a.htm.

To take one recent example from Venezuela's last presidential election, which the governing party candidate Nicolás Maduro won by 1.5 percentage points, there were violent opposition demonstrations claiming fraud. Washington refused to recognize the results, even though there was no question about the outcome. Venezuela has a dual voting system that former President Jimmy Carter—whose Carter Center is involved in election observations in dozens of countries—has called "the best in the world."[108] Voters press a touch screen, receive a paper receipt, and place the receipt in a ballot box. When the polls close, the paper ballots are counted and compared with the electronic tally at about half the polling places in the presence of observers from all parties, as well as neighborhood residents. Because of the huge sample, a statistical analysis showed that the probability of getting the official results, if the election were actually stolen, was less than one in 25,000 trillion.[109]

Yet US Secretary of State John Kerry refused to accept the results and joined the opposition's call for a "full recount." He managed to get only the right-wing government of Spain and the Secretary General of the OAS, José Miguel Insulza, to support him. But all of them had to back off after UNASUR, led by Brazil, reacted strongly against the US moves.[110]

108. "30 Years of The Carter Center," *The Carter Center* (video), 86:32, September 11, 2012, http://www.cartercenter.org/news/multimedia/Conversations/30-years-of-the-carter-center.html.

109. David Rosnick and Mark Weisbrot, "A Statistical Note on the April 14 Venezuelan Presidential Election and Audit of Results," Center for Economic and Policy Research, 2013, http://www.cepr.net/index.php/publications/reports/a-statistical-note-on-the-april-14-venezuelan-presidential-election-and-audit-of-results.

110. Shobhan Saxena, "South Americans Back Venezuela's Maduro, Blast US 'Interference,'" *The Times of India*, April 17, 2013, http://timesofindia.indiatimes.com/world/rest-of-world/South-Americans-back-Venezuelas-Maduro-blast-US-interference/articleshow/19602966.cms; see also Weisbrot, "The US Game in Latin America."

US-supported attempts to undermine left governments were met repeatedly with confrontations like these throughout the past 15 years, with increasing organization and solidarity among the Latin American governments, especially in South America. The military coup in June 2009 in Honduras was a turning point. The new president of the United States, Barack Obama, had been welcomed by the leftist presidents, who saw him as one of their own, even before he was elected. "Just as Brazil elected a metal worker, Bolivia elected an Indian, Venezuela elected Chávez, and Paraguay a bishop," said President Lula da Silva, "I think that it would be an extraordinary thing if, in the largest economy in the world, a black man were elected president of the United States."[111]

But their hopes were extinguished just hours after the Honduran military grabbed President Mel Zelaya and flew him to Costa Rica (in his pajamas), stopping at the US military base at Palmerola on the way to refuel.[112] The White House statement on the day of the coup did not condemn the action, merely calling on "all political and social actors in Honduras" to respect democracy.[113] Since US officials acknowledged that they were talking to the Honduran military right up to the day of the coup—allegedly to prevent it—they had time to think about what their immediate response would be if it the coup occurred. Their statement said it all: this was the twenty-first century, and the White House could not say "we support the military overthrow of this democratically

111. EFE, "Elección de Obama sería como las de Morales, Chávez y Lugo," *Diario ABC Color*, October 31, 2008, http://www.abc.com.py/edicion-impresa/internacionales/eleccion-de-obama-seria-como-las-de-morales-chavez-y-lugo-1116531.html.

112. Freddy Cuevas, "Top Aide Says U.S. Complicit in Honduras Coup," *Toronto Star* (AP), August 16, 2009, http://www.thestar.com/news/world/2009/08/16/top_aide_says_us_complicit_in_honduras_coup.html.

113. Adam Thomson and Agencies, "Honduran Leader Ousted by Army," *Financial Times*, June 28, 2009, http://www.ft.com/cms/s/0/409b94b4-6432-11de-a818-00144feabdc0.html?siteedition=uk#axzz3L305fpGv.

elected government." Neutrality was as far as they could go in public. But it was enough so that every diplomat in Washington—not to mention anyone in Honduras who was paying attention—knew immediately that this coup had the support of the US government at the highest level.

For the next six months, every step the Obama administration took to support the consolidation of the coup government was therefore predictable. This could be seen in its refusal to endorse Zelaya's return to office or to criticize widespread human rights violations during the dictatorship, despite documentation and denunciations from Human Rights Watch,[114] Amnesty International,[115] the OAS Inter-American Commission on Human Rights,[116] and Honduran, European, and other human rights organizations. The US government's lonely support for "elections" in November 2009 was another; not even the OAS or EU, Washington's closest allies, would send representatives to observe them.[117]

The coup put an end to a brief experiment in more progressive government in Honduras and restored the country to its traditional role, as a US military base with a repressive government. But it also gave an added push to the rest of the hemisphere to proceed with institutional changes that would step up their cooperation on

114. Human Rights Watch, "Honduras: Investigate Abuses, Repeal Repressive Measures," October 30, 2009, http://www.hrw.org/en/news/2009/10/30/honduras-investigate-abuses-repeal-repressive-measures.

115. Amnesty International, "Honduras: Abuses Escalate in Crackdown," September 25, 2009, http://www.amnesty.org/en/library/info/AMR37/006/2009/en.

116. Inter-American Commission on Human Rights, "IACHR Condemns Excessive Use of Force in Repression of Protests in Honduras," September 22, 2009, http://www.cidh.org/comunicados/english/2009/65-09eng.htm.

117. See Mark Weisbrot, "Obama's Latin America Policy: Continuity Without Change," *Latin American Perspectives* 38 (2011): 63–72, first published on May 11, 2011; and "Top Ten Ways You Can Tell Which Side the United States Government Is on with Regard to the Military Coup in Honduras," December 16, 2009, http://www.cepr.net/op-eds-&-columns/op-eds-&-columns/top-ten-ways.

common security and economic concerns. One of these was the creation of a new hemispheric organization, the Community of Latin American and Caribbean States, which includes all countries of the region, except the United States and Canada. This was a logical response to Washington's manipulation of the OAS to support the Honduran coup.[118]

Latin American countries would increasingly respond to regional problems while ignoring or teaming up against the United States. The one exception was the overthrow of Haiti's democratically elected government in 2004.[119] Regional norms and practices began to change so that even non-leftist governments—the few that remained in South America—would side with the left-wing majority on foreign policy issues. President Bush started out by trying to isolate Venezuela, but ended up isolating the United States; the Obama administration occasionally tried to patch diplomatic matters up, but repeatedly succumbed to pressure from hard-liners at home.[120] The result is that Obama's administration currently has worse relations with the region than those of his predecessor, despite a more favorable image in the regional media.[121]

118. In her 2014 book, *Hard Choices*, former US Secretary of State Hillary Clinton acknowledges her role in blocking Zelaya's return to office after the coup. See Mark Weisbrot, "Hard Choices: Hillary Clinton Admits Role in Honduran Coup Aftermath," Al Jazeera America, September 29, 2014, http://america.aljazeera.com/opinions/2014/9/hillary-clinton-honduraslatinamericaforeignpolicy.html.

119. In this case Washington helped overthrow the elected President Jean-Bertrand Aristide and flew him to Africa—a kidnapping by his and witness accounts—where he spent seven years in exile. Latin America did not oppose the coup, although some Caribbean states did. Brazil led a UN military mission that occupied the country while the constitutionally elected officials were jailed and thousands of people were killed. See Hallward, *Damming the Flood*.

120. See Weisbrot, "Obama's Latin America Policy: Continuity Without Change."

121. See, e.g., Brian Ellsworth, "Despite Obama Charm, Americas Summit Boosts U.S. Isolation," Reuters, April 16, 2012, http://www.reuters.com/article/2012/04/17/us-americas-summit-obama-idUSBRE83F0UD20120417; Mark Weisbrot, "The US Needs to Take the Hint from Dilma Rousseff's

Of course in Latin America, a strategy that zealously guards national sovereignty and promotes regional co-operation as well as independence from the United States, does not have to be led by left-wing governments. But for various historical and political reasons this has been the case. It is likely that both of these trends are here to stay, so long as the left can continue to deliver greater economic and social progress.

Still, the left governments have not been able to advance much in the area of industrial policy or moving up the development ladder to higher value-added areas of production. After nearly four decades of neoliberal policies, they do not have the institutional strength or administrative capacity, and in some cases the human capital, to even reach the higher rates of growth they obtained in the 1960s or 1970s. It is worth noting that the governments of Bolivia, Ecuador, and Venezuela claim to be building "twenty-first century socialism," despite the fact that their efforts look much more like a social democratic project. The governments don't use that label because it has been discredited by political parties who used it while they presided over decades of neoliberal failure. But whether we call it socialism or social democracy, there are many development policy options that were commonly deployed in the pre-neoliberal era in developing countries that have yet to be initiated under the new left governments of Latin America. Even in Venezuela, the private sector grew faster than the public sector from 1999 to 2012.[122] In Brazil, as noted above, there have been some moves toward establishing an industrial policy, and Ecuador

Snub," *The Guardian*, September 18, 2013, http://www.theguardian.com/commentisfree/2013/sep/18/us-hint-nsa-dilma-rousseff-snub.

122. See Jake Johnston, and Sara Kozameh, "Venezuelan Economic and Social Performance under Hugo Chávez, in Graphs," Center for Economic and Policy Research, March 13, 2013, http://www.cepr.net/index.php/blogs/the-americas-blog/venezuelan-economic-and-social-performance-under-hugo-chavez-in-graphs.

has a five-year plan that seeks to diversify away from its dependence on extractive industries. But these are just beginnings. On the positive side, they have stopped the drive toward privatization and deregulation, and in many cases reversed some of the worst macroeconomic policies, that contributed to Latin America's economic failure of the prior 20 years.

The experience of the past 15 years also shows that some of the new governments have not escaped the economic weaknesses of Latin America's past, especially regarding balance of payments problems. This is most clear in Venezuela, as noted above, although in this case the problems arise from of a dysfunctional exchange rate system, rather than a genuine shortage of dollars. Argentina is also confronting a similar but much less severe dynamic in which it is plagued by a sizable black market premium that went as high as 89 percent in 2014, before retreating to 50 percent, along with some capital flight and problems with high inflation that by some estimates reached 39 percent in 2014. The Argentine case is different in that it is partly due to having been largely shut out of international financial markets since its 2002 default. The debt was restructured, with about 76 percent of creditors accepting new bonds by 2005, and more than 92 percent by 2010. The government has made all payments on the restructured bonds on time. In 2012, a judge in the US District Court for the Southern District of New York, however, ruled that the Argentine government could not continue to pay these creditors unless it first paid plaintiff "vulture funds"—hedge funds that buy up defaulted debt and then sue for the full face value of the bond.[123] This was an unprecedented decision—taking 92 percent of the creditors hostage— in order to satisfy the claims of just a

123. See Mark Weisbrot, "The Debt Vultures' Fell Swoop," *New York Times*, June 22, 2014, http://www.nytimes.com/2014/06/23/opinion/the-debt-vultures-fell-swoop.html.

few, and it was based on legal reasoning that most experts found to be flawed.[124] But the decision was upheld by the US Supreme Court, and it threw a wrench into Argentina's plans to return to normal borrowing from international financial markets. This is despite the fact that the Argentine government settled with the Paris Club of official creditors in June 2014, as well as settling a number of disputes with foreign investors.

By the time this work is published, some arrangements will probably be reached to allow Argentina to return to international borrowing. Or Argentina will find a way to pay the restructured bondholders outside the reach of the New York judicial system. In any case, it is another example of the importance of national economic and financial independence. A New York judge of questionable competence[125] should not have been able to have this much impact on Argentina's economy, by forcing what much of the business press called "Argentina's second default in 12 years,"[126] even though Argentina had deposited its interest payments to bondholders on time. In this case, too, there was an interesting twist that showed once again how the far right in foreign policy circles can push the Obama administration to undermine the leftist governments they hate. In July 2013, IMF Managing Director Christine Lagarde announced that the IMF was going to file an amicus brief with the US Supreme Court supporting Argentina's case. There was

124. Brief for the United States of America as Amicus Curiae in Support of Argentina's Petition for Panel Rehearing and Rehearing En Banc, NML Capital, Ltd. v. Republic of Argentina, No. 12-105 cv(L) (2d Cir. Dec. 28, 2012), 2012 WL 6777132.

125. Floyd Norris, "Argentina's Case Has No Victors, Many Losers," *New York Times*, November 20, 2014, http://www.nytimes.com/2014/11/21/business/international/in-argentinas-debt-case-no-winners-but-a-lot-of-losers.html.

126. Luc Cohen, Benedict Mander, and Elaine Moore, "Investors Sanguine as Argentina Defaults," *The Financial Times*, July 31, 2014. Retrieved February 12, 2015, from http://www.ft.com/cms/s/0/5d7c8016-1832-11e4-a6e4-00144feabdc0.html?siteedition=uk.

no love lost between the Fund and Argentina, but the IMF recognized that the lower court's decision, upheld on appeal, could have a destabilizing impact on the international financial system: it could make it much more difficult for governments facing default to restructure their debt. But then, a week later, the Fund had to walk back from its commitment; the US Treasury Department had vetoed it. A reporter asked IMF spokesperson Bill Murray at a press conference why the Fund had reversed course. "Go to the U.S. Treasury and ask them to explain their decisions," he replied.[127] But apparently nobody did. The most likely explanation is that right-wing members of the US Congress threatened to hold up the IMF's funding increase.[128]

Whatever emerges in Argentina and Venezuela, their current difficulties also illustrate the crucial role of managing an exchange rate regime to avoid balance of payments crises and associated macroeconomic instability. Venezuela's use of a fixed, overvalued exchange rate with periodic devaluations is a crisis-prone system, which they were able to navigate so long as there were large current account surpluses, and they did not have much of a non-oil export sector to worry about. Argentina's use of a managed float, targeting a stable and competitive real exchange rate, worked very well for several years after the default. But they ran into trouble as inflation picked up after 2007. In both cases, relatively high inflation (Venezuela's averaged about 22 percent annually from 1999 to 2012) was not directly harmful to economic growth, but as noted previously, it becomes a problem as the inflation causes the real exchange rate to appreciate. The problem is worse in an era of very

127. IMF, "Transcript of a Press Briefing by William Murray, Deputy Spokesman, Communications Department, International Monetary Fund," Washington, DC, July 25, 2013, https://www.imf.org/external/np/tr/2013/tr072513.htm.

128. Mark Weisbrot, "Who Shot Argentina?" U.S. News & World Report, June 24, 2014, http://www.usnews.com/opinion/articles/2014/06/24/supreme-court-dismisses-case-between-argentina-and-us-vulture-funds.

low inflation internationally, as it is the difference between their own rate of inflation and that of their trading partners that determines the extent of real appreciation. Once there is a black market with a sizable premium, it can set in motion the harmful feedback loop between inflation, the black market premium, expected devaluation, and capital flight described above. This is a situation that must be avoided, and is better dealt with sooner rather than later.

As for the region, Nixon's nightmare has become a reality 40 years later. Washington failed to topple the first elected left government at the turn of the century, and the rush to achieve independence spread like an epidemic. During the 1990s, part of the Washington foreign policy establishment noticed the irony that Latin America had done vastly better economically under the dictatorships of the 1960s and 1970s than with the "Washington consensus," and worried that people would become nostalgic for authoritarian government. But instead, many Latin Americans opted for more inclusive democracy, which with free elections meant left-wing governments willing to implement new economic and social policies that have sharply reduced poverty and inequality for the first time in decades. They have still not returned to the growth rates of the 1960s and 1970s, but they have made a good start. Politically, there has been one brief reversal in Chile that brought in a right-wing government in 2010–2014, but the Socialist Party's Michele Bachelet was re-elected in 2014. Other than governments removed illegally, as in Paraguay in 2012, Honduras in 2009, and Haiti in 2004, all of the left-wing governments that were elected have been re-elected. It doesn't look like this progressive trend will be reversed any time soon.

Conclusion

Looking Ahead

Economists do not have a good track record in forecasting, even when there are glaring imbalances that flash huge red warning lights in front of everyone's face. My colleague Dean Baker was the first, and one of the few, economists to correctly analyze the United States' two biggest asset bubbles—in the stock market in the late 1990s, and in real estate beginning in 2002. The consequences of both are now much better known, yet the most prominent commentary and analysis continue to come from people who missed both of them.

In addition to unexplained blindness, there are many unforeseen events (such as the recent collapse of oil prices) and even predictable ones, the impacts of which are not easy to know in advance. The Fed will probably begin to raise short-term interest rates in the near future, and this will reduce capital flows to low- and middle-income countries—but how much impact it will have is not easy to know ahead of time.

With these provisos, what the "experts"—some of whom are actual experts and many of whom are not—have missed about some of the most important trends of the past few decades, as described in this book, can possibly tell us something about the future.

The analysis in this book shows the eurozone to be a special case, in which institutional constraints make political change possible only through an excruciatingly slow process of democratization. This is partly due to the removal of the most important decision-making powers from national governments, which would be at least somewhat more accountable to an abused and discontented electorate, and partly to the overall political agenda of the European authorities. The latter can be influenced, with great difficulty, by pressure from below. The European Central Bank's (ECB) changes in policy, including its putting an end to the financial crisis of the euro in July 2012 and its decision in 2015 to implement quantitative easing, are part of that unfortunately protracted process. So, too, is the rapid rise of new left parties such as Syriza in Greece and Podemos in Spain. It remains to be seen how much pressure can be generated from within the eurozone's member countries. But in the absence of any government actually leaving the eurozone—which could set off a domino effect if it were to result in a robust recovery for the first country to do so—this looks like the way in which positive change is going to take place.

Unless this pressure from below accelerates enormously, the next few years will bring considerable unnecessary unemployment and pain in Europe. The IMF is projecting that unemployment in the eurozone will still be more than 10 percent in 2017.[1] Even though fiscal austerity has wound down considerably, without a serious effort to tackle the region's mass unemployment, much unnecessary joblessness is likely to linger. Even worse, the authorities are redefining potential output (and therefore full employment) so that this mass unemployment could become the new normal. The IMF predicts that by 2019 Spain will have practically reached its potential output,[2] yet this will be accompanied by

1. IMF, "World Economic Outlook Database," April 2015, http://www.imf.org/external/pubs/ft/weo/2015/01/weorept.aspx?pr.x=53&pr.y=9&sy=2013&ey=2020&scsm=1&ssd=1&sort=country&ds=.&br=1&c=163&s=LUR&grp=1&a=1.

2. IMF, "Spain: Selected Issues," July 2014, http://www.imf.org/external/pubs/ft/scr/2014/cr14193.pdf.

an unemployment rate of 17.8 percent. This means that the IMF is defining more than 17 percent unemployment as full employment for Spain. The failure of most major political parties in the eurozone countries to offer any alternative to continued recession, stagnation, and high unemployment—or worse, their efforts to chip away at social protections won decades ago—has left many voters vulnerable to the appeal of far-right and even fascist politicians. The recent electoral gains of the National Front in France, Golden Dawn in Greece, and other right-wing parties are at least partly a result of this abject failure of leadership on the part of the center-left. Nonetheless, the far right is unlikely to get much further traction in Europe.

In the developing world, economic policy and the rate of increase of living standards are likely to show improvement in the foreseeable future. As the late economist Alice Amsden argued persuasively in her last book, "freedom of choice [makes] economic development a lot easier."[3] In the postwar period prior to 1980, many developing countries had more choices than they would subsequently enjoy, because of the United States' fear at the time of leftist alternatives, competition from the Soviet Union, and Washington's other strategic considerations. This is part of the reason for the faster growth observed in most developing countries in the 1950–1980 period.

Chapter 3 has argued that the twenty-first century rebound in the low- and middle-income countries is related to a new emergence of better policy choices. This, in turn, is partly due to the loss of US and IMF influence over many countries' economic policies and governments. China's role in the post-2000 recovery went beyond the rapid growth of its demand for the exports of many developing countries; it has also become an important alternative source of investment, lending, and development aid. If this analysis

3. Alice H. Amsden, *Escape from Empire: The Developing World's Journey Through Heaven and Hell* (Cambridge, MA: MIT Press, 2007).

is correct, we would expect to see the trends of the past 15 years toward increasing national independence (as in Latin America), better policy choices, and better economic and social outcomes in the developing world continue as China continues to increase its global economic weight and influence.

In January 2015, for example, China announced a $250 billion investment program in Latin America for the next decade.[4] It also announced a $7.5 billion investment commitment to Ecuador,[5] a country that is currently threatened by the drop in oil prices. China is continuing to loan money to Venezuela, which it considers to be a "strategic ally." In 2014 it initiated an $11 billion currency swap arrangement with Argentina,[6] which is relieving some of the pressure on that country's reserves as it grapples with an assault from vulture fund creditors that has recently blocked its return to international financial markets. China has also played a major role in Africa's growth rebound in the twenty-first century, through investment in infrastructure, loans, and development aid, which are often difficult to separate.[7]

Aid is often tied to purchases from Chinese companies, and there have been other criticisms of the Chinese foreign commercial policy. But if we look at it in practical and economic rather than

---

4. Reuters, "China's Xi Woos Latin America with $250 Billion Investments," *New York Times*, January 7, 2015, http://www.nytimes.com/reuters/2015/01/07/world/americas/07reuters-china-latam.html?ref=americas&_r=0.

5. Jonathan Kaiman, "China Agrees to Invest $20bn in Venezuela to Help Offset Effects of Oil Price Slump," *The Guardian*, January 8, 2014, http://www.theguardian.com/world/2015/jan/08/china-venezuela-20bn-loans-financing-nicolas-maduro-beijing.

6. Camila Russo, "Argentina Gets Reserves Boost from China Currency Swap," *Bloomberg*, October 30, 2014, http://www.bloomberg.com/news/2014-10-30/argentina-gets-reserves-boost-from-china-currency-swap.html.

7. See, e.g., Deborah Bräutigam, "Aid 'With Chinese Characteristics': Chinese Foreign Aid and Development Finance Meet the OECD-DAC Aid Regime," *Journal of International Development* 23 (2011): 752–764, doi: 10.1002/jid.1798.

moralistic terms, there are very big differences between China's practices and those of the West. Most important, China has a policy of noninterference in the domestic policies—including the economic policies—of the recipient countries. Its government has a long-term strategy of trying to build secure and reliable sources for the resources that they see as necessary to China's growth and development, and China's diplomatic and foreign policy goals are tied to commercial policy. But these are very limited indeed compared with the goals of the United States and its allies. The United States is probably the only country in the world that defines its "national security" interests broadly enough to include practically the entire globe and a whole set of policies that other countries, including China, consider to be the sovereign concern of individual countries. China's role in regions such as Latin America and Africa is therefore vastly different from that of the United States and institutions such as the IMF and World Bank that are under US leadership. The end result is that China's increasing role in the world economy means more choices for developing countries.

On a purchasing power parity basis, the Chinese economy is already bigger than that of the United States. A decade from now, the United States is projected to be a distant second, with China more than 50 percent larger. The weight of the developing world as a whole is increasing in the world economy, moreover. Politically, this is leading to an increasingly multipolar world, and this can only be good for developing countries.

This trend is obvious to most of the world, but not to most of the "experts" who dominate public opinion in the United States and its allies. For them, "Father Knows Best" is still the default mindset. Discussion of empire is practically taboo in the United States. Most intellectuals and policy analysts seem convinced that because the United States and its high-income allies have more developed systems of democracy and the rule of law than most developing countries, and profess to believe in universal human rights, a world order dominated by these governments is inherently better than one in which countries with less democratic governance, including China, have a bigger say. Of course it is questionable, given the never-ending wars, secret prisons, torture, mass surveillance, and other worldwide abuses perpetrated by Washington and its allies, how far the United States' commitment to democracy and the rule of law truly extends. But in any case, paradoxical as it may seem to some, democratization and the rule of the law at the international level in a world of nation-states will require a redistribution of power from the rich countries to the world's majority outside them. This is as true for economic policy as it is for politics, despite the fact that the United States still dominates the IMF and the World Bank, much as it did when these institutions were created 70 years ago. The formation of the G-20 in 1999 was a significant but mostly symbolic change.

Much more lies ahead. If the analysis in this book is correct, we would expect the IMF to continue to lose influence in developing countries, and that this loss of influence—as in the past 15 years—will dominate the process of harm reduction involving the Fund, rather than any changes in IMF policies. There is now a literature that sees the IMF as evolving into a different institution since the Great Recession,[8] based on changes in some of its research and public pronouncements. The changes in research, some of which are noted in Chapter 4, are welcome, as is Managing Director Christine Lagarde's call for Germany to pursue an expansionary fiscal policy to help revive the euro-zone economy.[9] But the German government doesn't really care what Christine Lagarde recommends. In the European countries that have to care what the IMF says—Spain, Greece, Italy,

8. See, e.g., Kevin P. Gallagher. "Contesting the Governance of Capital Flows at the IMF," *Governance* (2014), doi: 10.1111/gove.12100.

9. IMF, "Interview by Les Echos with Christine Lagarde, Managing Director, International Monetary Fund," September 2014, http://www.imf.org/external/np/vc/2014/090814.htm.

Portugal, Ireland—the IMF is still pushing austerity policies in the midst of mass unemployment.[10] The thousands of pages of IMF agreements, reviews, and Article IV consultations described in Chapter 4 show that the IMF remains a long way from any real transformation. This is only to be expected, since it is not an independent entity but is dominated by the United States and its allies. The latter governments have not changed their views on how low- and middle-income countries should run their economies; and the more powerful European directors have not yet changed their agenda for the eurozone.

All this is not to say that ideas do not matter—they do, but they matter much more when they are put into practice. The US Federal Reserve's unprecedented quantitative easing, for example, has had a sizable influence not only on the US recovery from the Great Recession but also likely on economic policy going forward. We have now come a considerable distance from 20 years ago, when Fed Vice Chair Alan Blinder had the temerity to suggest that the Fed should care not only about keeping inflation low but also about employment.[11] The storm of criticism that followed forced him to walk back from his remarks, but now this responsibility of the Fed, already in the law when Blinder dared to suggest it, is widely

10. For Spain, see IMF, "2014 Article IV Consultation—Staff Report; Staff Supplement; Press Release, 2014; and Statement by the Executive Director for Spain," July 2014, http://www.imf.org/external/pubs/ft/scr/2014/cr14192. pdf. For Greece, see IMF, "Greece: Letter of Intent," July 2013, http://www.imf. org/external/np/loi/2013/grc/071713.pdf. For Italy, see IMF, "2014 Article IV Consultation—Staff Report; Press Release; and Statement by the Executive Director for Italy," September 2014, http://www.imf.org/external/pubs/ft/ scr/2014/cr14283.pdf. For Portugal, see IMF, "Portugal: Letter of Intent, Memorandum of Economic and Financial Policies, and Technical Memorandum of Understanding," March 2014, http://www.imf.org/external/np/loi/2014/ prt/032814.pdf.

11. Keith Bradsher, "Fed Official Disapproves of Rate Policy," New York Times, August 28, 1994, http://www.nytimes.com/1994/08/28/us/fed-official-disapproves-of-rate-policy.html.

accepted. There is progress in history, and if we are lucky, maybe some of it will spread to the eurozone.

At the broader international level, some of this progress will, ironically, be reflected in a lack of progress within institutions that were set up with rules stacked in favor of the rich countries and their corporations, the World Trade Organization (WTO) being the most prominent example. The WTO's troubles—negotiations have hardly gone anywhere over the past 20 years—are the result of the increasing weight of developing countries in the world economy. The lopsided 1995 agreement would almost certainly never have been approved by many governments if it were to be put forward today.

In the absence of democratization of the current institutions of global economic governance, developing countries may choose to go around them altogether. A promising step in this direction was taken in July 2014, when the BRICS countries (Brazil, Russia, India, China, and South Africa) agreed to form a Contingent Reserve Arrangement (CRA) and New Development Bank (NDB). The CRA, which is to be created with $100 billion, is to provide balance of payments support and could therefore potentially provide an alternative to the IMF. The NDB, starting with a fund of $50 billion, would provide an alternative to borrowing from the World Bank. There is still some way to go before any of this becomes a reality. The BRICS countries were not quite ready to leave the IMF out of the picture, as a clause in their treaty would require an IMF agreement for countries borrowing more than 30 percent of their quota from the CRA.[12] But it is the first move toward creating competition for the IMF and World Bank in 70 years. Given that the United States and its allies are not likely to cede their power over the Bretton Woods institutions, the possibility of these new

---

12. Lidia Kelly, "BRICS to Launch New Development Bank Next Week—Russia," *Reuters*, July 9, 2014, http://www.reuters.com/article/2014/07/09/russia-brics-banks-idUSL6N0PJ33820140709.

entities growing into serious alternatives outside Washington's control is very real.

Regardless of whether change takes place through new international institutions or bilateral arrangements, the international economic order is changing irreversibly. It remains to be seen how long it will take for most developing countries—especially outside Asia—to return to the rates of growth and development that they had prior to the 1980s. As noted in Chapter 5, the newly independent Latin American governments have for the most part taken only small steps toward introducing industrial or long-term development policies. But they—along with most of the developing world—will have more choices going forward. The sustained economic failure that most low- and middle-income countries suffered during the last two decades of the twentieth century is over and will not be repeated. The ideas that facilitated that regrettable failure remain influential, but these, too, will become increasingly less relevant in time.

Bibliography

AFX News. "No Argentina/EU Aid Talks until Deal Signed with IMF—Ruckauf." AFX News, May 22, 2002.

Al Jazeera English. "South American Leaders Back Morales." September 16, 2008. Accessed November 29, 2014. http://www.aljazeera.com/news/americas/2008/09/200891641749670258.html.

Alarcón, Cristian. "Caballo y perro, parte del menú habitual en una zona de Paraná." *Página/12*, May 16, 2002. http://www.pagina12.com.ar/diario/sociedad/3-5190-2002-05-16.html.

Alarcón, Cristian. "Los chicos del país del hambre." *Página/12*, May 20, 2002. http://www.pagina12.com.ar/diario/sociedad/3-5341-2002-05-20.html.

Alesina, Alberto, Edward Glaeser, and Bruce Sacerdote. "Work and Leisure in the U.S. and Europe: Why So Different?" *National Bureau of Economic Research Macroeconomics Annual* 2005, Vol. 20. http://www.nber.org/chapters/c0073.

Alesina, Alberto, and Lawrence Summers. "Central Bank Independence and Macroeconomic Performance: Some Comparative Evidence." *Journal of Money, Credit and Banking* 25, no. 2 (May 1993): 151–162. http://www.econ.ucdenver.edu/smith/econ4110/Alesina%20Summers%20-%20Central%20Bank%20Independence%20and%20Macro%20Performance.pdf.

Amnesty International. "Bolivia: Victims of the Pando Massacre Still Await Justice." Press Release. September 9, 2009. Accessed November 28, 2014. http://www.amnesty.org/en/for-media/press-releases/bolivia-victims-pando-massacre-still-await-justice-20090909.

Amnesty International. "Honduras: Abuses Escalate in Crackdown." September 25, 2009. http://www.amnesty.org/en/library/info/ AMR37/006/2009/en.

Amsden, Alice H. *Escape from Empire: The Developing World's Journey Through Heaven and Hell.* Cambridge, MA: MIT Press, 2007.

Armstrong, Neal. "Italian Bond Yields Surge Past 7 Percent." Reuters, November 9, 2011. http://www.reuters.com/article/2011/11/09/ markets-bonds-euro-close-idUSL6E7M95J020111109.

Associated Press. "Bolivia Elects Evo Morales as President for Third Term." October 13, 2014. http://www.theguardian. com/world/2014/oct/13/bolivia-evo-morales—president- third-term.

Associated Press. "Leftists Fear Domino Effect of Honduras Coup." August 19, 2009. Accessed December 1, 2014. http://www.nbcnews. com/id/32478307/ns/world_news-americas/#.VHvLock3KpE.

Badawi, Zeinab, and William Kremer. "Greece's Life-Saving Austerity Medics." July 10, 2013. Accessed December 9, 2013. http://www. bbc.co.uk/news/magazine-23247914.

Baker, Dean. *The Conservative Nanny State: How the Wealthy Use the Government to Stay Rich and Get Richer.* Washington, DC: Center for Economic and Policy Research, 2006.

Baker, Dean. *The End of Loser Liberalism: Making Markets Progressive.* Washington DC: Center for Economic and Policy Research, 2011.

Baker, Dean. *False Profits: Recovering from the Bubble Economy.* Sausalito, CA: PoliPointPress, 2010.

Baker, Dean. "Issues in Trade and Protectionism." Washington, DC: Center for Economic and Policy Research, November 2009.

Baker, Dean. *Plunder and Blunder: The Rise and Fall of the Bubble Economy.* Sausalito, CA: PoliPointPress, 2009.

Baker, Dean. "Recession Looms for the U.S. Economy in 2007." Center for Economic and Policy Research. November 2006. http://www. cepr.net/index.php/publications/reports/recession-looms- for-the-us-economy-in-2007.

Baker, Dean. "The Run-Up in Home Prices: Is It Real or Is It Another Bubble?" Center for Economic and Policy Research. August 2002. Accessed February 12, 2015. http://www.cepr.net/index.php/reports/the- run-up-in-home-prices-is-it-real-or-is-it-another-bubble/.

Baker, Dean. *The United States since 1980.* Cambridge: Cambridge University Press, 2007.

Baker, Dean, and Jared Bernstein. *Getting Back to Full Employment.* Washington, DC: Center for Economic and Policy Research, 2013.

Baker, Dean, and David Rosnick. "Too Sunny in Latin America? The IMF's Overly Optimistic Growth Projections and Their Consequences." Center for Economic and Policy Research, September 16, 2003.

Banco Central de Ecuador. "Operaciones del Sector Público no Financiero-SPNF- Porcentaje del PIB (mensual)." 2014. http://www.bce.fin.ec/index.php/component/k2/item/295-operaciones-del-sector-p%C3%BAblico-no-financiero.

Barchfield, Jenny. "Brazil Expands Labor Rights for Domestic Workers." Associated Press, August 21, 2014. http://bigstory.ap.org/article/brazil-expands-labor-rights-domestic-workers.

Barry, Ellen, and Michael Schwirtz. "After Election, Putin Faces Challenges to Legitimacy." *New York Times*, March 5, 2012.

BBC. "Argentina Scraps Key Economic Law." May 30, 2002. http://news.bbc.co.uk/2/hi/business/2016410.stm.

BBC. "Asia-Pacific Inquiry Blames Army for Jakarta Riots." November 3, 1998. http://news.bbc.co.uk/2/hi/asia-pacific/207067.stm.

Beattie, Alan, and Adam Thomson. "Argentina Loan Rollover Delayed by Wrangling IMF Deal." *Financial Times*, September 8, 2003.

Bell, Michael W. et al. 1993. "China at the Threshold of a Market Economy." International Monetary Fund Occasional Paper 103, September 2014.

Berg, Janine. "Brazil: The Minimum Wage as a Response to the Crisis." ILO, 2009. http://www.ilo.org/wcmsp5/groups/public/---americas/---ro-lima/documents/article/wcms_limd3_11_en.pdf.

Bértola, L., and José Antonio Ocampo. "Latin America's Debt Crisis and Lost Decade." Institute for the Study of the Americas. February 20, 2012. http://www.ilas.sas.ac.uk/sites/default/files/files/filestore documents/events/Papers/Bertola_and_Ocampo_paper.pdf

Bevins, Vincent. "Brazil's Dilma Rousseff Is Popular, But Not among News Media." *Los Angeles Times*, March 3, 2013. http://articles.latimes.com/2013/mar/03/world/la-fg-brazil-hostile-media-20130304.

Bhalla, Surjit S. "Indian Economic Growth, 1950–2008: Facts and Beliefs, Puzzles and Policies." In *India's Economy: Performances and Challenges*, edited by Shankar Acharya and

Rakesh Mohan, pp. 39–81. New York: Oxford University Press, 2010.

Bigwood, Jeremy. "New Discoveries Reveal US Intervention in Bolivia." *Bolivia Matters*, October 11, 2008. Accessed December 4, 2014. https://boliviamatters.wordpress.com/2008/10/11/new-discoveries-reveal-us-intervention-in-bolivia/.

Birdsall, Nancy, Dani Rodrik, and Arvind Subramanian. "How to Help Poor Countries." *Foreign Affairs* 84, no. 4 (Jul–Aug 2005): 136–152.

Blanchard, Olivier, Giovanni Dell'Ariccia, and Paolo Mauro. "Rethinking Macroeconomic Policy." International Monetary Fund Staff Position Note 10/03, February 12, 2010.

Blanchard, Olivier, and Daniel Leigh. "Growth Forecast Errors and Fiscal Multipliers." International Monetary Fund Working Paper 13/1, January 2013.

Bloomberg. "Blanchard Says Global Economy Faces Enormous Risks." September 23, 2011. http://www.washingtonpost.com/business/blanchard-says-global-economy-faces-enormous-risks/2011/09/23/gIQAUCcyqK_video.html.

Bloomberg. "ItalyGenericGovernment10YYield," n.d. Accessed February 10, 2015. http://www.bloomberg.com/quote/GBTPGR10:IND/chart.

Board of Governors of the Federal Reserve System. "FOMC Statement," March 18, 2009. Accessed May 12, 2014. http://www.federalreserve.gov/newsevents/press/monetary/20090318a.htm

Boskin, Michael. "Why Does Chile Prosper While Neighbouring Argentina Flounders?" *The Guardian*, November 22, 2013. Accessed December 9, 2013. http://www.theguardian.com/business/economics-blog/2013/nov/22/chile-prosper-argentina-flounders.

Bradsher, Keith. "Fed Official Disapproves of Rate Policy," *The New York Times*, August 28, 1994. http://www.nytimes.com/1994/08/28/us/fed-official-disapproves-of-rate-policy.html.

Bradsher, Keith. "To Conquer Wind Power, China Writes the Rules." *New York Times*, December 14, 2010. http://www.nytimes.com/2010/12/15/business/global/15chinawind.html?_r=0.

Bräutigam, Deborah. "Aid 'With Chinese Characteristics': Chinese Foreign Aid and Development Finance Meet the OECD-DAC Aid Regime." *Journal of International Development* 23 (2011): 752–764. doi: 10.1002/jid.1798.

Brief for the United States of America as Amicus Curiae in Support of Argentina's Petition. http://www.americanbar. org/content/dam/aba/publications/supreme_court_preview/ briefs-v3/12-842_pet_amcu_usa.authcheckdam.pdf.

Buergin, Ranier, and Patrick Donahue. "Germany's Schaeuble Says Greece Could Be Model for Ukraine Aid." Bloomberg, March 24, 2014. Accessed February 5, 2015. http://www.bloomberg.com/news/ articles/2014-03-26/germany-s-schaeuble-says-greece-could-be-model-for-ukraine-aid.

Bureau of Economic Analysis. "Comparison of Personal Saving in the NIPAs with Personal Saving in the FFAs." 2015. Accessed February 12, 2015. http://www.bea.gov/national/nipaweb/nipa-frb.asp.

Bureau of Economic Analysis. "National Income and Product Accounts Tables: Table 1.1.5. Gross Domestic Product." Accessed August 4, 2014. http://www.bea.gov/iTable/index_nipa.cfm.

Bureau of Economic Analysis. "National Income and Product Accounts Tables." Accessed February 10, 2015. http://www.bea.gov/iTable/ iTable.cfm?ReqID=9&step=1#reqid=9&step=1&isuri=1.

Bureau of Labor Statistics. "Employment, Hours, and Earnings from the Current Employment Statistics survey (National)." Accessed August 5, 2014. http://www.bls.gov/ces/.

Camdessus, Michel. "The Asian Crisis and the International Response." Speech at the Institute of Advanced Business Studies, University of Navarra, November 28, 1997. Accessed February 9, 2015. https://www.imf.org/external/np/speeches/ 1997/mds9717.htm.

Candelaresi, Cledis. "Para dejar tranquilo a Singh." *Página/12*, April 19, 2002. http://www.pagina12.com.ar/diario/economia/ 2-4185-2002-04-19.html.

Carter Center. "30 Years of The Carter Center" (video), 86:32. September 11, 2012. http://www.cartercenter.org/news/multimedia/ Conversations/30-years-of-the-carter-center.html.

Casey, Michael. "Does Argentine Recovery Have Legs?" *The Wall Street Journal*, April 9, 2004. A7.

Center for Economic and Policy Research. "Press Release: U.S. Should Disclose its Funding of Opposition Groups in Bolivia and Other Latin American Countries." September 12, 2008. http://www.cepr.net/index.php/press-releases/press-releases/ us-should-disclose-its-funding-of-opposition-groups-in-bolivia-and-other-latin-american-countries/.

Centre for Economic and Policy Research. Euro Area Business Cycle Dating Committee. "June 2014—Euro Area Mired in Recession Pause." June 2014. Accessed February 5, 2015. http://www.cepr.org/content/euro-area-business-cycle-dating-committee.

Centers for Medicare & Medicaid Services. "National Health Expenditure Data." May 2014. http://www.cms.gov/Research-Statistics-Data-and-Systems/Statistics-Trends-and-Reports/NationalHealth ExpendData/NationalHealthAccountsHistorical.html.

Central Bank of Argentina. "Mercado de Cambio—Cotizaciones Cierre Vendedor: Peso," n.d. Accessed September 27, 2013. http://www.bcra.gov.ar/index.htm.

Central Bank of Ecuador. "Información Estadística Mensual." Online database. Accessed December 2014. http://www.bce.fin.ec/index.php/publicaciones-de-banca-central3.

Central Bank of Venezuela, CPI. http://www.bcv.org.ve/excel/4_5_2.xls?id=415.

Central Bank of Venezuela. "Indice nacional de precios al consumidor." Banco Central de Venezuela, n.d. Accessed February 12, 2015. http://bcv.org.ve/c2/indicadores.asp.

Centro de Estudios para el Desarrollo Laboral y Agrario. 2013. "El Sector Informal Urbano en Bolivia 2010–2011: Estadísticas del CEDLA." June 25, 2013. http://www.cedla.org/content/3467.

Chang, Ha-Joon. *Bad Samaritans: The Myth of Free Trade and the Secret History of Capitalism*. New York: Bloomsbury Press, 2007.

Chang, Ha-Joon. *Kicking Away the Ladder: Development Strategy in Historical Perspective*. New York: Anthem Press, 2002.

Chávez, Fran. "U.S. Ambassador Expelled for Allegedly Supporting Violent Opposition." Inter Press Service, September 11, 2008. Accessed December 1, 2014. http://www.ipsnews.net/2008/09/bolivia-us-ambassador-expelled-for-allegedly-su pporting-violent-opposition/.

Checa-Godoy A. "The Banking Sector and Media Ownership: The Case of Ecuador." *Revista Latina de Comunicación Social* 67 (2012): 125–147. La Laguna (Tenerife, Canary Islands): La Laguna University. Accessed December 4, 2014. http://www.revistalatinacs.org/067/art/950_Sevilla/06_ChecaEN.html.

Cohen, Luc, Benedict Mander, and Elaine Moore. "Investors Sanguine as Argentina Defaults." *The Financial Times*, July 31, 2014.

Accessed February 12, 2015. http://www.ft.com/cms/s/0/5d 7c8016-1832-11e4-a6e4-00144feabdc0.html?siteedition=uk.

Comisión Para la Auditoría Integral Del Crédito Público. "Informe Final de la Auditoría Integral de la Deuda Ecuatoriana," 2007. http://www.auditoriadeuda.org.ec/images/stories/documentos/ informe_final_CAIC.pdf.

Committee on Foreign Affairs. "Securing U.S. Interests Abroad: The FY 2014 Foreign Affairs Budget." 113th Congress, 1st session, April 17, 2013. http://www.gpo.gov/fdsys/pkg/CHRG-113hhrg80463/ html/CHRG-113hhrg80463.htm.

Cooper, Marc. "Many Oppose Trade Deal." *The Nation*, February 11, 2002. Accessed November 28, 2014. http://www.thenation.com/ article/many-oppose-trade-deal.

Cooper, William H. *The Russian Financial Crisis of 1998: An Analysis of Trends, Causes, and Implications*. Congressional Research Service, The Library of Congress, February 18, 1999. http://congressionalresearch. com/98-578/document.php?study=The+Russian+Financial+Crisis+of +1998+An+Analysis+of+Trends+Causes+and+Implications.

Cordero, José Antonio, and Juan Antonio Montecino. "Capital Controls and Monetary Policy in Developing Countries." Center for Economic and Policy Research, April 2010. http://www.cepr. net/documents/publications/capital-controls-2010-04.pdf.

Creswell, Julie, and Ben White. "The Guys from 'Government Sachs.'" *New York Times*, October 17, 2008. http://www.nytimes. com/2008/10/19/business/19gold.html?pagewanted=all.

Crooks, Nathan, and Corina Pons. "Chavez Mulls Revamping Currency Controls as Bolivar Plunges." Bloomberg, November 14, 2012. http://www.bloomberg.com/news/2012-11-14/chavez-mu lls-revamping-currency-controls-as-bolivar-plunges.html.

Cuevas, Freddy. "Top Aide Says U.S. Complicit in Honduras Coup." *Toronto Star* (AP), August 16, 2009. http://www.thestar.com/ news/world/2009/08/16/top_aide_says_us_complicit_in_hon-duras_coup.html.

Da Costa, Ana Nicolaci. "Investors Snub ECB Liquidity Promises, Bund Rallies." Reuters, August 4, 2011. http://www.reuters.com/ article/2011/08/04/markets-bonds-euro-idUSL6E7J42I620110804.

Damill, Mario, Roberto Frenkel, and Roxana Maurizio. "Macro-economic Policy for Full and Productive Employment and Decent

Work for All." International Labour Organization, Employment Working Paper No. 109, 2011, p. 48. Accessed December 2, 2013. http://www.ilo.org/employment/Whatwedo/Publications/ working-papers/WCMS_173147/lang--en/index.htm.

Dandan, Alejandra. "Quilmes, a pocos kilómetros de la Rosada." *Página/12*, June 6, 2002. http://www.pagina12.com.ar/diario/elpais/ 1-5965-2002-06-06.html.

Dávila, Sérgio. "EUA tentaram influenciar reforma política do Brasil." *Folha de São Paulo*, July 22, 2005. http://www1.folha.uol.com.br/ fsp/brasil/fc2207200820.htm.

Davis, Bob, and David Wessel. "World Bank, IMF at Odds over Asian Austerity." *Wall Street Journal*, January 8, 1998. Accessed December 14, 2014. http://www.nytimes.com/2010/12/15/business/global/ 15chinawind.html.

Departamento del Tesoro. "Departamento del Tesoro, Outstanding of Public Securities (Breakdown by Maturity)." Rome: Ministero dell'Economia e delle Finanze, December 31, 2011. Accessed February 10, 2015. http://www.dt.tesoro.it/export/sites/sitodt/modules/ documenti_en/debito_pubblico/scadenze_titoli_suddivise_ per_anno/Outstanding_public_securities_31-12-2011_GPO. pdf. http://www.dt.tesoro.it/export/sites/sitodt/modules/ documenti_en/debito_pubblico/scadenze_titoli_suddivise_per_ anno/Outstanding_public_securities_31-10-2011_GPO.pdf.

Department of Economic and Social Affairs, Population Division. "World Population Prospects: The 2012 Revision, Volume I: Comprehensive Tables." United Nations Department of Economic and Social Affairs, 2013, p. 2. Accessed February 13, 2015. http://esa.un.org/wpp/ documentation/pdf/WPP2012_Volume-I_Comprehensive-Tables.pdf.

Dhillon, A., J. García Fronti, S. Ghosal, and M. Miller. "Bargaining and Sustainability: The Argentine Debt Swap of 2005." CSGR Working Paper No. 189/06, 2005, p. 29.

Dobson, Paul. "Italian Bonds Rise on ECB Debt Purchases; French Spread Widens." Bloomberg, November 10, 2011. Accessed February 10, 2015. http://www.bloomberg.com/news/articles/ 2011-11-10/italian-5-year-government-notes-drop-yield-r ises-to-euro-era-record-7-80-.

Dolartoday. "Black Market Exchange Rate Time Series." Accessed February 12, 2015. https://d1phdof6oyl82t.cloudfront.net/ indicadores/.

Draghi, Mario. "Verbatim of the Remarks Made by Mario Draghi." Speech presented at the Global Investment Conference in London, July 26, 2014. Accessed February 5, 2015. http://www.ecb.europa.eu/press/key/date/2012/html/sp120726.en.html

Drajem, Mark. "Argentina Gets $100 Million World Bank Emergency Aid." Bloomberg, March 8, 2002.

Dunne, Nancy. "Knives Out in Washington for a Free Spirit. Joseph Stiglitz: He May Have Criticized the Institutional Consensus on Too Many Points." *Financial Times*, November 25, 1999, London ed. 2.

Easterly, William. *The Elusive Quest for Growth*. Cambridge, MA: MIT Press, 2001.

ECLAC (Economic Commission for Latin America and the Caribbean). CEPALSTAT Database. Santiago: United Nations Economic Commission for Latin American and the Caribbean, n.d. Accessed February 7, 2015. http://estadisticas.cepal.org/cepalstat/WEB_CEPALSTAT/estadisticasIndicadores.asp?idioma=i.

ECLAC. "Población en situación de indigencia y pobreza," 2014. Online database. Accessed February 6, 2014. http://interwp.cepal.org/sisgen/ConsultaIntegrada.asp?idIndicador=182&idioma=e.

ECLAC. "Social Panorama of Latin America 2013." March 2014. United Nations. http://repositorio.cepal.org/bitstream/handle/11362/36736/S2013869_en.pdf?sequence=1.

Economic Policy Institute. "The State of Working America, 12th Edition." Washington, DC: Economic Policy Institute, 2012. Accessed July 14, 2014. http://stateofworkingamerica.org/data/.

EFE. "Elección de Obama sería como las de Morales, Chávez y Lugo." *Diario ABC Color*, October 31, 2008. http://www.abc.com.py/edicion-impresa/internacionales/eleccion-de-obama-seria-como-las-de-morales-chavez-y-lugo-1116531.html.

EIA. "Henry Hub Natural Gas Spot Price 1997–2013." Accessed February 12, 2015. http://www.eia.gov/dnav/ng/hist/rngwhhdA.htm.

Eichengreen, Barry, and Poonam Gupta. "The Service Sector as India's Road to Economic Growth." National Bureau of Economic Research Working Paper. February 2011. http://www.nber.org/papers/w16757.pdf.

EIU. "Argentina: IMF Talks Suspended." Economist Intelligence Unit—Country Monitor. August 16, 2004.

El País. "El izquierdista Correa, favorito para ser el nuevo presidente de Ecuador según una encuesta," September 28, 2006. http://internacional.elpais.com/internacional/2006/09/28/actualidad/1159394401_850215.html.

Ellsworth, Brian. "Despite Obama Charm, Americas Summit Boosts U.S. Isolation." Reuters, April 16, 2012. http://www.reuters.com/article/2012/04/17/us-americas-summit-obama-idUSBRE83F0UD20120417.

EL.STAT. "02. Quarterly GDP—Seasonally Adjusted, Current Prices and Chain-Linked Volumes Reference Year 2010 (1st Quarter 1995–3rd Quarter 2014) (Provisional Data)." Hellenic Statistical Authority. Accessed February 10, 2015. http://www.statistics.gr/portal/page/portal/ESYE/PAGE-themes?p_param=A0704&r_param=SEL84&y_param=TS&mytabs=0.

EL.STAT. "Population 15+ (Employment Status, Age, Sex [Greece, Total]) (1st Quarter 2001–3rd Quarter 2014)." Hellenic Statistical Authority. Retrieved February 10, 2015. http://www.statistics.gr/portal/page/portal/ESYE/PAGE-themes?p_param=A0101&r_param=SJO01&y_param=TS&mytabs=0.

Epstein, Gerald. "Central Banks as Agents of Economic Development." United Nations University World Institute for Development Economics Research (UNU-WIDER). May 2006. Accessed February 11, 2013. http://www.wider.unu.edu/stc/repec/pdfs/rp2006/rp2006-54.pdf.

European Central Bank. "ECB Decides on Measures to Address Severe Tensions in Financial Markets." May 10, 2010. http://www.ecb.europa.eu/press/pr/date/2010/html/pr100510.en.html.

European Central Bank. "Introductory Statement to the Press Conference (with Q&A)." September 8, 2011. http://www.ecb.europa.eu/press/pressconf/2011/html/is110908.en.html.

European Central Bank. "Verbatim of the Remarks Made by Mario Draghi." July 26, 2012. https://www.ecb.europa.eu/press/key/date/2012/html/sp120726.en.html

European Commission. Eurostat Database. Accessed February 5, 2015. http://ec.europa.eu/eurostat/data/database.

Eurostat. "Hourly Labour Costs." Accessed May 2014. http://epp.eurostat.ec.europa.eu/portal/page/portal/labour_market/labour_costs/database.

Eurostat. "Unemployment Rate by Sex and Age Groups—Annual Average,%."AccessedApril25,2014.http://epp.eurostat.ec.europa. eu/portal/page/portal/employment_unemployment_lfs/data/ database.

Eurostat. "Unemployment Rate by Sex and Age Groups—Monthly Average, %." 2014. Accessed May 2014. http://epp.eurostat. ec.europa.eu/portal/page/portal/employment_unemployment_ lfs/data/database. Ewing, Jack. "Central Bank Chief Hints at Stepping Up Euro Support." *New York Times*, December 1, 2011. http://www.nytimes.com/2011/12/02/business/global/ draghi-hints-again-at-rate-cut-in-europe.html?pagewanted=all.

Faiola, Anthony. "Argentina's Peso Is Freed to Float, and Quickly Sinks; Protests Against Economic Changes Become Violent in Buenos Aires." *Washington Post*, January 12, 2002. http://www. highbeam.com/doc/1P2-335669.html.

Faiola, Anthony. "Despair in Once Proud Argentina." *Washington Post*, August 6, 2002, p. A01.

Faiola, Anthony. "Growing Crisis Leaves Argentines Feeling Helpless." *Washington Post*, May 3, 2002, p. A01.

Feenstra, Robert C., Hong Ma, J. Peter Neary, and D. S. Prasada Rao. "Who Shrunk China? Puzzles in the Measurement of Real GDP." *Economic Journal, Royal Economic Society* 123, no. 12 (December 2013): 1100–1129. http://www.nber.org/papers/w17729.

Ferguson, Charles H. *Predator Nation: Corporate Criminals, Political Corruption, and the Hijacking of America*. New York: Random House, 2012.

Frankel, Jeffrey, Carlos Végh, and Guillermo Vuletin. "On Graduation from Procyclicality." NBER Working Paper 17619, 2011, p. 4.

Frenkel, Roberto, and Martín Repetti. "Argentina's Monetary and Exchange Rate Policies after the Convertibility Regime Collapse." Center for Economic and Policy Research (CEPR) and Political Economy Research Institute (PERI), 2007. Accessed April 25, 2014. http://www.cepr.net/documents/publications/argentina_ 2007_04.pdf.

Friedman-Rudovsky, Jean, and Brian Ross. "Peace Corps, Fulbright Scholar Asked to 'Spy' on Cubans, Venezuelans." ABC News, February 8, 2014. Accessed December 1, 2014. http://abcnews. go.com/Blotter/Story?id=4262036&page=1.

Gaffney, Frank. "Bush Is Asked to Prevent Hemispheric 'Axis of Evil' and Back Ouster of Venezuela's Chavez." Center for Security Policy, October 25, 2002. http://www.centerforsecuritypolicy. org/2002/10/25/bush-is-asked-to-prevent-hemispheric-axis-of-evil-and-back-ouster-of-venezuelas-chavez-2/.

Gallagher, Kevin P. "Contesting the Governance of Capital Flows at the IMF." *Governance*, 2014. Accessed January 12, 2015, doi: 10.1111/gove.12100.

Gargan, Edward A. "Asian Nations Affirm I.M.F. as Primary Provider of Aid." *New York Times*, November 19, 1997. http://www.nytimes.com/1997/11/20/business/asian-nations-affirm-imf-as-primary-provider-of-aid.html.

Goldman Sachs. "The 'Lulameter.'" *Emerging Markets Strategy: Bonds, Currencies, and Interest Rates*, June 6, 2002. GS Global Economics Website. http://moya.bus.miami.edu/~sandrade/Lulameter_GS.pdf.

Goldstein, Morris. "IMF Structural Conditionality: How Much Is Too Much?" Peterson Institute for International Economics, Revision of Paper Presented at NBER Conference on "Economic and Financial Crises in Emerging Market Economies." Woodstock, Vermont. October 2000. http://www.petersoninstitute.org/publications/wp/01-4.pdf.

Greek Ministry of Finance. "Greece: Medium-Term Fiscal Strategy 2012–15." June 2011. http://www.minfin.gr/content-api/f/binaryChannel/minfin/datastore/24/a9/69/24a9692f9ed208ecd6625e492f789bb868f038a0/application/pdf/Greece+MTFS+Eurogroup+20110614.pdf.

Greenspan, Alan. "Remarks by Chairman Alan Greenspan at the Haas Annual Business Faculty Research Dialogue, University of California, Berkeley, California," Speeches of Federal Reserve Board Officers, September 4, 1998. http://www.federalreserve.gov/boarddocs/speeches/1998/19980904.htm.

Guinane, Timothy W. "The Historical Fertility Transition: A Guide for Economists." *Journal of Economic Literature* 49, no. 3 (2011): 589–614.

Hallward, Peter. *Damming the Flood: Haiti and the Politics of Containment.* New York: Verso Books, 2010.

Hellenic Statistical Authority. "Gross Domestic Product—Timeseries." 2014. Accessed May 15, 2014. http://www.statistics.gr/portal/page/portal/ESYE/PAGE-themes?p_param=A0704&r_param=SEL84&y_param=TS&mytabs=0.

Helliwell, John F., Richard Layard, and Jeffrey D. Sachs. "World Happiness Report 2013." Sustainable Development Solutions Network, September 2013. http://unsdsn.org/wp-content/uploads/2014/02/WorldHappinessReport2013_online.pdf.

Heredia, Lourdes. "Agonizing Week for the Peso." BBC, March 16, 2002.

Howard, Greg, Robert Martin, and Beth Anne Wilson. *Are Recoveries from Banking and Financial Crises Really So Different?* Federal Reserve Board, 2011.

Hufbauer, Gary, and Jeffrey J. Schott. "Payoff from the World Trade Agenda." Peterson Institute for International Economic. June 2013. http://www.piie.com/publications/papers/hufbauerschott20130422.pdf.

Human Rights Watch. "Honduras: Investigate Abuses, Repeal Repressive Measures." October 30, 2009. http://www.hrw.org/en/news/2009/10/30/honduras-investigate-abuses-repeal-repressive-measures.

IEO. *The IMF and Recent Capital Account Crises: Indonesia, Korea, Brazil.* Washington, DC: Independent Evaluation Office, International Monetary Fund, 2003. Accessed February 5, 2015. http://www.imf.org/external/np/ieo/2003/cac/pdf/all.pdf

IMF (International Monetary Fund). "2011 Triennial Surveillance Review," October 2011. https://www.imf.org/external/np/spr/triennial/.

IMF. "2014 Article IV Consultation—Staff Report; Press Release; and Statement by the Executive Director for Italy," September 2014. http://www.imf.org/external/pubs/ft/scr/2014/cr14283.pdf.

IMF. "2014 Article IV Consultation—Staff Report; Staff Supplement; Press Release; and Statement by the Executive Director for Spain," July 2014. http://www.imf.org/external/pubs/ft/scr/2014/cr14192.pdf.

IMF. "Argentina, Memorandum of Economic Policies of the Government of Argentina for a Transitional Program in 2003," January 16, 2003. http://www.imf.org/external/np/loi/2003/arg/01/index.htm.

IMF. "Bolivia: Fourth Review under the Stand-By Arrangement and Request for Waiver of Nonobservance of Performance Criteria," November 4, 2004. Accessed December 9, 2013. http://www.imf.org/external/pubs/cat/longres.aspx?sk=17827.0.

IMF. "Bolivia: Staff Report for the 2013 Article IV Consultation—Staff Report," February 2014, p. 5. http://www.imf.org/external/pubs/ft/scr/2014/cr1436.pdf.

IMF. "Brazil: Letter of Intent, Memorandum of Economic Policies, and Technical Memorandum of Understanding," August 29, 2002. http://www.imf.org/external/np/loi/2002/bra/04/index.htm.

IMF. "Brazil: Technical Note on Consumer Credit Growth and Household Financial Stress," June 6, 2013. https://www.imf.org/external/pubs/cat/longres.aspx?sk=40591.0.

IMF. "Direction of Trade Statistics." Online database. Accessed November 1, 2011. http://elibrary-data.imf.org/.

IMF. "France: 2009 Article IV Consultation—Staff Report; Public Information Notice on the Executive Board Discussion; and Statement by the Executive Director for France," 2009, p. 20.

IMF. "Greece: 2009 Article IV Consultation," August 6, 2009, p. 11. Accessed December 9, 2013. http://www.imf.org/external/pubs/cat/longres.aspx?sk=23169.0.

IMF. "Greece: Fifth Review under the Stand-By Arrangement," December 2011, p. 48. Accessed December 9, 2013. http://www.imf.org/external/pubs/cat/longres.aspx?sk=25429.0.

IMF. "Greece: Fourth Review under the Stand-By Arrangement," July 13, 2011, p. 9. Accessed December 9, 2013. http://www.imf.org/external/pubs/cat/longres.aspx?sk=25038.0.

IMF. "Greece Needs Deeper Reforms to Overcome Crisis," *IMF Survey Magazine*, December 16, 2011. Accessed December 9, 2013. http://www.imf.org/external/pubs/ft/survey/so/2011/car121611a.htm.

IMF. "Greece: Request for Stand-By Arrangement,: May 2010. http://www.imf.org/external/pubs/ft/scr/2010/cr10111.pdf.

IMF. "Greece: Staff Report on Request for Stand-By Arrangement," 2010, p. 140. Accessed February 6, 2015. http://www.imf.org/external/pubs/ft/scr/2010/cr10110.pdf.

IMF. "IMF Approves €30 Bln Loan for Greece on Fast Track," IMF Survey online, May 9, 2010. https://www.imf.org/external/pubs/ft/survey/so/2010/NEW050910A.htm.

IMF. "IMF Approves Augmentation of Argentina's Stand-By Credit to US$14 Billion and Completes Second Review," Press Release 01/3, January 12, 2001. http://www.imf.org/external/np/sec/pr/2001/pr0103.htm.

IMF. "IMF Lending Arrangements as of April 30, 2011." Accessed February 19, 2015. http://www.imf.org/external/np/fin/tad/extarr11.aspx?memberKey1=ZZZZ&date1key=2011-04-30.

IMF. "IMF Performance in the Run-up to the Financial and Economic Crisis: IMF Surveillance in 2004–07." Evaluation Report, Independent Evaluation Office, 2011, p. vii, 1. http://www. ieo-imf.org/ieo/pages/CompletedEvaluation107.aspx.

IMF. "IMF Policy on Lending into Arrears to Private Creditors," June 14, 1999. www.imf.org/external/pubs/ft/privcred/.

IMF. "IMF's Financial Resources and Liquidity Position, 2009–May 2011." Accessed February 19, 2015. http://www.imf.org/external/ np/tre/liquid/2011/0511.htm.

IMF. "IMF Standing Borrowing Arrangements," 2014. Accessed February 19, 2015. http://www.imf.org/external/np/exr/facts/ gabnab.htm.

IMF. "Interview by Les Echos with Christine Lagarde, Managing Director, International Monetary Fund." September 2014. http:// www.imf.org/external/np/vc/2014/090814.htm.

IMF. "Introductory Remarks on the Role of the IMF Mission in Argentina." Press briefing, Buenos Aires, April 10, 2002. Accessed December 9, 2013. http://www.imf.org/external/np/tr/2002/tr020410.htm.

IMF. "Korea—Memorandum on the Economic Program," December 3, 1997. http://www.imf.org/external/np/loi/120397.htm#memo.

IMF. "People's Republic of China: 2014 Article IV Consultation-Staff Report; Press Release; and Statement by the Executive Director for the People's Republic of China," July 30, 2014, Table 1. http:// www.imf.org/external/pubs/cat/longres.aspx?sk=41799.0

IMF. "Portugal: Letter of Intent, Memorandum of Economic and Financial Policies, and Technical Memorandum of Understanding." March 2014. http://www.imf.org/external/np/ loi/2014/prt/032814.pdf.

IMF. "Spain: 2010 Article IV Consultation—Staff Statement; Staff Supplement; Staff Report," 2010. https://www.imf.org/external/ pubs/ft/scr/2010/cr10254.pdf.

IMF. "Spain: Selected Issues." July 2014. http://www.imf.org/external/ pubs/ft/scr/2014/cr14193.pdf.

IMF. "Statement of the Interim Committee on the Liberalization of Capital Movements Under an Amendment of the Articles," Report of the Managing Director to the Interim Committee on Strengthening the Architecture of the International Monetary System, October 1, 1998. http://www.imf.org/external/np/ omd/100198.htm#attach.

IMF. "Total Fund Credit and Loans Outstanding," and "SDR/USD Exchange Rate." International Financial Statistics Database. Accessed February 19, 2015. https://stats.ukdataservice.ac.uk/index.aspx?r=662533&DataSetCode=IFS#.

IMF. "Transcript of a Press Briefing by William Murray, Deputy Spokesman, Communications Department, International Monetary Fund," July 25, 2013. https://www.imf.org/external/np/tr/2013/tr072513.htm

IMF. "Ukraine: Request for Stand-by Arrangement." May 1, 2014. https://www.imf.org/external/pubs/cat/longres.aspx?sk=41516.0.

IMF. "World Economic Outlook, April 2014," Accessed May 9, 2014. http://www.imf.org/external/pubs/ft/weo/2014/01/weodata/index.aspx,

IMF. "World Economic Outlook: Legacies, Clouds, Uncertainties," October 2014. http://www.imf.org/external/pubs/ft/weo/2014/02/pdf/text.pdf.

IMF. "World Economic Outlook, October 2010." Accessed November 27, 2013. http://www.imf.org/external/pubs/ft/weo/2010/02/weodata/index.aspx.

IMF. "World Economic Outlook, October 2012." http://www.imf.org/external/pubs/ft/weo/2012/02/weodata/index.aspx.

IMF. "World Economic Outlook, October 2014." Accessed February 6, 2015. http://www.imf.org/external/pubs/ft/weo/2014/02/weodata/index.aspx.

Independent Evaluation Office. "The IMF and Recent Capital Account Crises: Indonesia, Korea, Brazil." Evaluation Report, Independent Evaluation Office, 2003, pp. 17, 38, 107.

Instituto Nacional de Estadística y Censos (INEC). "Reporte Laboral," June 2014. http://www.ecuadorencifras.gob.ec/documentos/web-inec/EMPLEO/Empleo_junio_2014/15Anios/Informe%20Econom%eda%20laboral%20-%20jun14%28rev%29.pdf.

Instituto Nacional de Estadística y Censos (INEC). "Resultados principales," September 2014. http://www.ecuadorencifras.gob.ec/pobreza/.

Instituto Nacional de Estadística y Censos (INEC). "Crecimiento de la Formación Bruta Capital Fijo a Precios Constantes," 2014. Accessed November 28, 2014. http://www.ine.gob.bo/indice/general.aspx?codigo=40310.

Instituto Nacional de Estadísticas y Censos (INEC). "Encuesta Permanente de Hogares, Incidencia de la Pobreza y de la Indigencia, Resultados del segundo semestre 2011." Buenos Aires: Instituto Nacional de Estadísticas y Censos, April 25, 2012.

Instituto Nacional de Estadística y Censos (INEC). "Exportaciones," 2014. Accessed November 28, 2014. http://www.ine.gob.bo/indice/general.aspx?codigo=50101.

Instituto Nacional de Estadisticas y Censos (INEC). "Pobreza por línea de ingreso, 1er semestre 1997–2do semestre 2013." Accessed February 5, 2015. http://www.ine.gov.ve/index.php?option=com_content&view=category&id=104&Itemid=45#.

Instituto Nacional de Estudos e Pesquisas Educacionais Anísio Teixeira (INEP). "Censo da Educação Superior," 2014. http://portal.mec.gov.br/index.php?option=com_docman&task=doc_details&gid=14154& Itemid=.

Inter-American Commission on Human Rights. "IACHR Condemns Excessive Use of Force in Repression of Protests in Honduras." September 22, 2009. http://www.cidh.org/comunicados/english/2009/65-09eng.htm.

IPCC. "Fifth Assessment Report: Climate Change 2014: Synthesis Report." Intergovernmental Panel on Climate Change, 2014, Table 2.1, p. 63. Accessed February 16, 2015. http://www.ipcc.ch/pdf/assessment-report/ar5/syr/SYR_AR5_LONGERREPORT_Corr2.pdf.

IPEA. "Salário mínimo real." IPEA Data. Accessed November 28, 2014. http://www.ipeadata.gov.br/.

ITN News. "Chaos in Ecuador as Police Protest in Streets." ITN News. http://www.dailymotion.com/video/xf0rc6_chaos-in-ecuador-as-police-protest_news.

Jácome, Luis Ignacio. "The Late 1990s Financial Crisis in Ecuador: Institutional Weaknesses, Fiscal Rigidities, and Financial Dollarization at Work." January 1, 2004. International Monetary Fund. https://www.imf.org/external/pubs/cat/longres.aspx?sk=17127.0.

Johnson, Simon, and James Kwak. *13 Bankers: The Wall Street Takeover and the Next Financial Meltdown*. New York: Random House, 2010.

Johnston, Jake, and Sara Kozameh. "Venezuelan Economic and Social Performance under Hugo Chávez, in Graphs." Center for Economic and Policy Research, March 13, 2013. http://www.cepr.net/index.php/blogs/the-americas-blog/venezuelan-economic-and-social-performance-under-hugo-chavez-in-graphs.

Johnston, Jake, and Stephan Lefebvre. "Bolivia's Economy under Evo in 10 Graphs." *The Americas Blog*, a blog on the Center for Economic and Policy Research site. October 8, 2014. http://www.cepr.net/index.php/blogs/the-americas-blog/bolivias-economy-under-evo-in-10-graphs.

Jones, Bart. "U.S. Funds Aid Chávez Opposition." *National Catholic Reporter*, April 2, 2004. http://natcath.org/NCR_Online/archives2/2004b/040204/040204a.htm.

Jones, Claire. "ECB Raises Heat on Athens with Curb on Cash for Banks." *Financial Times*, February 4, 2015. http://www.ft.com/intl/cms/s/0/c3a1a602-acaf-11e4-beeb-00144feab7de.html?siteedition=intl#axzz3QjJojaYm.

Kaiman, Jonathan. "China Agrees to Invest $20bn in Venezuela to Help Offset Effects of Oil Price Slump." *The Guardian*, January 8, 2014. http://www.theguardian.com/world/2015/jan/08/china-venezuela-20bn-loans-financing-nicolas-maduro-beijing.

Kapur, Muneesh, and Rakesh Mohan. "India's Recent Macroeconomic Performance: An Assessment and Way Forward." No. 14-68. Washington, DC: International Monetary Fund. Accessed February 10, 2015. https://www.imf.org/external/pubs/ft/wp/2014/wp1468.pdf.

Kelly, Lidia. "BRICS to Launch New Development Bank Next Week—Russia." *Reuters*, July 9, 2014. http://www.reuters.com/article/2014/07/09/russia-brics-banks-idUSL6N0PJ33820140709.

Kinzer, Stephen. *Overthrow: America's Century of Regime Change from Hawaii to Iraq.* New York: Times Books, 2006.

Kitsantonis, Niki, and Rachel Donadio. "Anxieties Stir as Greece Plans Referendum on Latest Europe Aid Deal." *New York Times*, October 31, 2011. http://www.nytimes.com/2011/11/01/world/europe/greece-to-hold-referendum-on-new-debt-deal.html.

Klein, Naomi. *The Shock Doctrine: The Rise of Disaster Capitalism.* New York: Picador, 2008.

Kondilis, Elias, Stathis Giannakopoulos, Magda Gavana, Ioanna Ierodiakonou, Howard Waitzkin, and Alexis Benos. "Economic

Crisis, Restrictive Policies, and the Population's Health and Health Care: The Greek Case." *American Journal of Public Health* 103, no. 6 (2013): 973.

Kornbluh, Peter. *The Pinochet File: A Declassified Dossier on Atrocity and Accountability* (New York: The New Press, 2013), pp. 24–25.

Kotwal, Ashok, et al. "Economic Liberalization and Indian Economic Growth: What's the Evidence?" *Journal of Economic Literature* 49, no. 4 (2011): 1152–1199. http://mypage.siu.edu/lahiri/Econ429/kotwal%28JEL%29.pdf.

Kotz, David M., and Fred Weir. *Revolution from Above: The Demise of the Soviet System*. New York: Routledge, 1997.

Kristoff, Nicolas. "Asia Feels Strain Most at Society's Margins." *New York Times*. June 8, 1998, p. 1.

Krueger, Anne O. "Transcript of a Press Briefing on Argentina." International Monetary Fund, January 11, 2001. http://www.imf.org/external/np/tr/2002/tr020111.htm.

Lally, Kathy, and Will Englund. "Putin Heads Toward Russia's Presidency." *Washington Post*, March 3, 2012. http://www.washingtonpost.com/pb/world/europe/putin-heads-toward-russias-presidency/2012/03/03/gIQArCC4oR_story.html.

Lam, David. "How the World Survived the Population Bomb: Lessons from 50 Years of Extraordinary Demographic History." *Demography* 48, no. 4 (2011): 1231–1262.

Latvijas Statisika. "Gross Domestic Product—Quarterly Data," 2014. Accessed May 16, 2014. http://www.csb.gov.lv/en/dati/statistics-database-30501.html. Leahy, Joe. "Arminio Fraga Offers Brazil an Orthodox Path." *Financial Times*, September 17, 2014. http://www.ft.com/cms/s/5982c43c-3e5e-11e4-b7fc-00144feabdc0,Authorised=false.html?_i_location=http%3A%2F%2Fwww.ft.com%2Fcms%2Fs%2F0%2F5982c43c-3e5e-11e4-b7fc-00144feabdc0.html%3Fsiteedition%3Duk&siteedition=uk&_i_referer=#axzz3KUNdpFVQ.

Lewis, Michael. *The Big Short: Inside the Doomsday Machine*. New York: W. W. Norton, 2010.

Lewis, Paul. "Mexican Rescue Plan: Financial Markets; Wall Street and Its Latin Counterparts Respond with Relief and a Wave of Higher Prices." *New York Times*, February 1, 1995. A16.

Lissakers, Karin. *Review of the Operations of the International Monetary Fund, Before the Subcommittee on General Oversight and*

Investigations, Committee on Banking and Financial Services, April 21, 1998 (statement of Karin Lissakers, U.S. Executive Director, International Monetary Fund).

MacKenzie, Kate. "Greece: Preliminary Debt Sustainability Analysis." Alphaville (*Financial Times*), February 21, 2012, p. 1. Accessed December 8, 2013. http://ftalphaville.ft.com//2012/02/21/889521/that-greek-debt-sustainability-analysis-in-full/.

Mackey, Robert. "Dramatic Video of a Standoff in Ecuador." *The Lede*, a blog in the *New York Times*. October 1, 2010. Accessed December 1, 2014. http://thelede.blogs.nytimes.com/2010/10/01/dramatic-video-of-a-stand-off-in-ecuador/.

McCrum, Dan. "European Banks Face Shortsellers' Fire." *Financial Times*, August 8, 2011. http://www.ft.com/intl/cms/s/0/21550128-bf9b-11e0-90d5-00144feabdc0.html?siteedition=intl#axzz2zGm4N52N.

McHale, John. "Brazil in the 1997–1999 Financial Turmoil." *Fourth Country Meeting of the NBER Project on Exchange Rate Crises in Emerging Market Countries*. National Bureau of Economic Research, April 14–15, 2000. http://www.nber.org/crisis/brazil_report.html

Meakin, Lucy, and Emma Charlton. "Spanish Yield Reaches Euro-Era Record on Regional Concern." Bloomberg, July 23, 2012. http://www.bloomberg.com/news/2012-07-23/german-bonds-rise-on-debt-crisis-as-spanish-yield-reaches-record.html.

"Measurement of Economic Performance and Social Progress." Commission on the Measurement of Economic Performance and Social Progress, September 2009. http://www.stiglitz-sen-fitoussi.fr/documents/rapport_anglais.pdf.

Ministerio de Hidrocarburos y Energía. Separata Nacional, May 2014. http://www2.hidrocarburos.gob.bo/index.php/prensa/separatas.html?download=388:separata-nacional-ministerio-de-hidrocarburos-y-energia-1ro-de-mayo-2014.

Ministerio de Trabajo, Empleo y Seguridad Social. "Mercado de Trabajo," 2014. Accessed May 8, 2014. http://www.trabajo.gob.ar/left/estadisticas/bel/index.asp.

Mulligan, Mark. "Time Is Running Out, Argentina Admits." *Financial Times*, May 9, 2002, p. 7.

Muntaner, Carles, et al. "History Is Not Over: The Bolivarian Revolution, 'Barrio Adentro,' and Health Care in Venezuela." In *The Revolution in Venezuela*, edited by Thomas Ponniah and

Jonathan Eastwood. Cambridge, MA: Harvard University Press, 2011, pp. 225–256.

Mydans, Seth. "Pressed By I.M.F., Indonesia Accepts Economic Reforms." *New York Times*, January 18, 1998. http://www.nytimes.com/1998/01/15/world/pressed-by-imf-indonesia-accepts-economic-reforms.html.

Netherlands Environmental Agency. "Developing Countries' Contributions to Climate Change Approach 50%." PBL Netherlands Environmental Assessment Agency, October 31, 2013. http://www.pbl.nl/en/news/newsitems/2013/developing-countries%E2%80%99-contribution-to-climate-change-approach-50.

Norris, Floyd. "Argentina's Case Has No Victors, Many Losers." *The New York Times*, November 20, 2014. http://www.nytimes.com/2014/11/21/business/international/in-argentinas-debt-case-no-winners-but-a-lot-of-losers.html.

OECD (Organisation for Economic Co-operation and Development). "Greece." in *OECD Economic Outlook*, Volume 2011, Issue 2. Paris: OECD Publishing, 2011.OECD. "Level of GDP per Capita and Productivity," 2012. Accessed May 2014. http://stats.oecd.org/Index.aspx?DataSetCode=PDB_LV.

OECD. *OECD Economic Surveys: Brazil 2013*. http://dx.doi.org/10.1787/eco_surveys-bra-2013-en.

OECD. "Quarterly Growth Rates of Real GDP, Change over Previous Quarter." Accessed May 2014. https://stats.oecd.org/index.aspx?queryid=350#. Panagariya, Arvind, "India in the 1980s and 1990s: A Triumph of Reforms." Washington, DC: International Monetary Fund, 2004.

Panel Rehearing and Rehearing En Banc, NML Capital, Ltd. v. Republic of Argentina, No. 12-105-cv(L) (2d Cir. Dec. 28, 2012), 2012 WL 6777132.

Petkoff, Teodoro. "A Watershed Moment in Venezuela." *Inter-American Dialogue Working Paper*, July 2008. http://www.thedialogue.org/PublicationFiles/A%20Watershed%20Moment%20in%20Venezuela%20-%20Teodoro%20Petkoff%20(July%202008).pdf.

Piketty, Thomas. *Capital in the Twenty-first Century*. Cambridge, MA: Belknap Press, 2014.

Poe, Abigal. "President Bush Suspends Bolivia's Trade Preferences under ATPDEA." *Security Assistance Monitor*, October 6, 2008. http://justf.org/blog/president-bush-suspends-bolivias-trade-preferences-under-atpdea.

Pollard, P. S. "Central Bank Independence and Economic Performance," *Federal Reserve Bank of St. Louis Review*, July 1993, pp. 21–36. http://research.stlouisfed.org/publications/review/93/07/Bank_ Jul_Aug1993.pdf.

Pomerleano, Michael. Public Policy for the Private Sector, Note No. 155, "Corporate Finance Lessons from the East Asian Crisis." World Bank, October 1998. http://siteresources.worldbank.org/ EXTFINANCIALSECTOR/Resources/282884-1303327122200/1 55pomer.pdf.

Prasad, Eswar, ed. "China's Growth and Integration into the World Economy," 2004. International Monetary Fund Occasional Paper 232, September 2014. http://www.imf.org/external/pubs/ft/ op/232/op232.pdf

Radelet, Steven, and Jeffrey Sachs. "The Onset of the East Asian Financial Crisis." In *Currency Crises*, edited by Paul Krugman, pp. 105–153. Chicago: University of Chicago Press, 2000.

Ray, Rebecca, and Sara Kozameh. "Ecuador's Economy since 2007." Center For Economic and Policy Research, May 2012. http:// www.cepr.net/index.php/publications/reports/ecuadors- economy-since-2007.

Ray, Rebecca, and Mark Weisbrot. "The Scorecard on Development, 1960–2010: Closing the Gap?" Center for Economic and Policy Research, April 2011. http://www.cepr.net/documents/publications/ scorecard-2011-04.pdf.

Reid, Paula. "Goldman Sachs' Revolving Door." CBS News, April 8, 2010. https://www.google.com/url?sa=t&rct=j&q=&esrc=s&source =web&cd=1&cad=rja&uact=8&ved=0CB4QFjAA&url=http% 3A%2F% 2Fwww.cbsnews.com%2Fnews%2Fgoldman-sachs- revolving-door%2F&ei=XL1TVayWNJLBgwSHpYCIAg& usg=AFQjCNHm6zein 2MtoxkuM44HWkUUO_LaqQ&sig2= 3KYJj5vWo6Gg-_Gn8gDCLA&bvm =bv.93112503,d.eXY.

Reinhart, Carmen, and Kenneth S. Rogoff. "The Aftermath of Financial Crises." National Bureau of Economic Research Working Paper No. 14656, 2009. http://www.nber.org/papers/ w14656.

Reinhart, Carmen M., and Kenneth Rogoff. "The Aftermath of Financial Crises," *American Economic Review* 99 (2009): 466–472.

Reinhart, Carmen M., and Kenneth Rogoff. *This Time Is Different: Eight Centuries of Financial Folly.* Princeton, NJ: Princeton University Press, 2009.

Reserve Bank of India. "Handbook of Statistics on the Indian Economy." http://www.rbi.org.in/scripts/annualPublications.asp x?head=Handbook+of+Statistics+on+Indian+Economy.

Reuters. "China's Xi Woos Latin America with $250 Billion Investments." *New York Times*, January 7, 2015. http://www.nytimes.com/reuters/2015/01/07/world/americas/07reuters-china-latam.html?ref=americas&_r=0.

Reuters. "IMF's Blanchard Says No Need for More U.S. Stimulus," October 8, 2010. http://in.reuters.com/article/2010/10/08/idINIndia-52065220101008.

Rodrik, Dani. "The Real Exchange Rate and Economic Growth." *Brookings Papers on Economic Activity* 2 (Fall 2008), 365–412.

Rohter, Larry. "Argentina's Chief Is Sworn In and Comes Out Fighting." *New York Times*, May 26, 2003. https://www.google.com/url?sa=t&rct=j&q=&esrc=s&source=web&cd=1&cad=rja&uact=8&ved=0CB8QFjAA&url=http%3A%2F%2Fwww.nytimes.com%2F2003%2F05%2F26%2Fworld%2Fargentina-s-chief-is-sworn-in-and-comes-out-fighting.html&ei=ib1TVaiXPIGmgwTx_oHIBA&usg=AFQjCNFBGDopvmCrq1wmbeEbdBibu7csdA&sig2=o8F0o23ynNkJiSnqZljAUw&bvm=bv.93112503,d.eXY.

Rohter, Larry. "Brazilians Find Political Cost for Help from I.M.F." *New York Times*, August 11, 2002. http://www.nytimes.com/2002/08/11/world/brazilians-find-political-cost-for-help-from-imf.html.

Rohter, Larry. "The Homes of Argentines Are at Risk in I.M.F. Talks." *New York Times*, June 23, 2003. http://www.nytimes.com/2003/06/23/world/the-homes-of-argentines-are-at-risk-in-imf-talks.html.

Rojas Calizaya, Juan. "Agrarian Transformation in Bolivia at Risk." *Bolivia Information Forum Bulletin*, September 2012. http://boliviarising.blogspot.com/2012/10/agrarian-transformation-in-bolivia-at.html.

Rojas Calizaya, Juan Carlos. *Resultados de la Reconducción Comunitaria de la Reforma Agraria en Bolivia II: la tierra vuelve a manos indígenas y campesinas.* La Paz: Instituto Nacional de Reforma Agraria (INRA), 2010.

Rosnick, David. "The Consequences of Increased Population Growth for Climate Change." Center for Economic and Policy Research, 2014. http://www.cepr.net/documents/Climate-population-2014-12.pdf

Rosnick, David. "Reduced Work Hours as a Means of Slowing Climate Change." Center for Economic and Policy Research, February 2013. http://www.cepr.net/index.php/publications/reports/reduced-work-hours-as-a-means-of-slowing-climate-change

Rosnick, David, and Mark Weisbrot. "Are Shorter Work Hours Better for the Environment?" Washington, DC: Center for Economic and Policy Research, 2006.

Rosnick, David, and Mark Weisbrot. "Latin American Growth in the 21st Century: The 'Commodities Boom' That Wasn't." Center for Economic and Policy Research, May 2014. http://www.cepr.net/documents/terms-of-trade-2014-05.pdf.

Rosnick, David, and Mark Weisbrot. "Political Forecasting? The IMF's Flawed Growth Projections for Argentina and Venezuela." Center for Economic and Policy Research, 2007. Accessed December 2, 2013. http://www.cepr.net/index.php/publications/reports/political-forecasting-the-imfs-flawed-growth-projectio ns-for-argentina-and-venezuela.

Rosnick, David, and Mark Weisbrot. "A Statistical Note on the April 14 Venezuelan Presidential Election and Audit of Results." Center for Economic and Policy Research, 2013. http://www.cepr.net/index.php/publications/reports/a-statistical-note-on-the-ap ril-14-venezuelan-presidential-election-and-audit-of-results.

Russo, Camila. "Argentina Gets Reserves Boost from China Currency Swap." *Bloomberg*, October 30, 2014. http://www.bloomberg.com /news/2014-10-30/argentina-gets-reserves-boost-from-china-currency-swap.html.

Sachs, Jeffrey D. *Common Wealth: Economics for a Crowded Planet*. New York: Penguin Press, 2008.

Sachs, Jeffrey D. *The End of Poverty: Economic Possibilities for Our Time*. New York: Penguin Books, 2005.

Sachs, Jeffrey. "The IMF and the Asian Flu." *The American Prospect*, March/April 1998, p. 16.

Sachs, Jeffrey. "With Friends Like IMF . . ." *Cleveland Plain Dealer*, June 6, 1998, p. 9.

Salmon, Felix. "Lessons from Ecuador's Bond Default," Reuters, May 29, 2009. Accessed December 1, 2014. http://blogs.reuters.com/felix-salmon/2009/05/29/lessons-from-ecuadors-bond-default/.

Sanger, David E. "IMF Reports Plan Backfired, Worsening Indonesia Woes." *New York Times*, January 14, 1998.

Saxena, Shobhan. "South Americans Back Venezuela's Maduro, Blast US 'Interference.'" *The Times of India*, April 17, 2013. http://timesofindia.indiatimes.com/world/rest-of-world/South-Americans-back-Venezuelas-Maduro-blast-US-interference/articleshow/19602966.cms.

Schipani, Andres. "Bolivia Facing Up to Lower Gas Export Prices," *BeyondBRICS*, a blog in the *Financial Times*. October 23, 2014. Accessed November 28, 2014. http://blogs.ft.com/beyond-brics/2014/10/23/bolivia-facing-up-to-lower-gas-export-prices/?Authorised=false.

Shah, Ajay, and Ila Patnaik. "India's Experience with Capital Flows: The Elusive Quest for a Sustainable Current Account Deficit," NBER Chapters. In *Capital Controls and Capital Flows in Emerging Economies: Policies, Practices and Consequences*, pp. 609–644. National Bureau of Economic Research, Cambridge, 2007.

Singh, Anoop. "Introductory Remarks on the Role of the IMF Mission in Argentina." Press Briefing, Buenos Aires, April 10, 2002. http://www.imf.org/external/np/tr/2002/tr020410.htm.

Sistema de Indicadores Sociales de Venezuela, n.d. http://sisov.mppp.gob.ve/indicadores/SS0100300000000/.

Smith, Tony. "Argentina Defaults on $3 Billion I.M.F. Debt." *New York Times*, September 10, 2003. http://www.nytimes.com/2003/09/10/business/argentina-defaults-on-3-billion-imf-debt.html.

Smith, Tony. "Argentina Reaches Deal on 3-Year Aid Package." *New York Times*, September 11, 2003. http://www.nytimes.com/2003/09/11/business/argentina-reaches-deal-on-3-year-aid-package.html.

Socio-Economic Database for Latin America and the Caribbean (CEDLAS and the World Bank). "Poverty." Accessed May 2014. http://sedlac.econo.unlp.edu.ar/eng/statistics.php.

Socio-Economic Database for Latin America and the Caribbean (CEDLAS and The World Bank). "Incomes," February 2014. Accessed December 4, 2014. http://sedlac.econo.unlp.edu.ar/eng/statistics.php.

"Statement by the Executive Director for Spain; and Public Information Notice on the Executive Board Discussion." Washington, DC: International Monetary Fund, July 2010, p. 13.

Stiglitz, Joseph, Amartya Sen, and Jean-Paul Fitoussi. "Report by the Commission on the Measurement of Economic Performance and Social Progress. http://www.stiglitz-sen-fitoussi.fr/documents/rapport_anglais.pdf.

Stone, Oliver. *South of the Border*. 2010. http://www.southoftheborderdoc.com/

Subramanian, Arvind. "Greece's Exit May Become the Euro's Envy." *The Financial Times*, May 14, 2012. Accessed December 9, 2013. http://www.ft.com/intl/cms/s/0/4bdda8a0-9dad-11e1-9a9e-00144feabdc0.html.

Summa, Ricardo. "Mercado de trabalho e a evolução dos salários no Brasil." Instituto de Economia, Universidade Federal do Rio de Janeiro, 2014. http://www.ie.ufrj.br/index.php/index-publicacoes/textos-para-discussao.

Tagaris, Karolina "Greek Health System Crumbles under Weight of Crisis." Reuters, June 15, 2013. Accessed December 9, 2013. http://www.reuters.com/article/2012/06/15/greece-health-idUSL5E8HF17O20120615.

The Times. "Fund Managers in a Surrey State." *The Times* (London), December 5, 1997.

Thomson, Adam. "Argentina and IMF Lock Horns as Deal Expires." *Financial Times*, September 2, 2003.

Thomson, Adam. "Argentina Pays Dollars 3.1bn IMF bill." *Financial Times*, March 10, 2004.

Thomson, Adam, and Agencies. "Honduran Leader Ousted by Army." *Financial Times*, June 28, 2009. http://www.ft.com/cms/s/0/409b94b4-6432-11de-a818-00144feabdc0.html?siteedition=uk#axzz3L305fpGv.

Toyer, Julien, and Ilona Wissenbach. "'Shock and Awe' Euro Rescue Lifts Global Markets." Reuters, May 10, 2010. http://www.reuters.com/article/2010/05/10/us-eurozone-idUSTRE6400PJ20100510.

Tseng, Wanda, et al. "Economic Reform in China: A New Phase," 1994. International Monetary Fund Occasional Paper 114. Washington, DC, November 2014.

UNDP. "Human Development Report 2009." http://hdr.undp.org/en/content/human-development-report-2009. UNDP. "Human Development Report 2014." http://hdr.undp.org/en/2014-report/download.

UNDP. "Human Development Report 2010." http://hdr.undp.org/en/content/human-development-report-2010.

UNESCO Institute for Statistics Database, n.d. http://data.uis.unesco.org/.

US Census Bureau. "CPS Historical Time Series Tables: Table A-2. Percent of People 25 Years and Over Who Have Completed High School or College, by Race, Hispanic Origin and Sex: Selected Years 1940 to 2013." Accessed July 14, 2014. http://www.census.gov/hhes/socdemo/education/data/cps/historical/.

US Census Bureau. "Foreign Trade, US Trade in Goods by Country." www.census.gov/foreign-trade/balance/.

US Senate. "Covert Action in Chile, 1963–1973." Staff Report of the Select Committee to Study Governmental Operations with Respect to Intelligence Activities. United States Senate, 1975. http://fas.org/irp/ops/policy/church-chile.htm.

US Senate Banking, Housing, and Urban Affairs Committee. "Reform of the International Monetary Fund" (Hearing before the Subcommittee on International Trade and Finance), 106th Congress, 2nd session. Washington, DC: Government Printing Office, April 27, 2000.

US Centers for Disease Control and Prevention. "Life Expectancy." February 13, 2014. Accessed July 14, 2014. http://www.cdc.gov/nchs/fastats/life-expectancy.htm.

VTV. "Logros de la Educación venezolana en Revolución," December 25, 2013. http://www.vtv.gob.ve/articulos/2013/12/25/logros-de-la-educacion-venezolana-en-revolucion-8607.html.

Vyas, Kejal. "Venezuela to Use Diamonds to Boost International Reserves." *Wall Street Journal*, December 4, 2014. http://online.wsj.com/articles/venezuela-to-use-diamonds-to-boost-international-reserves-1417735501.

Wearden, Graeme. *The Guardian*. "EU Debt Crisis: Greece Forced to Wait for Crucial Bailout Funds—as It Happened." September 16, 2011. http://www.theguardian.com/business/2011/sep/16/euro-debt-crisis-finance-ministers.

Weisbrot, Mark. "The Debt Vultures' Fell Swoop." *New York Times*, June 22, 2014. http://www.nytimes.com/2014/06/23/opinion/the-debt-vultures-fell-swoop.html.

Weisbrot, Mark. "Hard Choices: Hillary Clinton Admits Role in Honduran Coup Aftermath." *Al Jazeera America*, September 29, 2014. http://america.aljazeera.com/opinions/2014/9/hillary-clinton-honduraslatinamericaforeignpolicy.html.

Weisbrot, Mark. "Honduras Needs Help from the South." *The Guardian*, November 18, 2011. http://www.cepr.net/index.php/op-eds-&-columns/op-eds-&-columns/honduras-needs-help-from-the-south.

Weisbrot, Mark. "Italy Pushed to the Brink by ECB Fiscal Orthodoxy." *The Guardian*, November 9, 2011. http://www.theguardian.com/commentisfree/cifamerica/2011/nov/09/italy-pushed-brink-ecb-fiscal-orthodoxy.

Weisbrot, Mark. "Obama's Latin America Policy: Continuity Without Change." Center for Economic and Policy Research, May 2011. http://www.cepr.net/documents/publications/obamas-latin-america-policy-2011-05.pdf.

Weisbrot, Mark. "Obama's Latin America Policy: Continuity Without Change." *Latin American Perspectives* 38 (July 2011): 63–72; first published on May 11, 2011.

Weisbrot, Mark. "Ten Years After: The Lasting Impact of the Asian Financial Crisis." Center for Economic and Policy Research, 2007. Accessed February 11, 2015. http://www.cepr.net/index.php/publications/reports/ten-years-after-the-lasting-impact-of-the-asian-financial-crisis.

Weisbrot, Mark. "Top Ten Ways You Can Tell Which Side the United States Government Is on with Regard to the Military Coup in Honduras." Center for Economic and Policy Research, December 16, 2009. http://www.cepr.net/op-eds-&-columns/op-eds-&-columns/top-ten-ways.

Weisbrot, Mark. "Ukraine May Face Disillusionment with Europe if It Follows IMF/EU Prescriptions." *Al Jazeera America*, May 7, 2014. http://america.aljazeera.com/opinions/2014/5/ukraine-economy-imfeuropeanunionrussia.html

Weisbrot, Mark. "Ukraine's IMF Agreement Could Worsen the Country's Problems." *The Chicago Tribune*, May 29, 2014. http://www.chicagotribune.com/sns-mct-bc-ukraine-con-20140529,0,6610877.story

Weisbrot, Mark. "The United States and Bolivia: A New Beginning?" *The Guardian*, February 25, 2009. http://www.cepr.net/index.php/op-eds-&-columns/op-eds-&-columns/the-united-states-and-bolivia-a-new-beginning/.

Weisbrot, Mark. "The US Game in Latin America." *The Guardian*, January 29, 2010. http://www.theguardian.com/commentisfree/cifamerica/2010/jan/29/us-latin-america-haiti-honduras.

Weisbrot, Mark. "The US Needs to Take the Hint from Dilma Rousseff's Snub." *The Guardian*, September 18, 2013. http://www. theguardian.com/commentisfree/2013/sep/18/us-hint-nsa-di lma-rousseff-snub.

Weisbrot, Mark. "Venezuela in the Chávez Years: Its Economy and Influence on the Region." In *The Revolution in Venezuela: Social and Political Change under Chávez*, edited by Thomas Poniah and Jonathan Eastwood. Cambridge, MA: Harvard University Press, 2011, Chapter 6.

Weisbrot, Mark. "Venezuela's Election Provides Opportunity for Washington to Change Course." McClatchy Tribune Information Services, December 6, 2006. http://www.cepr.net/index.php/ op-eds-&-columns/op-eds-&-columns/venezuelas-election-provides-opportunity-for-washington-to-change-course/.

Weisbrot, Mark. "What Next for the Eurozone? Macroeconomic Policy and the Recession." Center for Economic and Policy Research, April 17, 2013. http://www.cepr.net/index.php/ events/events/what-next-for-the-eurozone-macroecon omic-policy-and-the-recession.

Weisbrot, Mark. "When Surrender Isn't Good Enough." Knight-Ridder/ Tribune Information Services, April 22, 2002. http://www. cepr.net/index.php/op-eds-&-columns/op-eds-&-columns/ when-surrender-isnt-good-enough.

Weisbrot, Mark. "Who Shot Argentina?" U.S. News & World Report, June 24, 2014. http://www.usnews.com/opinion/ articles/2014/06/24/supreme-court-dismisses-case-between-argentina-and-us-vulture-funds.

Weisbrot, Mark, et al. "The Greek Economy: Which Way Forward?" Center for Economic and Policy Research, January 2015. http://www.cepr.net/index.php/publications/reports/the-gr eek-economy-which-way-forward.

Weisbrot, Mark, et al. "IMF-Supported Macroeconomic Policies and the World Recession: A Look at Forty-One Borrowing Countries." Center for Economic and Policy Research, October 2009. http:// www.cepr.net/documents/publications/imf-2009-10.pdf

Weisbrot, Mark, Jake Johnston, and Stephan Lefebvre. "The Brazilian Economy in Transition: Macroeconomic Policy, Labor and Inequality." Center for Economic and Policy Research, September 2014. http://www.cepr.net/documents/brazil-2014-09.pdf.

Weisbrot, Mark, Jake Johnston, and Stephan Lefebvre. "Ecuador's New Deal: Reforming and Regulating the Financial Sector." Center For Economic and Policy Research, February 2013. http://www.cepr.net/index.php/publications/reports/ecuadors-new-deal-reforming-and-regulating-the-financial-sector.

Weisbrot, Mark, Jake Johnston, and Stephan Lefebvre. "The Scorecard on Development, 1960–2010: Closing the Gap?" Center for Economic and Policy Research, 2014. Accessed February 6, 2015. http://www.cepr.net/documents/brazil-2014-09.pdf.

Weisbrot, Mark, and Helene Jorgensen. "Macroeconomic Policy Advice and the Article IV Consultations: A European Union Case Study." Center for Economic and Policy Research, January 2013. http://www.cepr.net/index.php/publications/reports/macroeconomic-policy-advice-and-the-article-iv-consultations.

Weisbrot, Mark, Stephan Lefebvre, and Joseph Sammut. "Did NAFTA Help Mexico? An Assessment after 20 Years." Center for Economic and Policy Research, February 2014. http://www.cepr.net/index.php/publications/reports/nafta-20-years.

Weisbrot, Mark, and Juan Montecino. "Alternatives to Fiscal Austerity in Spain." Center for Economic and Policy Research, July 2010. http://www.cepr.net/index.php/publications/reports/alternatives-to-fiscal-austerity-in-spain.

Weisbrot, Mark, and Rebecca Ray. "Latvia's Internal Devaluation: A Success Story?" Center for Economic and Policy Research, 2011. http://www.cepr.net/index.php/publications/reports/latvias-internal-devaluation-a-success-story.

Weisbrot, Mark, and Rebecca Ray. "The Scorecard on Development, 1960–2010: Closing the Gap?" Center for Economic and Policy Research, April 2011. http://www.cepr.net/index.php/publications/reports/the-scorecard-on-development-1960-2010-closing-the-gap.

Weisbrot, Mark, Rebecca Ray, and Jake Johnston. "Bolivia: The Economy during the Morales Administration." Center for Economic and Policy Research, December 2009. http://www.cepr.net/documents/publications/bolivia-2009-12.pdf.

Weisbrot, Mark, R. Ray, J. Johnston, J. A. Cordero, and J. A. Montecino. "IMF-Supported Macroeconomic Policies and the World Recession: A Look at Forty-one Borrowing Countries." Center for Economic and Policy Research, October 2009. Accessed February 5,

2015. http://www.cepr.net/index.php/publications/reports/imf-supported-macroeconomic-policies-and-the-world-recession.

Weisbrot, Mark, Rebecca Ray, Juan Montecino, and Sara Kozameh. "The Argentine Success Story and Its Implications." Center for Economic and Policy Research, 2011. Accessed December 2, 2013. http://www.cepr.net/documents/publications/argentina-success-2011-10.pdf.

Weisbrot, Mark, and Luis Sandoval. "The Distribution of Bolivia's Most Important Natural Resources and the Autonomy Conflicts." Center for Economic and Policy Research, July 2008. http://www.cepr.net/index.php/publications/reports/the-distribution-of-bolivias-most-important-natural-resources-and-the-autonomy-conflicts.

Weisbrot, Mark, and Luis Sandoval. "Update on the Ecuadorian Economy." Center for Economic and Policy Research, June 2009. http://www.cepr.net/index.php/publications/reports/update-on-the-ecuadorian-economy.

Weiss, Martin A. "International Monetary Fund: Selecting a Managing Director." Congressional Research Service, Library of Congress, R41828, May 20, 2011.

White House. "Memorandum of Understanding, National Security Council Meeting—Chile," November 6, 1970. Accessed February 12, 2015. http://www.gwu.edu/~nsarchiv/news/20001113/701106.pdf.

White House Office of Management and Budget. "Historical Tables: Table 1.2—Summary of Receipts, Outlays, and Surpluses or Deficits (-) as Percentages of GDP: 1930–2019." Accessed May 2014. http://www.whitehouse.gov/sites/default/files/omb/budget/fy2015/assets/hist01z2.xls.

Williamson, John. "The Strange History of the Washington Consensus." Journal of Post Keynesian Economics 27, no. 2 (Winter 2004–2005): 195. http://www.jstor.org/stable/4538920?seq-1#page_scan_tab_contents.

Wilson, Scott. "Scott Wilson on US Involvement in Venezuela Coup." Washington Post. Youtube video by Center for Economic and Policy Research, July 30, 2010. https://www.youtube.com/watch?v=KzSnH4_p0PY.

World Bank. "New Data Show 1.4 Billion Live on Less Than US$1.25 a Day, But Progress Against Poverty Remains Strong." September 2008.

http://www.worldbank.org/en/news/press-release/2008/09/16/
new-data-show-14-billion-live-less-us125-day-progress-aga
inst-poverty-remains-strong.

World Bank. "Press Release: World Bank Continues Support," July 19,
2002. http://web.worldbank.org/WBSITE/EXTERNAL/NEWS/0
,,contentMDK:20055157~menuPK:34466~pagePK:34370~piPK:
34424~theSitePK:4607,00.html.

World Bank. "Quarterly Update." Beijing: World Bank, November 2010.
http://siteresources.worldbank.org/CHINAEXTN/Resources/
318949-1268688634523/cqu_Nov_2010.pdf.

World Bank. "World Databank: World Development Indicators," 2014.
Online database. Accessed July 14, 2014. http://databank.world-
bank.org/data/views/variableselection/selectvariables.aspx?sou
rce=World-Development-Indicators.

World Bank. "World Development Indicators: Gross Capital Formation
(% of GDP)." Accessed February 9, 2015. http://data.worldbank.
org/indicator/NE.GDI.TOTL.ZS.

Xie, Yu, and Xiang Zhou. "Income Inequality in Today's China."
Proceedings of the National Academy of Sciences, February 20, 2014.
http://www.pnas.org/content/111/19/6928.short.

Zettelmeyer, Jeromin, Christoph Trebesch, and G. Mitu Gulati. "The
Greek Debt Restructuring: An Autopsy." Peterson Institute for
International Economics Working Paper No. 2013-13-8, August
1, 2013, p. 15.

Index

Afghanistan, 154, 223
Allende, Salvador, 167–68, 170
Amsden, Alice, 236
Andean Trade Promotion and Drug Eradication Act, 198
Argentina: Asian financial crisis contagion and, 130, 142; austerity measures in, 59–60, 66, 145, 147, 152; balance of payments and, 68, 232; bonds issued by, 230–31; capital flows and, 60, 65, 75, 142–43, 148, 230; Central Bank in, 68; China's currency swap arrangement with, 237; "commodities boom" argument regarding, 7, 15, 64–66, 75, 174; consumer price index in, 62n11; currency devaluation in, 7–8, 61–62, 65–68, 75, 78, 142, 145–46, 152, 172; current account deficit in, 60, 142–43; debt defaults by, 7–8, 13, 60–62, 65–67, 69, 75, 105, 141, 145–46, 148, 153–55, 172, 230–32; debt restructuring agreement (2005) and, 67, 230–31; economic recovery (early 2000s) in, 7–8, 15, 58, 62–66, 68–69, 75, 78, 149, 152–54, 172, 174; economic stagnation during late twentieth century in, 59, 71; economic subversion law in, 148; election of left-wing governments in, 14, 169; emergency mortgage foreclosure protection in, 151–52; exchange rate policies in, 59–61, 68–69, 93, 105, 141–43, 145–46, 152, 232; exports from, 7–8, 59, 64–67, 75–76, 141; financial crisis (2001-2002) in, 7–8, 13, 58, 60–62, 66, 105, 141–52; fiscal policy in, 143–45, 147; fixed currency exchange rate in, 59–61, 69, 93, 105, 141–43, 145–46, 152; foreign exchange controls in, 67; foreign exchange levels in, 145; GDP per capita in, 58, 62–63; Great Recession and, 62, 68; inflation in, 59–60, 62, 68, 141, 147, 151–54, 230, 232; Inter-American Development Bank and, 66; interest rates in, 60, 66, 141–43, 150; internal devaluation strategy in, 60;

Argentina: Asian financial crisis contagion and (*Cont.*)
International Monetary Fund
and, 8, 13, 60–61, 64, 66, 69,
141–43, 145–55, 231–32; monetary policy in, 147, 152, 154;
pensions in, 147; poverty levels
in, 7, 58–59, 61–62, 146–47;
privatization in, 144; public debt
levels in, 60; social security program in, 63, 144, 152; taxes in,
67, 144; trade balance in, 7, 141;
unemployment in, 7, 59, 61–64,
68, 146, 149; World Bank and,
66, 144, 149
Article IV consultations
(International Monetary
Fund): calls for healthcare spending cuts and, 5–6, 45–46, 164;
calls for pension cuts and, 5–6,
45–46, 164; calls for public sector
cuts in, 6, 164; eurozone countries and, 5–6, 41–42, 45–47, 164
Articles of Agreement (International
Monetary Fund), 45
Asian financial crisis
(1997-1998): austerity measures
after, 135; capital flows and, 13,
105, 130–35, 172; China and,
132; currency collapses and, 59,
77–78, 131–32; export strategies
and, 129–30; financial contagion
from, 59–60, 130, 142; foreign
exchange reserves and, 13, 105,
130–32, 135; Indonesia and, 13,
59, 71, 78, 131, 133–34, 136–37;
International Monetary Fund
and, 12–13, 106, 129, 131–37,
139–40, 154, 157; Japan and,
132; South Korea and, 13, 59, 71,
78, 131, 133, 135; Thailand and,
13, 71, 78, 131–32, 135; United
States and, 132–34, 136, 139

Asian Infrastructure Investment
Bank, x
Asian Monetary Fund proposal, 132
austerity. *See also* neoliberalism: in
Argentina, 59–60, 66, 145, 147,
152; Asian financial crisis and,
135; economic growth and, 32;
European Central Bank and
European Commission's imposi-
tions of, 5, 36, 41, 46, 55, 72,
74, 77, 81, 135–36; eurozone
and, 22, 24, 28, 34–36, 38–39,
41–44, 46–47, 51, 54–55, 85,
135, 145, 164, 176, 235, 239–40;
in Greece, 29–31, 35–36, 43, 58,
70, 72, 74–75, 77, 79, 81, 164,
239–40; internal devaluation
strategy and, 43; International
Monetary Fund and, 8, 12,
35–36, 41–42, 46–47, 55, 77, 81,
105–6, 117, 125, 133, 135–36,
146–47, 149, 152, 157, 160–61,
163–64, 239–40; in Ireland, 36,
240; in Italy, 35–37, 239–40; in
Portugal, 36, 43, 240; in Spain,
36, 43, 239–40
Austria, 46

Bachelet, Michele, 233
Baker, Dean, 158–59, 234
balance of payments: Argentina
and, 68, 232; Bolivia and,
195; Contingency Reserve
Arrangement and, 241; crises
in, 8, 31; Greece and, 76–77;
International Monetary Fund
and, 31; in Latin America, 15,
173, 175, 230; Latin America
and, 15
Bank of England, 4, 31, 40
Beni province (Bolivia), 196
Berlusconi, Silvio, 35, 37
Bértola, L., 172

Birdsall, Nancy, 109
Blanchard, Olivier, 162–63
Blinder, Alan, 240
Boccara, Bruno, 61–62
Bolívar, Simón, 222
Bolivia: Andean Trade Promotion and Drug Eradication Act and, 198; balance of payments and, 195; economic growth in, 16, 126, 193–95, 199; education in, 200; election of left-wing governments in, 14–15, 126, 169, 226, 229; exports from, 15, 175, 192, 194, 196; foreign exchange reserves in, 195; foreign investment in, 194–95; Great Recession and, 194; healthcare in, 198–200; indigenous population in, 15, 192, 196, 200; inequality in, 191–92; inflation in, 195–96; International Monetary Fund and, 15, 126–27, 191–92; land redistribution in, 16, 196, 200; media bias in, 195; "Media Luna" provinces in, 196; minimum wage in, 15, 199; monetary policy in, 195; nationalization of industries in, 15, 127, 192–94, 222; natural gas and oil sector in, 15, 126–27, 192–96, 201, 222; pensions in, 15, 194, 200; poverty in, 126, 191–92, 196, 199, 201; privatization in, 126; public investment in, 194; remittances to, 194; retirement age in, 200; separatist movement in, 196–97; Spanish colonial era in, 191; United States and, 191, 194, 197–99
Bolsa Familia (Brazilian social spending program), 181–82
bonds: Argentina and, 230–31; Brazil and, 177–78; collateral requirements and, 36; European Central Bank and, 4–5, 30–31, 33–34, 36–40, 53, 73, 80–81, 235; eurozone and, 4–5, 25, 30–34, 36–41, 49–50, 53, 73, 80–81, 235; France and, 49; Germany and, 41, 49; Greece and, 26, 30–31, 34, 49, 73, 80–81; "haircuts" and, 26, 30, 73; Ireland and, 30–31, 36, 49; Italy and, 32–34, 36–37, 39, 41, 49, 80–81; Mexico and, 127; Portugal and, 30–31, 36, 49; quantitative easing (QE) policy and, 22–23, 50, 81, 235, 240; short-selling of, 32–34; Spain and, 30, 32–33, 39–41, 49, 80–81; United States and, 22–23, 36; Venezuela and, 209; yield rates and, 5, 31–34, 36–41, 80–81, 209
BPC (Brazilian social welfare program), 182
Brazil: Asian financial crisis contagion and, 60, 130, 142, 147; bonds issued by, 177–78; capital flows and, 179; Central Bank in, 178–79; "commodities boom" argument regarding, 175; consumer credit in, 183, 187–88; Contingent Reserve Arrangement and, x, 241; corruption in, 189; currency appreciation in, 178–79; currency collapses in, 60, 105, 142, 178; economic growth in, 89–90, 180–81, 184, 186–88; economic stagnation during late twentieth century in, 180–81; economic stagnation (2010s) in, 186–88; education in, 91; election of left-wing governments in, 14, 16–17, 169, 176, 226; eurozone bond purchases and, 25; exports from, 175, 179, 187; financial crisis (2002-2003) in, 177–78;

Brazil: Asian financial crisis contagion and *(Cont.)* fiscal policy in, 17, 178, 180, 186, 188; fixed currency exchange rate in, 93, 105, 154; floating currency exchange regime in, 178–79; foreign currency reserves in, 179; GDP per capita in, 17, 25, 89–90; Great Recession and, 17, 186–87; Haiti and, 228n119; Human Development Index indicators in, 90–91; income distribution in, 184–85; industrial policy in, 183, 229; inequality in, 17, 184–86; infant mortality in, 91; inflation in, 147, 178–79, 188; interest rates in, 178–79, 187–88; International Monetary Fund and, ix, 13, 154, 177–78, 180; labor market dynamics in, 185–86; land reform policies in, 177; media bias in, 189–90; minimum wage in, 17, 183, 186; monetary policy in, 180, 188; New Development Bank and, x, 241; oil industry in, 188; pensions in, 183; poverty and poverty reduction in, 17, 83, 91, 180–83; services sector in, 184; social spending programs in, 181–82, 186; taxes in, 184; unemployment in, 17, 184, 186; unemployment insurance in, 183; United States and, 18, 177, 223–25; wages in, 186–87

Brazilian Development Bank (BNDES), 183

Bretton Woods system, 11, 125, 241. *See also* International Monetary Fund (IMF); World Bank

BRICS countries (Brazil, Russia, India, China, and South Africa), x, 25, 241

Buffet, Warren, 4

Bulgaria, 104

Bush, George W., 144n37, 223–24, 228

Camdessus, Michel, 134

Canada, 18, 88, 228

capital flows: Argentina and, 60, 65, 75, 142–43, 148, 230; Asian financial crisis and, 13, 105, 130–35, 172; Brazil and, 179; Ecuador and, 205; Indonesia and, 131; inflation and, 232–33; interest rates and, 114, 234; International Monetary Fund and, 133, 162; neoliberalism and, 93, 100, 125, 130; South Korea and, 131, 133; Thailand and, 131; Venezuela and, 216, 220, 230, 233; volatility of, 9

Capital in the Twenty-first Century (Piketty), 84

Cardoso, Fernando Henrique, 180, 190

Carter, Jimmy, 225

Castro, Fidel, 176

central banks. *See also* European Central Bank; Federal Reserve Bank: democratic deficit in the governance of, 9; independence of, 22, 52, 93, 100, 178, 204; "lender of last resort" function of, 4, 206; neoliberalism and, 93, 100, 204

Central Intelligence Agency (CIA), 224

Chad, 13

Chávez, Hugo: on Bush, 223; coup attempt (2002) against, 197, 211–13, 224; death of, 221–22; election (1999) of, 210, 213, 226; Hyde on, 176; media coverage of, 221–22, 224; nationalization of oil industry and, 17; referendum election (2003) and, 212–13; socioeconomic policies of, 218–20; United States and, 221–22

Cheney, Richard, 138

child mortality. *See also* infant mortality: comparisons between low-, middle-, and high-income countries regarding, 98–99; the "demographic transition" and, 123; diminishing returns to improvements in, 98; in low- and middle-income countries, 8–9; medical advances and, 98

Chile: Chávez and, 222; election of left-wing governments in, 14, 169, 233; exports from, 175; military dictatorship in, 168; U.S.-sponsored coup (1973) in, 167–68, 170

China: Africa and, 237–38; Asian financial crisis (1997-1998) and, 132; Asian Infrastructure Investment Bank and, x; Contingent Reserve Arrangement, x, 241; counter-cyclical economic policies in, 11; currency exchange policies in, 107; departures from neoliberalism in, x, 10–11, 97, 102, 109–11, 117; economic growth in, x, 10–11, 97, 100, 102, 108–9, 111, 117, 171; eurozone bond purchases and, 25; exports from, 101, 108, 110, 114, 236; foreign currency reserves in, 25, 76, 195; foreign investment in, 10, 109–11; GDP per capita in, 25; Great Recession and recovery from, 10–11, 108–9, 117, 174; imports to, 100–102, 108; inequality in, 85; International Monetary Fund and, 165; Latin

American investments of, 76, 102, 237–38; low-income countries' trade with, 100–101, 107, 236–37; market-oriented reform in, 109–10; middle-income countries' trade with, 100–101, 107, 236–37; New Development Bank and, x, 241; noninterference policy in foreign investment by, 238; poverty reduction in, 85; Special Economic Zones in, 110; state-managed investment and economic development in, 108–11; state-owned enterprises in, 10, 107–8, 110; technology transfer and, 110; trade policies in, 109; trade surplus in, 114; Venezuela's loans from, 76, 217, 237; wind turbine industry in, 111; World Trade Organization and, 111

Church committee, 168

climate change, 3, 11, 117, 119–22

Clinton, Hillary, 228n118

Cold War, 137, 170–71, 236

Colombia, 71, 162, 170, 175

Community of Latin American and Caribbean States (CELAC), 18, 222, 228

Congo, Republic of, 160

Congress. *See* United States Congress

Contingent Reserve Arrangement (CRA), x, 241

Correa, Rafael: biographical background of, 201; on Bush, 223; coup attempt (2010) against, 201–2; Ecuador's debt default and, 16; election (2006) of, 201, 223; financial sector reforms of, 16, 204–7; re-election (2013) of, 202; U.S. military expelled from Ecuador by, 223

Cuba, 76

da Silva, Lula: approval ratings of, 189; biographical background of, 176–77; on Chávez, 222; corruption scandals and, 189–90; election (2002) of, 16, 169, 176, 180; fiscal policies of, 178; Free Trade Area of the Americas opposed by, 177; Hyde on, 176; International Monetary Fund and, ix, 177; neoliberalism opposed by, 169; on Obama, 226; Wall Street opposition to, 177
debt. *See* public debt
the "demographic transition," 122–23
Denmark, 46
deregulation, neoliberalism's advocacy for, 9, 93, 125, 230
Draghi, Mario, 4–5, 38–41

Eastern Europe, 104, 157. *See also specific countries*
economic growth: in Argentina, 7–8, 15, 58, 62–66, 68–69, 75, 78, 149, 152–54, 172, 174; austerity and, 32; in Bolivia, 16, 126, 193–95, 199; in Brazil, 89–90, 180–81, 184, 186–88; in China, x, 10–11, 97, 100, 102, 108–9, 111, 117, 171; climate change and, 11; diminishing returns in, 94–95; in Ecuador, 203, 208; environmental impact of, 119; in high-income countries, 95–96, 103–4; in India, 11, 97, 111–13, 115–16; internal devaluation strategy and, 43; in low-income countries, x, 8, 11, 86, 95–96, 98, 100, 103–5, 116, 236, 242; in Mexico, 89; in middle-income countries, x, 8, 11, 14, 86–87, 95–96, 98, 100, 104–5, 116, 125, 236, 242; Piketty on, 84;

population growth and, 11, 87, 121; poverty-reducing aspects of, 85–88; productivity and, 11, 121, 123; social indicators of, 8–9; social progress linked to, 91–92, 98–99; in South Korea, vii, 89–90, 94, 171; in the United States, 88, 97, 103–4; in Venezuela, 210–14, 218
Ecuador: capital flows and, 205; Central Bank in, 203–6; China's investment in, 76, 237; commercial banks' political power in, 206; consumer credit in, 203, 205; coup attempt (2010) in, 201–2; debt default by, 16, 207; economic growth in, 203, 208; election of left-wing governments in, 14, 169, 201, 229; exports from, 175, 202; financial sector reform in, 16, 204–7, 209; fiscal policy in, 203; Great Recession and aftermath in, 202–3; inequality reduced in, 16, 208; interest rates in, 205; liquidity fund in, 206; monetary policy in, 203, 205; oil industry in, 202, 208, 222, 229–30; poverty and poverty reduction in, 16, 208; public investment in, 208; remittances to, 202; social security system in, 208; taxes in, 205–6, 208; U.S. dollar as currency for, 203, 205–6, 209; U.S. military expelled from, 223
education: economic stagnation's impact on spending for, 9, 119; Human Development Index and, 90–91; impact on fiscal policy of, 23–24; Latin America's expansions of, 170; women and, 123
Egypt, 95
El Salvador, 14, 169

Estonia, 104

euro currency. *See also* eurozone: efforts to preserve, 4–5, 36, 40–41, 235; euroskeptics' criticisms of, 48, 51; exchange rates for, 36, 43

European Central Bank (ECB): austerity and, 5, 36, 41, 46, 55, 72, 74, 77, 81, 135–36; bond markets and, 4–5, 30–31, 33–34, 36–40, 53, 73, 80–81, 235; currency markets and, 4–5, 33, 40–41, 43–44, 235; dollar reserves and, 33; failures of, 4–6, 22–23, 37–38, 44, 50–51; inflation and, 52–53; interest rates and, 22; "lender of last resort" function and, 40–41, 53; mandate of, 38–40, 52; monetary policy and, 22–23, 31, 51; neoliberalism and, 20, 47, 52–53; Outright Monetary Transactions program and, 40; quantitative easing and, 50, 81, 235; Securities Market Program (SMP) and, 33, 40

European Commission. *See also* eurozone: austerity and, 5, 36, 41, 46, 55, 72, 74, 77, 81, 135–36; currency markets and, 43–44; neoliberalism and, 20, 47

European Union (EU). *See also* European Commission; eurozone: democratic deficit in governance of, 5; formal democratic guarantees in, 82; Honduras coup (2009) and, 227; loans to developing countries from, 127; political left's support for, 54; Ukraine and, 2, 161–62

"euroskeptics," 48, 51

eurozone. *See also specific countries*: austerity measures in, 22, 24, 28, 34–36, 38–39, 41–44, 46–47, 51, 54–55, 85, 135, 145, 164, 176, 235, 239–40; average hours worked in, 119–20; bond markets and, 4–5, 25, 30–34, 36–41, 49–50, 53, 73, 80–81, 235; countries' consideration of leaving, 6–8, 52, 76–77, 79–82, 235; currency policy strictures in, 20; democratic deficit in governance of, 3–6, 20–21, 34, 39, 47, 55, 79, 234–35; double-dip recession (2010s) in, 163; economic bubble of early 2000s and, 4; efforts to preserve euro currency in, 4–5; energy consumption in, 120; euro currency in, 20–21; exports between countries in, 48–49; fascist parties in, 82, 236; financial markets and, 33; fiscal policy in, 20–21, 27–28, 51, 53–54; GDP per capita in, 25; Great Recession and aftermath in, 1–3, 5–8, 20–21, 24, 50–51, 57–58, 106, 172; healthcare spending in, 5–6, 43, 46, 81, 164; inflation in, 23, 52–53; interest rates in, 22–23, 31, 34, 36, 38–41, 49, 53, 73, 80–81, 104; "internal devaluation" policies approach and, 42–43, 60; International Monetary Fund and, ix, 5–6, 11, 13, 20, 25, 28–31, 35–36, 40–43, 45–47, 60, 106, 125–29, 135, 157, 163–65, 235–36, 239–41; neoliberalism and, 24, 34–35, 51–53, 109, 125–26; pensions in, 5–6, 24, 43, 45–46, 81, 164; political left's support for, 54; private sector borrowing in, 49; privatization in, 24; productivity differences among members of, 48–50; public debt levels and "crisis" in, viii, 7, 22–32, 35–36,

eurozone (*Cont.*)
44–45, 47, 50–51, 53–54, 73, 76, 80–81, 145, 172, 235; public sector employment cuts in, 6, 24, 29–30; trade balances in, 48–49; unemployment in, 1, 3, 5, 8, 21, 24, 43–44, 46, 52, 55–57, 82, 85, 235–36, 240
exchange rate policies: in Argentina, 59–61, 68–69, 93, 105, 141–43, 145–46, 152, 232; in Brazil, 93, 105, 154, 178–79; in China, 107; fixed exchange rates and, 11, 59–60, 67, 69, 93, 105, 125, 132, 138, 141–43, 145, 152, 154, 214, 220, 232; floating exchange rates and, 132, 178–79, 216–18, 220, 232; in India, 113–14; in Russia, 93, 105, 138, 154; in Thailand, 132; in Venezuela, 216–18, 220, 230, 232

Fedecamaras (business association in Venezuela), 213
Federal Reserve Bank (United States): Great Recession and, 22; inflation and unemployment strategy of, 179; interest rates and, 22, 141, 178–79, 234; "lender of last resort" function of, 4, 40, 53; mandate regarding employment of, 52, 240; monetary policy and, 22–23, 31; quantitative easing (QE) policy and, 22–23, 50, 81, 235, 240
fertility rates, 122–23
Finland, 27, 71, 78
foreign exchange reserves: Asian financial crisis and, 13, 105, 130–32, 135; balance of payments crises and, 67; in Bolivia, 195; in China, 25, 76, 195; controls and, 67; European Central Bank and, 33; global markets in, 67; in Russia, 76, 138; in Venezuela, 217
Fraga, Arminio, 189
France: Asian Infrastructure Investment Bank and, x; bonds issued by, 49; election (2012) in, 41; eurozone public debt issues and, 35; fascist party in, 82, 236; interest rates in, 49; International Monetary Fund and, 46
Frankel, Jeffrey, 107
free markets. *See* neoliberalism
Free Trade Area of the Americas (FTAA), 177

G-7, 138, 165
G-20, 239
Georgia, 78
Germany: Asian Infrastructure Investment Bank and, x; bonds issued by, 41, 49; current account surpluses in, 48–49; euro currency exit question and, 52; eurozone public debt issues and, viii, 23, 27, 35, 47, 80; exports from, 27; fertility rates and life expectancy in, 123; fiscal policy in, 239; inflation in, 50, 53; interest rates in, 49; International Monetary Fund and, 239; wages in, 49–50
Ghana, 95
Gini coefficients, 85, 220
global warming. *See* climate change
Goldberg, Phillip, 197
Golden Dawn (Greek political party), 82, 236
Goldman Sachs, 159, 177
Great Depression, 69, 71, 172–73
Great Recession: Argentina and, 62, 68; Bolivia and, 194; Brazil and, 17, 186–87; China's impact on the recovery from, 10–11, 108–9,

117, 174; Ecuador and, 202–3; eurozone countries and, 1–3, 5–8, 20–21, 24, 50–51, 57–58, 106, 172; Greece and, 2, 6–8, 21, 27, 69–72, 77–79, 172; human capital wasted in, 124; India and, 112–14; International Monetary Fund and, 12, 105–6, 156–62, 239; Italy and, 6–7, 22, 172; Latin America and, 16, 174, 212; Portugal and, 6–7, 172; Spain and, 6–8, 21–22, 172; United Kingdom and, 50; United States and, 3, 12, 21–22, 49–51, 57–58, 104, 157–58, 160, 163, 202, 212, 240; Venezuela and, 210, 212–13

Greece: austerity cuts in, 29–31, 35–36, 43, 58, 70, 72, 74–75, 77, 79, 81, 164, 239–40; authoritarian pre-eurozone era in, 7, 81–82; balance of payments and, 76–77; bonds issued by, 26, 30–31, 34, 49, 73, 80–81; capital flight from, 80; current account deficit in, 49; debt default proposal regarding, 76; election (2015) in, 79; euro currency as overvalued in, 59; eurozone exit proposal regarding, 76–77, 79–81; eurozone fiscal policy strictures and, 20; exports and, 8, 75, 77; fascist party in, 82, 236; GDP per capita in, 29; Great Recession and aftermath in, 2, 6–8, 21, 27, 69–72, 77–79, 172; healthcare spending and public health in, 70–72; imports to, 217; inequality in, 75; interest rates in, 23, 34, 49, 73, 80; internal devaluation strategy and, 43; International Monetary Fund and, 26, 28–30, 35, 72–75, 77, 79, 81, 126, 164, 172, 239–40; left-wing Syriza party in, 6, 79–80, 235;

minimum wage in, 74–75; population growth in, 70; poverty rates in, 75; public debt levels and "crisis" in, viii, 7, 23–30, 32, 35, 37, 44, 50, 58, 73, 76, 79, 81, 172; public debt restructuring in, 73–74; public opinion regarding euro currency in, 81; public sector layoffs in, 29–30; retirement age in, 34; Stand-By Arrangement (2010) and, 74, 79; tax evasion and collection in, 27, 72, 76; unemployment in, 2, 21, 58, 69–70, 74–75, 79

greenhouse gases (GHGs), 11, 119–21, 124. *See also* climate change

Greenspan, Alan, 130, 139

Gulf States, 76

Haiti: GDP per capita in, 86; Great Recession and, 160; International Monetary Fund and, 160; poverty in, 83; U.S.-backed coup (2004) in, 171, 228, 233

Hamilton, Alexander, viii

healthcare: economic stagnation's impact on spending for, 9, 119; in eurozone countries, 5–6, 43, 46, 81, 164; IMF calls to cut spending in, 5–6, 45–46, 164; Latin America's expansions of, 170

high-income countries. *See also specific countries*: balance of payment crises in, 31; child mortality in, 98–99; the "demographic transition" and, 122–23; economic growth in, 95–96, 103–4; inequality in, 84; International Monetary Fund and, ix, 11, 31, 126, 157, 162–64; neoliberalism's failures in, 20; state-sponsored development in, vii

Hollande, François, 41

Honduras: coup (2009) in, 18, 171, 201, 226–28, 233; election of left-wing governments in, 14, 169, 233; human rights violations in, 227; United States and, 18, 171, 226–28

Hong Kong, 71, 132

Human Development Index (HDI), 90–91

Hungary, 104, 160

Hyde, Henry, 176

Iceland, 78

India: capital controls in, 115; capital formation in, 115; Contingent Reserve Arrangement and, x, 241; counter-cyclical economic policies in, 11, 113–14; departures from neoliberalism in, 97, 113–14, 116; economic growth in, 11, 97, 111–13, 115–16; eurozone bond purchases and, 25; exchange rate policy in, 113–14; exports from, 114; foreign investment in, 112, 115; GDP per capita in, 25; Great Recession and, 112–14; interest rates in, 112–14; monetary policy in, 113; Monopolies and Restrictive Trade Practices Act in, 112; New Development Bank and, x, 241; public debt levels in, 113; service sector in, 114; tariffs in, 112; trade deficits in, 114–15

Indonesia: Asian financial crisis (1997-1998) and, 13, 59, 71, 78, 131, 133–34, 136–37; bank closures in, 136; capital flows and, 131; corruption in, 134; currency collapse in, 59, 78, 131; foreign investment and, 133; International Monetary Fund and, 13, 133–34, 136–37; regime change (1998) in, 134

inequality: in Bolivia, 191–92; in Brazil, 17, 184–86; in China, 85; in Ecuador, 16, 208; Gini coefficient as a measure of, 85, 220; in Greece, 75; high-income countries and, 84; means of reducing, 83; minimum wage and, 84; Piketty on, 84; population growth and, 84; public policy debates regarding, 83–84; taxation and, 84; in the United States, 85–87; in Venezuela, 17, 200

infant mortality. See also child mortality: the "demographic transition" and, 123; diminishing returns regarding improvement in, 94, 98; in low- and middle-income countries, 8–9

inflation: in Argentina, 59–60, 62, 68, 141, 147, 151–54, 230, 232; black market currency premium and, 232–33; in Bolivia, 195–96; in Brazil, 147, 178–79, 188; capital flows and, 232–33; central banks' policies regarding, 9; European Central Bank and, 52–53; in Germany, 50, 53; International Monetary Fund and, 162–64; in Russia, 137; in Spain, 53; in the United States, 23; in Venezuela, 17, 209, 214–15, 217, 220–21, 232

Insulza, José Miguel, 225

intellectual property, 9, 93, 111

Inter-American Commission on Human Rights, 227

Inter-American Development Bank, 66, 105, 126

interest rates: in Argentina, 60, 66, 141–43, 150; in Brazil, 178–79, 187–88; capital flows and, 114, 234; in Ecuador, 205; in the eurozone, 22–23, 31, 34, 36, 38–41,

49, 53, 73, 80–81, 104; in France, 49; in Germany, 49; in Greece, 23, 34, 49, 73, 80; in India, 112–14; in Ireland, 36, 49; in Italy, 22, 26, 32–34, 36–37, 39, 41, 49, 80–81; in Portugal, 36, 49; in Spain, 22, 31, 39–41, 49, 80–81; in Thailand, 135; unemployment and, 179; in the United States, 22, 141, 178–79, 234; in Venezuela, 209

Intergovernmental Panel on Climate Change, 122

internal devaluation policies, 42–43, 60

International Monetary Fund (IMF): Argentina and, 8, 13, 60–61, 64, 66, 69, 141–43, 145–55, 231–32; Article IV consultations and, 5–6, 41–42, 45–47, 164, 240; Articles of Agreement of, 45; Asian financial crisis (1997-1998) and, 12–13, 106, 129, 131–37, 139–40, 154, 157; austerity and conditionality of loans from, 8, 12, 35–36, 41–42, 46–47, 55, 77, 81, 105–6, 117, 125, 133, 135–36, 146–47, 149, 152, 157, 160–61, 163–64, 239–40; Bolivia and, 15, 126–27, 191–92; capital flow policies and, 133, 162; China and, 165; declining influence of, ix, 11, 13–14, 105–7, 117, 125, 127, 129, 131, 139–40, 154–58, 166, 170, 236, 239; democratic deficit in the governance of, 128–29, 164–66, 241; eurozone and, ix, 5–6, 11, 13, 20, 25, 28–31, 35–36, 40–43, 45–47, 60, 106, 125–29, 135, 157, 163–65, 235–36, 239–41; Great Recession and, 12, 105–6, 156–62, 239; Greece and, 26, 28–30, 35, 72–75, 77, 79, 81, 126, 164, 172, 239–40; high-income countries and, ix, 11, 31, 126, 157, 162–64; Independent Evaluation Office of, 12–13, 136–37, 157–58; Indonesia and, 13, 133–34, 136–37; inflation and, 162–64; internal devaluation strategy and, 43; labor market policy and, 45–46; Latin America and, ix, 105, 157, 170, 173, 222–23; "lender of last resort" function and, 131–32, 148–49, 155; lend into arrears policy and, 150–51; low-income countries and, ix, 12, 31, 106, 117, 126, 162, 236, 239–40; middle-income countries and, ix, 11–12, 31, 105–6, 117, 125–26, 129, 156–57, 175, 236, 239–40; neoliberalism and, ix, 20, 34–35, 47, 92–93, 106, 117, 125, 155–56; Portugal and, 31, 126, 172, 240; poverty and, 46; reform proposals regarding, 131; Russia and, 105, 127 , 137, 139, 145, 154, 157; Spain and, 47, 126, 172, 239–40; Special Drawing Rights (SDRs) and, 162; Ukraine and, 2; United States and, ix, 12, 47, 106, 126–29, 132–34, 140, 157, 161–66, 170, 172–73, 177, 236, 238–42; World Bank and, 105, 126, 128, 149

Iran, 78, 223

Iraq, 13, 223

Ireland: austerity cuts in, 36, 240; bonds issued by, 30–31, 36, 49; bubble-driven economic growth in, 27; current account deficit in, 49; eurozone fiscal policy strictures and, 20; interest rates in, 36, 49; International Monetary Fund and, 31, 240; public debt levels in, 37; real estate bubble (2000s) in, 104

Italy: austerity cuts in, 35–37, 239–40; bonds issued by, 32–34, 36–37, 39, 41, 49, 80–81; currency devaluation (1992) by, 78; eurozone fiscal policy strictures and, 20, 28; Great Recession and aftermath in, 6–7, 22, 172; interest rates in, 22, 26, 32–34, 36–37, 39, 41, 49, 80–81; International Monetary Fund and, 172, 239–40; public debt levels and "crisis" in, 25–26, 30–32, 37, 172; retirement age in, 34; tax evasion in, 27

Japan: Argentina crisis (early 2000s) and, 150; Asian financial crisis and, 132; central bank in, 4; economic downturn (1992) and, 71; fertility rates and life expectancy in, 123; International Monetary Fund and, 128
Johnson, Simon, 135–36

Kantor, Mickey, 132, 136
Katari, Túpac, 191
Kerry, John, 168, 225
Keynesian economic policy, 1, 92, 101
Kirchner, Néstor: Argentina's debt default and, 13, 154; International Monetary Fund and, 13, 69, 151, 154–55; neoliberalism opposed by, 150
Kissinger, Henry, 167–68
Klein, Naomi, 47
Korea. See South Korea
Korry, Edward, 167
Krueger, Anne, 146
Kwak, James, 135–36

Lagarde, Christine, 164, 231, 239
Lasso, Guillermo, 206
Latin America. See also specific countries: austerity policies in, 176; balance of payments crises in, 15, 173, 175, 230; capital flows and, 172; Chávez and, 222; China's investment and trade in, 76, 102, 237–38; Cold War and, 170–71; "commodities boom" argument regarding, 15, 174–75; counter-cyclical policies in, 175–76; debt crisis (1980s) in, 172; economic rebound in early 2000s in, 14–15, 84, 173–75; economic stagnation during late twentieth century in, 1, 14, 84, 169, 171–73, 176, 230, 233; election of left-wing governments in, 14, 168–70, 225–26, 229, 233; exports and, 15, 174–75; foreign exchange reserve levels in, 175; GDP per capita in, 14, 171; Great Depression and, 172–73; Great Recession and, 16, 174, 212; inequality in, 173, 233; inflation in, 173; interest rates in, 172; International Monetary Fund and, ix, 105, 157, 170, 173, 222–23; neoliberalism opposed in, 14, 169–70, 229; poverty in, 14, 84, 173–75, 233; "second independence" of, 18, 170–71, 209, 222–23; tariffs in, 109; United States policy in, 18, 167–68, 170–71, 173, 177, 197–99, 221–33
Latvia, 71, 104, 160
LCH Clearnet, 36
Leal Filho, Laurindo, 189–90
Lehman Brothers collapse (2008), 21, 36
Leigh, Daniel, 163
life expectancy: the "demographic transition" and, 122–23; diminishing returns regarding

improvement in, 94, 98; in low-
and middle-income countries,
8–9, 116
Lincoln, Abraham, viii
Lissakers, Karin, 128
Lithuania, 104
low-income countries. *See also specific
countries*: capital flows and, 234;
child mortality in, 98–99, 116;
China's trade with, 100–101, 107,
236–37; counter-cyclical policies
in, 107, 175; economic growth in,
x, 8, 11, 86, 95–96, 98, 100, 103–5,
116, 236, 242; International
Monetary Fund and, ix, 12, 31,
106, 117, 126, 162, 236, 239–40;
life expectancy in, 8–9, 116;
neoliberalism's failures in, 8–9,
92, 102, 116, 242; socioeconomic
progress in, 92
Lula. *See* da Silva, Lula

Maastricht Treaty (1992), 20, 53
Maduro, Nicolás, 210, 213, 225
Malaysia, 13, 71, 78, 131
Mali, 95
Manta (Ecuador), 223
market fundamentalism. *See*
neoliberalism
Media Luna region (Bolivia), 196
Menem, Carlos, 150
Merkel, Angela, 35
Mexico: bonds issued by, 127; economic growth and GDP per capita
in, 89; illegal immigration and,
89; International Monetary Fund
and, 162; NAFTA and, 88–89;
peso crisis (1995-1996) in, 59, 78,
127, 141
middle-income countries. *See also
specific countries*: capital flows
and, 234; child mortality in,
98–99, 116; China's trade with,
100–101, 107, 236–37; choices

regarding consumption *versus*
leisure in, 120; counter-cyclical
policies in, 107, 175–76; economic
growth in, x, 8, 11, 14, 86–87,
95–96, 98, 100, 104–5, 116, 125,
236, 242; economic redistribution
in, 87; foreign exchange reserve
levels and, 13, 175; International
Monetary Fund and, ix, 11–12,
31, 105–6, 117, 125–26, 129,
156–57, 175, 236, 239–40; life
expectancy in, 8–9, 116; neoliberalism's failures in, 8–9, 92,
102–3, 116, 242; socioeconomic
progress in, 92
Misión Barrio Adentro program
(Venezuela), 218–19
Monopolies and Restrictive Trade
Practices Act (India), 112
Morales, Evo: economic record of,
15, 194–95, 201; election (2005)
of, 126, 191, 226; indigenous ethnic identity of, 15, 126, 191, 226;
International Monetary Fund
and, 192; land reform policies
of, 196–97; media opposition to,
195; nationalization of hydrocarbon industries and, 15, 193;
re-elections (2009 and 2014) of,
199; United States and, 198
Movement Toward Socialism
(Bolivian political party), 198
Murray, Bill, 232

National Front (French political
party), 82, 236
neoliberalism. *See also* austerity: capital flows and, 93, 100,
125, 130; central banks and, 93,
100, 204; China's departures
from, x, 10–11, 97, 102, 109–11,
117; comparative advantage
and, 111; "creation myths" of,
vii; deregulation and, 9, 93, 125,

neoliberalism (*Cont.*)
230; eurozone and, 24, 34–35, 51–53, 109, 125–26; failures of, ix–x, 8–11, 14, 18–20, 92–93, 96–97, 99–100, 102–3, 105, 116–18, 124–26, 208–9, 242; fiscal policy and, 94, 97, 100; intellectual property and, 93; International Monetary Fund and, ix, 20, 34–35, 47, 92–93, 106, 117, 125, 155–56; labor market policy and, 94; Latin America's opposition to, 14, 169–70, 229; monetary policy and, 93, 97, 100; trade and, 93, 97, 100, 125

The Netherlands, 46
Neves, Aécio, 190
New Development Bank (NDB), x, 241
Nicaragua, 14, 169
Nixon, Richard, 167–68, 233
North American Free Trade Agreement (NAFTA), 88–89
Norway, 71

Obama, Barack: Argentina and, 231; eurozone financial policy and, 41; Honduras coup (2009) and, 226–27; Latin American public opinion and, 228; on Lula, 189; Lula on, 226
Ocampo, José Antonio, 172
Occupy Wall Street, 84
oil prices: "commodities boom" argument and, 15; Ecuador and, 202, 237; oil shocks (1970s) and, 97; Venezuela and, 212–13, 216–17
Organization for Economic Co-operation and Development (OECD), 100
Organization of American States (OAS), 18, 212, 225, 227–28

Outright Monetary Transactions program (European Central Bank), 40

Paine, Thomas, 221
Panama, 170
Pando region (Bolivia), 196–97
Papandreou, George, 35
Paraguay, 14, 169, 226, 233
Paris Club, 126, 231
PDVSA (Venezuelan oil company), 210–11
pensions: in Argentina, 147; in Bolivia, 15, 194, 200; in Brazil, 183; in eurozone countries, 5–6, 24, 43, 45–46, 81, 164; IMF calls to cut, 5–6, 45–46, 164; in Venezuela, 18, 220
Peru, 175
Petkoff, Teodoro, 211
Petrobras (Brazilian oil company), 188–90
pharmaceuticals, 93, 166
The Philippines, 13, 71, 131
PIIGS countries (Portugal, Italy, Ireland, Greece, and Spain), 20, 25, 49
Piketty, Thomas, 84
Pinochet, Augusto, 168
Podemos (Spanish political party), 6, 235
Poland, 100n27, 104, 138, 162
population growth: climate change and, 11, 121–22; the "demographic transition" and, 122–23; economic growth and, 11, 87, 121; inequality and, 84
Portugal: austerity cuts in, 36, 43, 240; authoritarian pre-eurozone era in, 7, 81–82; bonds issued by, 30–31, 36, 49; current account deficit in, 49; euro currency as overvalued in, 59; eurozone

fiscal policy strictures and, 20; Great Recession and aftermath in, 6–7, 172; interest rates in, 36, 49; internal devaluation strategy and, 43; International Monetary Fund and, 31, 126, 172, 240; public debt level in, 37, 172; public opinion regarding euro currency in, 81

poverty: in Argentina, 7, 58–59, 61–62, 146–47; in Bolivia, 126, 191–92, 196, 199, 201; in Brazil, 17, 83, 91, 180–83; in China, 85; economic growth as means of reducing, 85–88; in Ecuador, 16, 208; Great Recession and global levels of, 3, 56; in Greece, 75; in Haiti, 83; IMF recommendations regarding, 46; in Latin America, 14, 84, 173–75, 233; redistribution as a means of reducing, 86–87; in Russia, 137; in South Korea, 91; in the United States, 83; in Venezuela, 17, 218–19

Prat-Gay, Alfonso, 153

privatization, neoliberalism's advocacy for, 9, 93, 97, 230

productivity: climate change and, 11, 121; economic growth and, 11, 121, 123; eurozone countries' varying levels of, 48–50; leisure *versus* consumption as result of, 119; technological change and, 121; wages and, 87

public debt: in Argentina, 60; in eurozone, viii, 7, 22–32, 35–36, 44–45, 47, 50–51, 53–54, 73, 76, 80–81, 145, 172, 235; in Greece, viii, 7, 23–30, 32, 35, 37, 44, 50, 58, 73–74, 76, 79, 81, 172; in Italy, 25–26, 30–32, 37, 172; in Portugal, 37, 172; in Spain, 25, 37, 172

Putin, Vladimir, 138–39

quantitative easing (QE): European Central Bank and, 50, 81, 235; expansionary fiscal impact of, 22–23; Federal Reserve Bank (United States) and, 22–23, 50, 81, 235, 240

Rand, Ayn, 3

Reinhart, Carmen, 57, 71

renewable energy, 121

Renta Dignidad program (Bolivia), 200

Republican Party (United States), 3

Rio de Janeiro (Brazil), 83, 185, 190

Rodrik, Dani, 109, 113

Rogoff, Kenneth, 57, 71

Romney, Mitt, 22

Roosevelt, Franklin D., 69

Rousseff, Dilma: Brazilian media opposition to, 190; corruption scandals and, 189–90; economic record of, 186–88; election (2014) of, 188, 191

Rubin, Robert, 139

Russell, Bertrand, 221

Russia: Asian financial crisis contagion and, 60, 130, 137, 142; Contingent Reserve Arrangement and, x, 241; currency collapse (1995) in, 127; currency collapse (1998) in, 60, 105, 142; currency devaluation in, 138; currency exchange peg in, 93, 105, 138, 154; economic boom (2000s) in, 138–39; economic decline during the 1990s and, 137; election (2012) in, 138–39; eurozone bond purchases and, 25; foreign exchange reserves in, 76, 138; inflation in, 137; International Monetary Fund and, 105, 127, 137, 139, 145, 154, 157; life expectancy in, 137; neoliberalism

Russia: Asian financial crisis
contagion and (Cont.)
and "shock therapy" policies in,
105, 110; New Development Bank
and, x, 241; oil industry in, 138;
poverty in, 137; price liberalization in, 110; privatization in, 110;
Ukraine and, 161; United States
and, 138

Sachs, Jeffrey, 137–38, 140
Santa Cruz region (Bolivia),
196–97, 199
Santiago summit (2008), 197
Sarkozy, Nicolas, 35, 41
Schäuble, Wolfgang, 2
Securities Market Program (SMP;
European Central Bank), 33, 40
The Shock Doctrine (Klein), 47
"shock therapy" (Russia), 105, 110
short-selling, 32–34
Singapore, 132
Singh, Anoop, 60, 147–48
Socialist Workers Party (Spain), 36
South Africa, x, 25, 241
South Korea: Asian financial crisis
(1997-1998) and, 13, 59, 71, 78,
131, 133, 135; capital flows and,
131, 133; currency collapse in,
59, 78, 131; economic growth
in, vii, 89–90, 94, 171; education in, 91; exports from, 114;
foreign exchange controls in,
133; Human Development Index
indicators in, 90–91; infant
mortality in, 91; interest rates
in, 135; International Monetary
Fund and, 13; poverty rates in,
91; state-sponsored development
in, vii; trade surplus in, 114
Soviet Union, 236
Spain: austerity cuts in, 36,
43, 239–40; authoritarian

pre-eurozone era in, 7, 81–82;
bonds issued by, 30, 32–33,
39–41, 49, 80–81; current
account deficit in, 48–49; election
(2011) in, 36; euro currency as
overvalued in, 59; eurozone fiscal
policy strictures and, 20; Great
Recession and aftermath in,
6–8, 21–22, 172; inflation in, 53;
interest rates in, 22, 31, 39–41,
49, 80–81; internal devaluation
strategy in, 43; International
Monetary Fund and, 47, 126,
172, 239–40; public debt levels
and "crisis" in, 25, 37, 172; public
opinion regarding euro currency
in, 81; real estate bubble (2000s)
in, 27, 104, 202; retirement
age in, 34; stock market bubble
(2000s) in, 104; unemployment in, 21, 235–36; Venezuela
and, 225
Special Drawing Rights (SDRs), 162
Special Economic Zones (China), 110
Stiglitz, Joseph, 139–40
Strauss-Kahn, Dominique, 29,
156, 164–65
Subramanian, Arvind, 77, 109
Sudan, 154
Suharto, 134
Summers, Lawrence, 132, 139–40
Sweden, 71, 78
Syriza (Greek political party), 6,
79–80, 235

Taiwan, 114, 132
Tanzania, 95
tariffs, vii–viii, 109, 112. *See also*
World Trade Organization
Tarija region (Bolivia), 196
Thailand: Asian financial crisis
(1997-1998) and, 13, 71, 78,
131–32, 135; capital flows and,

131; currency collapse in, 78, 131–32; economic growth in, 95; fixed currency exchange rate in, 132; interest rates in, 135; International Monetary Fund and, 13

Thirteen Bankers (Johnson and Kwak), 135–36

trade: balances and, 15, 43, 48; currency exchange rates' impact on, 43; between eurozone countries, 48–49; internal devaluation policies and, 43; Latin America and, 15; neoliberal approaches to, 93, 97, 100, 125; volatility of, 9

Treasury Department (United States): Argentina debt restructuring and, 232; Asian financial crisis and, 132, 139–40; bonds issued by, 23; International Monetary Fund and, 47, 127, 157, 164, 232

Trichet, Jean-Claude, 52–53

the troika. *See* European Central Bank (ECB); European Commission; International Monetary Fund (IMF)

Tsipras, Alexis, 80

Turkey, 100n27

Ukraine, 2, 160–61

unemployment: in Argentina, 7, 59, 61–64, 68, 146, 149; in Brazil, 17, 184, 186; central banks' policies regarding, 9; in eurozone countries, 1, 3, 5, 8, 21, 24, 43–44, 46, 52, 55–57, 82, 85, 235–36, 240; financial crises' impact on, 57, 81; Great Recession and, 56–57; in Greece, 2, 21, 58, 69–70, 74–75, 79; interest rates' impact on, 179; in Spain, 21, 235–36; in the United States, 21, 57, 163; in

Venezuela, 218; welfare spending to alleviate, 6, 45

Union of South American Nations (UNASUR), 197, 222, 225

United Kingdom: Asian Infrastructure Investment Bank and, x; central bank in, 4, 31, 40; currency devaluation in, 78; fiscal policy and, 51; Great Recession and, 50; International Monetary Fund and, 165; monetary policy in, 31; private sector borrowing in, 49; real estate bubble (2000s) in, 104; state-sponsored development in, vii; tariffs in, vii

United States: Argentina-related court cases in, 230–32; Asian financial crisis and, 132–34, 136, 139; Asian Infrastructure Investment Bank and, x; average hours worked in, 119–20; Bolivia and, 191, 194, 197–99; bonds issued by, 22–23, 36; Brazil and, 18, 177, 223–25; budget deficit in, 23, 53–54, 72; child mortality in, 88; Chile and, 167–68, 170; Cold War and, 137, 170–71, 236; definition of national security interests by, 238; economic expansion of 1990s in, 97; economic growth in, 88, 97, 103–4; education in, 88; energy consumption in, 120; fiscal policy in, 23, 53–54; GDP per capita in, 86, 88; Great Depression in, 69, 71; Great Recession and, 3, 12, 21–22, 49–51, 57–58, 104, 157–58, 160, 163, 202, 212, 240; healthcare in, 118; Honduras and, 18, 171, 226–28; household savings rate in, 104; imperial foreign policy of, 238–39; inequality in, 85–87; inflation in, 23; interest rates in, 22, 141, 178–79, 234;

United States: Argentina-related
court cases in (Cont.)
International Monetary Fund
and, ix, 12, 47, 106, 126–29,
132–34, 140, 157, 161–66, 170,
172–73, 177, 236, 238–42; Iraq
and Afghanistan wars and, 223;
Latin American policy and,
18, 167–68, 170–71, 173, 177,
197–99, 221–33; life expectancy
in, 88; monetary policy in, 22–23,
31; NAFTA and, 88; neoliberalism and, 3, 106, 132–34; poverty
in, 83; private sector borrowing
in, 49; productivity levels in, 87;
quantitative easing (QE) policy
in, 22–23, 50, 81, 240; real estate
bubble (2000s) in, 3, 12, 49, 57,
103–4, 151, 158–59, 202, 234;
recession (2001) in, 103, 174;
recession (early 1980s) in, 172;
Russia and, 138; stimulus measures in, 57; stock market bubble
(early 2000s) in, 12, 103, 130, 158,
174, 234; tariffs in, viii; tax cuts
in, 23; trade balances and, 129;
Ukraine and, 161–62; unemployment in, 21, 57, 163; Venezuela
and, 221–25, 228; wages in, 87;
World Bank and, 129, 140, 166,
238–39, 241–42; World Trade
Organization and, 166
United States Congress: House
International Relations
Committee and, 176; IMF
funding debates in, 140, 232;
IMF hearings (1998) of, 128;
neoliberalism and, 3
Uruguay, 14, 169, 220
USAID, 198–99

Varoufakis, Yanis, 80
Végh, Carlos, 107

Venezuela: balance of payments in,
17, 217, 230, 232; black market
exchange rate in, 209, 214–17;
bonds issued by, 209; capital flows
and, 216, 220, 230, 233; China's
loans to, 76, 217, 237; consumer
goods shortages in, 209, 215–16;
consumer price index in, 221;
corruption in, 215–16; coup
attempt (2002) in, 197, 211–13,
224; currency devaluations in,
214; economic growth during the
twenty-first century in, 210–14,
218; economic stagnation of late
twentieth century in, 18, 210–11;
education in, 18, 219–20; election
of left-wing governments in, 14,
169, 225–26, 229; exchange rate
policies in, 216–18, 220, 230, 232;
exports from, 175, 214, 217–18,
232; fixed exchange rate in, 214,
220, 232; foreign exchange reserves
in, 217; Great Recession and, 210,
212–13; healthcare in, 18, 218–19;
housing in, 214; imports to, 217;
inequality reduced in, 17, 220;
inflation in, 17, 209, 214–15, 217,
220–21, 232; interest rates in, 209;
media coverage of, 221–22, 224;
nationalization of oil industry in,
17; oil sector in, 210–14, 222–23;
oil strike (2002-2003) in, 211–13;
pensions in, 18, 220; poverty and
poverty reduction in, 17, 218–19;
referendum election (2003) in,
212–13; unemployment in, 218;
United States and, 221–25, 228
Vietnam War, 168
Vuletin, Guillermo, 107

Walpole, Robert, vii
Washington Consensus, 92,
180, 233

Wilson, Scott, 224
Wolfowitz, Paul, 138
Workers' Party (PT, Brazil): Brazilian media opposition to, 189–90; consumer credit expansion and, 183; corruption and, 189; economic priorities and record of, 179–84, 191; election (2003) and, 16, 176; election (2014) and, 188; industrial policy and, 183; International Monetary Fund and, ix; land reform policies of, 177; social spending programs of, 181–82; U.S. opposition to, 223–24
World Bank: Argentina and, 66, 144, 149; conditionality of loans from, 12; International Monetary Fund and, 105, 126, 128, 149; neoliberalism and, ix, 92, 109, 117; United States and, 129, 140, 166, 238–39, 241–42
World Trade Organization (WTO): China and, 111; democratic deficit in the governance of, 241; developing countries' voting blocs in, 165–66; intellectual property rights and, 111; neoliberalism and, ix, 111, 117; United States and, 166

Zapatero, José Luis Rodríguez, 36
Zelaya, Mel, 201, 226–27